Pilgrims and Sultans

Pilgrims and Sultans

The Hajj under the Ottomans 1517–1683

SURAIYA FAROQHI

I.B.Tauris & Co Ltd
Publishers
London · New York

For Andreas Tietze
with respect and affection

Published in 1994 by
I.B.Tauris & Co Ltd
45 Bloomsbury Square
London WC1A 2HY

175 Fifth Avenue
New York
NY 10010

In the United States of America
and Canada distributed by
St Martin's Press
175 Fifth Avenue
New York
NY 10010

A full CIP record for this book is available from the British Library

A full CIP record for this book is available from the Library of Congress

ISBN 1–85043–606–1

Typeset by Photoprint, Torquay, Devon
Printed and bound in Great Britain by
WBC Ltd, Bridgend, Mid Glamorgan

Contents

Preface vii
Note on Transliteration and Abbreviations ix
List of Tables xi

Introduction 1

1 The Pilgrimage to Mecca in Pre-Ottoman Times 13

2 Caravan Routes 32

3 Caravan Security 54

4 The Finances of the Holy Cities 74

5 In Praise of Ruler and Religion: Public Buildings in Mecca and Medina 92

6 The Pilgrimage as a Matter of Foreign Policy 127

7 The Pilgrimage in Economic and Political Contexts 146

Conclusion 174

Chronology 188
Notes 191
Bibliography 214
Index 236

Preface

Every book is ultimately a collective work, and cooperation begins at an early stage, when the author begins to develop the chosen topic. Not all those who at some point suggested directions to take, and aspects to cover, will necessarily agree with the final result. Nevertheless, I am grateful to a number of people who helped along my thinking – such as it is – and suggested sources to consult. Of course, none of them can be held to the slightest degree responsible for the deficiencies of this book.

Doris Behrens-Abouseif helped with the Arabic sources, and gave generously of her time and patience. Time and again, I have profited from the rich experience and erudition of Andreas Tietze. I owe references to many Ottoman sources to Mehmet Genç; more importantly, I am grateful for his pertinent observations on the functioning of Ottoman state and society. Engin Akarlı, Halis Akder, Cornell Fleischer, Christoph Neumann and Isenbike Togan read through individual chapters and made valuable suggestions. Rifa'at Abou-El-Haj redirected my attention to the forest when the trees pressed too close; I have also profited from his ability to 'brush the fur of a text against the nap', teasing out information that the author of a given primary source may have included without being aware of the fact.

Among the people who helped me locate sources, the officials of the Başbakanlık Arşivi-Osmanlı Arşivi in Istanbul deserve special mention; they have helped in many different ways. I am especially grateful to my old teacher Mithat Sertoğlu, former director-general of the archives; he first made me feel the excitement of working with a rich and underexploited body of documentary evidence. Veli Tola and

Mesude Çorbacıoğlu were also very helpful. Hafez K. Shehab (Princeton), Tosun Arıcanlı (Harvard) and Winfried Riesterer (Munich) helped me locate important printed sources, while Andreas Tietze made it possible to procure microfilms from the Vienna National Library.

The present book is somewhat different from the German edition which preceded it. The introduction is rather more explicit. Profiting from the counsel of reviewers, I have gladly eliminated the last chapter, which took the story to the present day but was based exclusively on published material. The space thus gained allowed me to discuss financial affairs in a more detailed fashion, and to treat Meccan society as reflected in the Ottoman documents somewhat more fully. The book's new title reflects these various changes.

Christl Catanzaro and Giorgios Salakides produced the index, and I am grateful to them.

Note on Transliteration and Abbreviations

TRANSLITERATION

The present transcription is that employed by the *Encyclopedia of Islam*. Long vowels are marked by a line: ā, ī, ū. To maintain consistency, composite names such as Sa'd al-Dīn or 'Abd al-Raḥīm have also been spelt according to *EI* rules, although in Turkish they are pronounced Sadettin and Abdürrahim. But otherwise the *EI* convention of treating Arabic or Persian loans in Turkish as if they were still part of their original languages has not been followed. An Ottoman would therefore be called Aḥmed or Meḥmed, while a non-Ottoman bearing this name is referred to as Aḥmad or Muḥammad. Certain doubtful cases exist, in which I have normally adopted Turkish pronunciation.

Geographical terms still in use today have been spelt according to common usage. Names no longer in use have been transcribed. Words like shaykh, Sultan or Pasha which have entered the English language have been spelt in the customary fashion.

ABBREVIATIONS

EI *Encyclopedia of Islam*
IA *Islam Ansiklopedisi*
IFM *Istanbul Üniversitesi Iktisat Fakültesi Mecmuası*

MD Mühimme Defterleri (section in the Prime Minister's Archives in Istanbul)
MM Maliyeden Müdevver (section in the Prime Minister's Archives in Istanbul)
MZ Mühimme Zeyli (section in the Prime Minister's Archives in Istanbul)

List of Tables

1 Payments to Beduins from Egyptian Provincial Budgets, to Facilitate Hajj Travel 56
2 Payments to Beduins from Syrian Provincial Budgets, to Facilitate Hajj Travel 57
3 Bāyezīd II's Gifts to the Hejazis 77
4 Expenditure for Pilgrims and the Holy Cities from the Central Administration's Budget 78
5 Expenditure on Behalf of the Holy Cities According to the Egyptian Budget of 1596–7 (in *pāra*) 79
6 Expenditure on Behalf of the Holy Cities According to Early Seventeenth-century Egyptian Budgets (in *pāra*) 81

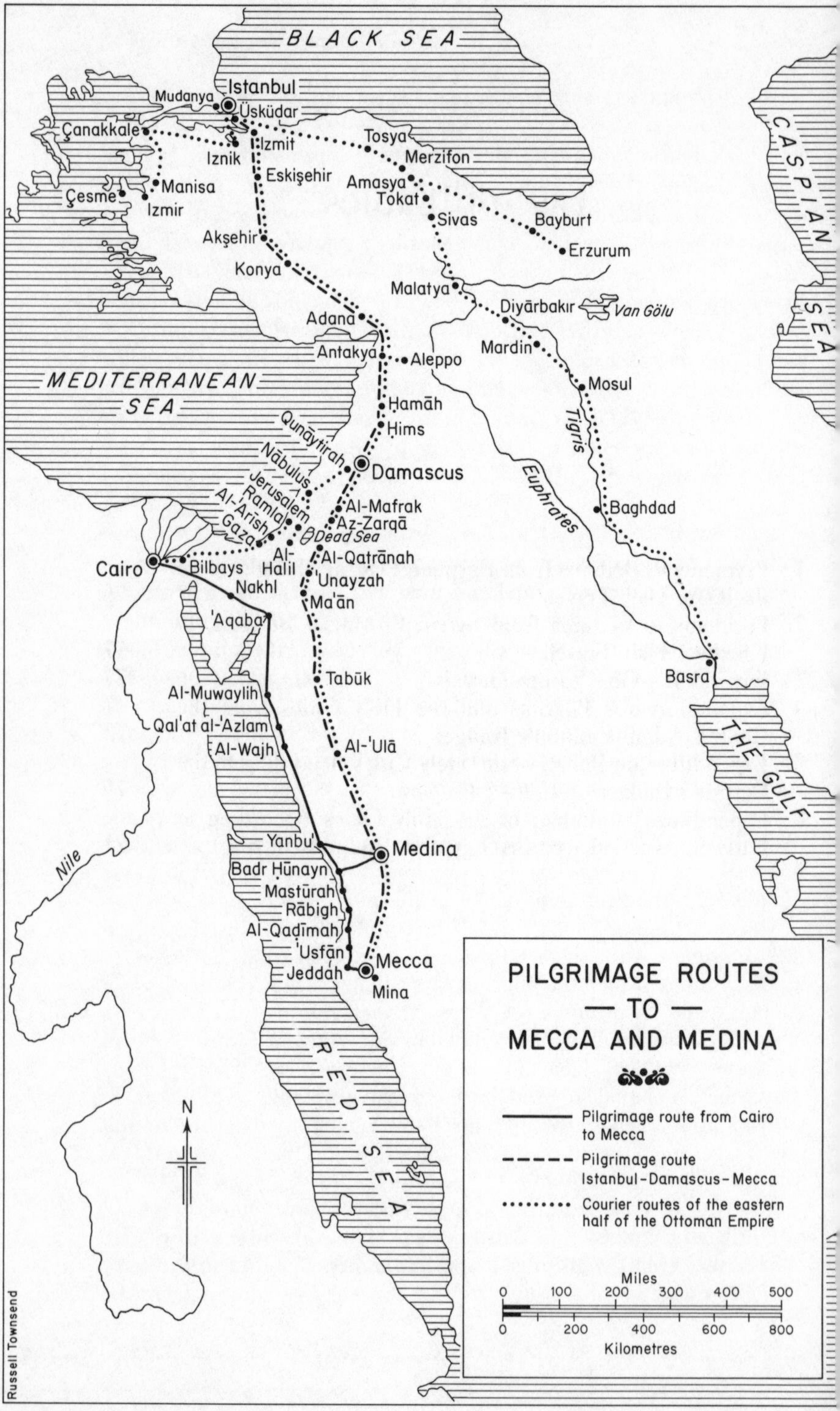

BLACK SEA
CASPIAN SEA
MEDITERRANEAN SEA
RED SEA
THE GULF
Istanbul
Mudanya
Üsküdar
Çanakkale
Iznik
Izmit
Tosya
Merzifon
Eskişehir
Amasya
Tokat
Manisa
Çesme
Izmir
Sivas
Bayburt
Erzurum
Akşehir
Konya
Malatya
Diyārbakır
Van Gölu
Adana
Mardin
Antakya
Aleppo
Mosul
Ḥamāh
Ḥims
Tigris
Qunayṭirah
Nābulus
Damascus
Jerusalem
Ramla
Al-'Arīsh
Gaza
Al-Mafrak
Az-Zarqā
Dead Sea
Euphrates
Baghdad
Al-Ḥalīl
Al-Qaṭrānah
Cairo
Bilbays
'Unayzah
Nakhl
Ma'ān
'Aqaba
Tabūk
Basra
Al-Muwaylih
Qal'at al-'Azlam
Al-Wajh
Al-'Ulā
Yanbu'
Medina
Nile
Badr Ḥūnayn
Mastūrah
Rābigh
Al-Qadīmah
'Usfān
Mecca
Jeddah
Mina
N
PILGRIMAGE ROUTES
— TO —
MECCA AND MEDINA
Pilgrimage route from Cairo to Mecca
Pilgrimage route Istanbul-Damascus-Mecca
Courier routes of the eastern half of the Ottoman Empire
Miles
0 100 200 300 400 500
0 200 400 600 800
Kilometres
Russell Townsend

Introduction

European and American readers who first encounter the word 'pilgrimage' will think of medieval men and women on their way to Rome, Santiago da Compostela or Jerusalem, or possibly of modern Catholics visiting Lourdes and Fatima. But for a Muslim, pilgrimage to Mecca plays a much more central role in the practice of his or her belief. Apart from a limited number of instances in which pilgrimage was prescribed for the atonement of sins by the medieval and early modern Catholic Church, Christian pilgrimages to Jerusalem are voluntary. In Islam, however, pilgrimage to Mecca is obligatory for all believers wealthy enough to afford it, even though at all times the majority of Muslims have been unable to fulfil this obligation for financial and other reasons. This practical difficulty does not however diminish the religious importance of the pilgrimage.

Moreover, the pilgrimage in Islam is fundamentally different from the experience with which Christians are familiar. The Ka'aba with its Black Stone, which the pilgrims kiss whenever they can come close enough, is by no means a relic, even though the pilgrims commemorate Abraham/Ibrāhīm, the builder of the 'Ancient House', one of the names of the Ka'aba. The latter structure possesses a religious significance unequalled even by the most venerated holy places in Christianity. When devoting himself or herself to the rites of the pilgrimage, the Muslim meditates the might and mercy of God, and also forswears the devil and all his works.

The rites of visitation are also quite different from those practised by Christian churches. The Muslim pilgrim does not necessarily enter the Ka'aba, even though this is possible at certain times of the year. The pilgrimage is valid even if the Ka'aba was beheld only from the outside, while in most Christian places of pilgrimage, pious visitors are expected to enter the church or shrine. A visit to the grave of the Prophet Muḥammad in Medina is by no means an obligation, even though many pilgrims will combine a stay in the second Holy City of the Hejaz with their pilgrimage to Mecca, and some will even affirm that they had a more profound religious experience in Medina. Before the nineteenth century most pilgrims who came to Medina probably visited the graves of members of the Prophet's family and those of various venerated figures from the first centuries of Islam, and many do so even today. But quite a few religious scholars disapprove of such visits, as detracting from the veneration due to God alone. Moreover, these visits have no connection with the pilgrimage itself. There is no cult of relics connected with the Ka'aba, even though many pilgrims expect certain blessings when they drink water from the well Zamzam located inside the Meccan sanctuary. Many religious scholars even disapprove of the popular custom of carrying back a bit of Meccan earth as a pilgrimage memento.[1]

THE PILGRIMAGE AS A SOCIAL AND POLITICAL PHENOMENON

The present study has a fairly modest aim. In the first place, it is meant to deal with the pilgrimage as a political and social, rather than a religious phenomenon. These different aspects were of course closely linked in real life; to quote just one example among thousands, the pilgrimage caravans travelled at a greater or lesser speed according to the amount of time left until the prayer meeting on the plateau of 'Arafat. For if that was missed, the entire pilgrimage was invalid, and the pilgrims' effort wasted. This latter consideration is without doubt a religious phenomenon, but greater speed on the part of tardy pilgrims might lead to a severe loss of camels. This, in turn, could give rise not only to economic difficulties, when replacements had to be purchased, but also to political conflict, if the caravan commander tried to force desert dwellers to supply the caravan with riding animals. We also need to keep in mind that pilgrims of the sixteenth century did not separate the economic and social aspects of their activities from the religious side, which to them doubtlessly constituted the essential reason for undergoing the trouble and sacrifices entailed by the journey. But for today's researcher, this division into socio-economic and religious domains is a great convenience, if only because religious and legal texts concerning the pilgrimage demand different skills from the researcher trying to evaluate them than do archival materials. Given the limitations of most specialists, including the present author, the two sets of skills are rarely encountered in the same person.

Secondly, we are concerned with a fairly limited period, namely the first two centuries of Ottoman control over the Hejaz. Our study begins in 922/1517, the year in which Sultan Selīm I conquered Cairo; for the purposes of this study, this event will be taken as the end of the medieval period and the beginning of the early modern age. The first two centuries of Ottoman control merit detailed study for a variety of reasons. First of all, we have become accustomed to view this period of extraordinary political and cultural florescence almost exclusively either from the perspective of Istanbul and the central Ottoman lands, or from the 'national history' point of view. In the latter perspective, Ottoman history is regarded as important because it forms a necessary preliminary to Syrian, Hungarian or of course Turkish national history. Yet such a perspective is especially inappropriate when applied to the pilgrimage cities of Mecca and Medina, whose enduring religious significance far outweighs their role in the formation of the modern state of which they form a part. In discussing relations of the Ottoman central government with a remote province, we are thus induced to study problems which have little relation to future nation building, but touch a number of issues crucial for the functioning of the Ottoman Empire during the sixteenth and seventeenth centuries.

TRAVEL AND COMMUNICATION

When we study the pilgrimage as a phenomenon of political and social history, it forms part of the history of human communication, of the transfer of both material and immaterial resources; the relative economic strengths and weaknesses of different regions also have a major part to play in such a model. Communication took place at different levels: on the basic level, the pilgrims during their stay in the Holy Cities had a unique opportunity to affirm their faith and to communicate this experience to their fellow pilgrims. The importance of this aspect emerges most clearly from the pilgrimage account of Ibn Djubayr, an Andalusian of the late twelfth century CE.[2] Less visible in the surviving sources, but certainly not of less importance, is the communication between returning pilgrims and their neighbours who did not have a chance to visit the Holy Cities. Remote little towns of fifteenth-century Anatolia often boasted very large numbers of people who called themselves hajjis, that is, returned pilgrims. For our purposes it is quite irrelevant whether these people had really been to Mecca. If they had not, if most hajjis owed their title to the fact that it had become part of a given name, or was accorded out of general respect for age and experience, the message was even clearer: the pilgrimage constituted something uniquely blessed and desirable, which people hoped their children might accomplish even if they themselves had not had the opportunity.[3] Or if an outlying Ottoman town somewhere in the Balkans housed a modest foundation benefiting the poor of Medina, this must have brought home to the townsmen that there was in fact such a city, with men and women living in it who no doubt spent their days in pious meditation. In an otherwise highly localized society, in which most people cultivated a garden and produced for a limited market, this message must have broadened horizons considerably.

The transfer of immaterial resources should be viewed in the same context: to the inhabitants not only of Cairo, but also of fairly remote Anatolian towns, the annual return of the pilgrims was a major event, to be celebrated by a procession that at times became so exuberant that the authorities issued prohibitions.[4] It would appear that the fellow townsmen of the pilgrims thought that the latter brought something valuable into the community, something that was worth welcoming by a special feast. And that this valuable, albeit immaterial resource was brought in from a distant place again counterbalanced all those elements in the lifestyle of Ottoman towns which made for extreme localization.

FOOD, PRECIOUS METALS AND POLITICS

Other transfers concerned material resources such as food and money. If twentieth-century historians dealing with the seventeenth-century rebel Ḳaṭırdjıoghlu have correctly read the evidence, this local magnate was well aware of the transfer aspect of the pilgrimage.[5] He was supposedly much opposed to the outflow of gold and silver carried to the Hejaz by the hajjis, and therefore robbed their caravans with special relish. Since we do not know who attributed this bullionist motivation to Ḳaṭırdjıoghlu, whether it was invented by his enemies or whether he himself espoused it, this story should not be made to carry the weight of excessive interpretation. But it can still serve as a warning that popular approval for the transfer of money and grain to the Hejaz was perhaps not as unanimous as one might assume.

In spite of the possibility of occasional protests, the transfer of gold, silver and grain to the Beduins of the Syrian and Arabian deserts and to the inhabitants of the Holy Cities continued apace. In the Ottoman core lands of Anatolia and Rumelia, gold was not much used even in the larger transactions of the townsmen, and European traders, too, mainly dealt in silver. Therefore the gold was probably supplied largely by the Ottoman government, which received it in the shape of tributes, or by the Egyptian treasury and Egyptian taxpayers; for in this province, access to the gold of Africa was easier than elsewhere. As we shall see, however, these resources sometimes were insufficient, and then silver was remitted, much to the dissatisfaction of the Hejazi recipients. This preference for gold may be connected with the growing importance in the commercial exchanges of the Arabian peninsula of Indian traders, who usually demanded payment in gold.[6]

In the Middle Ages, Mecca apparently sometimes received supplies from Yemen, but by the time of the Ottoman conquest, Egypt was almost the sole source of grain consumed in the Hejaz. In the later fifteenth century, when the Egyptian economy and particularly its agriculture were in crisis, this should have made food supplies in the Hejaz precarious.[7] Yet contemporary sources apparently did not regard the matter in those terms, or else the public foundations which supplied most of the grains exported to the Hejaz were under less fiscal pressure and therefore more productive than ordinary Egyptian villages. On the other hand, it is assumed that the first century of Ottoman rule over Egypt was a time in which abandoned villages were resettled, and population increased – but this fact is not reflected in the supply situation of Mecca, either: the chronicler Ḳuṭb al-Dīn complained of the declining yields of Egyptian foundation villages. Was Ḳuṭb al-Dīn a partisan of the Mamluks or simply an elderly man who thought everything was better in his youth, or is there something wrong with the assessments of present-day historians?[8]

The overwhelming importance of Egypt in supplying the Hejaz was due to the productivity of the region, and, more importantly, to the fact that water-borne transport was available most of the way. In spite of the atrocious reputation of Red Sea ships and their owners, documented from the twelfth up to the nineteenth century, land transport of major quantities of supplies was avoided as far as possible. This is true even though a large share of the grain was donated and not sold, making minimization of costs theoretically less important than in the commercial sector.[9] Presumably Syrian grain was of limited importance, as there was no Suez Canal – even though Ottoman administrators of the sixteenth century once planned to dig one, and the seventeenth-century traveller Ewliyā Čelebi waxed enthusiastic over the possibility of such an undertaking.[10] The spurts of activity observed in the town of Suez, which possessed a well-frequented port even though its lack of water made permanent habitation difficult, are nevertheless connected with the need to transport grain by ship.

ANCIENT PROBLEMS AND NEW DEPARTURES

Many of the problems of Ottoman administrators had confronted earlier rulers as well, and continue to demand solution today. To begin with, there was the question of supplies. Pilgrims normally were responsible for their own food, mounts and other necessities. But since the pilgrims could not possibly bring all they needed from their often remote home towns, the Ottoman administration had to ensure that they could purchase grain, blankets and riding gear along the way. Water had to be supplied in wells and cisterns along the main routes; this was not only a technical but also a political problem, as the Beduins inhabiting the desert equally needed water, and could not be persuaded to share it without some compensation. Pilgrims whose resources gave out had to be accorded some emergency aid; in the Holy Cities, a degree of provision had to be made for those people who were unable to find shelter for themselves, as well as for the sick. The safety of desert routes and sea lanes could not be procured by individuals at all, even though some groups, particularly the Maghribis, made efforts in that direction.

Certain solutions to these problems had been worked out before the Ottomans arrived, and were modified according to changing circumstances. Thus, even in Mamluk times, the needs of the permanent inhabitants of the Holy Cities had been taken care of by supplying them with grain from public foundations located in Egypt. But by the early sixteenth century these no longer sufficed, and new ones were instituted by Süleymān the Lawgiver, also known as the Magnificent, and some of his successors.[11] A contemporary chronicler indicated that this was due to declining tax yields in Egypt, but it is also possible that the number of pilgrims to Mecca increased during the expansive years of the mid-sixteenth century. A quite new problem, on the other hand, was posed by the Ottoman *'ilmiye* (juridical and religious scholars), who by the sixteenth century had become strongly bureaucratized. The *ḳāḍī*s of Mecca and Medina were high-level functionaries of an imperial state whose centre was situated thousands of miles away. To a member of the religious and juridical establishment of the time, taking a position in the Hejaz might appear as an obstacle to further advancement. To ensure that officials of standing accepted these positions nonetheless, in the seventeenth century former *ḳāḍī*s of the Holy Cities were offered special inducements in the form of seniority rights, which allowed many of these high-level officials rapid promotion after their return from the Hejaz.[12] Thus Ottoman rule meant both novel departures and the continuation of policies devised centuries before, and this imbrication of old and new arrangements will be a recurrent topic of the present study.

PILGRIMS AND RULERS: THE PROBLEM OF LEGITIMACY

All pilgrims, both male and female, were responsible for their own sustenance during the pilgrimage. Therefore, wives could not demand to be taken along as a matter of course if their husbands decided to travel to the Hejaz. In the *ḳāḍī* registers of certain Ottoman towns we occasionally find wives who promised their husbands a piece of property in return for being taken along on the pilgrimage.[13] Sometimes we also encounter the complaints of women who had been abandoned en route in spite of such a payment. Even for wealthy inhabitants of Anatolian or Rumelian towns, a pilgrimage entailed grave financial sacrifices. Wealthy people tried to earn extra money by taking along trade goods, while poor pilgrims were sometimes reduced to beggary. In case of calamities such as droughts, food scarcities and Beduin attacks, many pilgrims perished of thirst, hunger and exposure.

As long as the Ummayad and Abbasid caliphs held power (661–750 and 750–1258 CE), these rulers claimed the protection of the pilgrims as both a duty and a right. This function involved the setting of rules the pilgrims were expected to follow. In extreme cases the caliph might even proclaim that no pilgrimage would take place in a given year, and absolve the faithful from their obligation for the time being. This happened in 1047 and 1048 CE, when a famine in the Hejaz made it impossible to accommodate any further influx of people. But whether such an admission of failure undermined the legitimacy of the ruling caliph remains an open question.[14]

From the sixteenth century onward, the failure of a pilgrimage caravan to reach Mecca and return home safely constituted a severe political liability to the Sultan currently occupying the Ottoman throne. The same applied to major Beduin attacks or uprisings in the Holy Cities. To put it differently, such events occasioned a crisis of legitimacy. Sultanic legitimacy was also upheld by the construction and repair of pious foundations. The mere right to put up public buildings in Mecca and Medina was considered a privilege.[15] The local rulers of Mecca (known as Sherifs due to their descent from the Prophet Muḥammad), who controlled the city's day-to-day destinies from the tenth to the twentieth century, in pre-Ottoman times demanded a fee from every aspiring donor which equalled the sum of money to be spent on the construction itself. This state of affairs indicates a degree of competition between the Sherifs and their suzerains the Sultans residing in Cairo until 1517, and in Istanbul thereafter. Many Mamluk and Ottoman Sultans were surely motivated by reasons of personal piety when they put up magnificent buildings in Mecca and Medina. But, in addition, they were also staking their claim to a preeminent political position in the Holy Cities. Construction activities therefore are treated at some length in this book, which focuses on the ways and means of legitimizing sultanic power through the pilgrimage.

Ottoman Sultans' activities and responsibilities in the Hejaz are discussed in official documents with some frequency, but practically no texts have come to my attention which link the Sultan's role in this matter to his responsibilities as caliph. While the example of certain Mamluk Sultans is sometimes cited, Ottoman documents of the sixteenth and seventeenth centuries never evoke the image of Hārūn al-Rashīd and his consort Zubayda, who built the water conduits that Ottoman Sultans spent much time and money repairing. This is all the more remarkable as the munificence of the royal couple Süleymān the Lawgiver and Khurrem Sultan (Roxolana), who instituted major foundations in Mecca and Medina, would seem to have invited such a comparison. Ottoman official discourse was oriented toward the present and recent past, rather than toward the already very remote history of early Islam.

The annual preparation of the pilgrimage and public construction in the Holy Cities were very costly; and for at least part of the year they also demanded the concerted efforts of numerous Ottoman officials. We may visualize pilgrimage affairs as a set of interlocking mechanisms, whose component parts were meant to balance one another. Thus the Sherif in Ottoman times was allowed many of the trappings of an independent ruler, but his authority was counterbalanced by the Ottoman governor of Jeddah, a highly prestigious official. The Ottoman central administration instituted a complicated set of measures, some of which (such as gifts and tax exemptions) were meant to ensure the support of Beduins residing near the pilgrimage route.[16] Free deliveries of grain secured the cooperation of the year-round inhabitants of the Holy Cities. These measures could only be effective if their application was properly supervised, and the bureaucratic positions needed for this purpose were a source of patronage and therefore a further means of mobilizing support.

When the linkages between different socio-political groups and fields of activity were so numerous, a single failure could make the whole mechanism grind to a standstill. If gifts to Beduin tribes along the desert routes were omitted or not paid in full, or if disputes within the provincial governments of Egypt or Syria prevented the mobilization of support to the caravan from among the desert tribes, the pilgrims had to prepare to protect themselves – and they did not always succeed in doing this.[17] If discontented Beduins attacked the caravans, food scarcities in Mecca and Medina might be the result, and the pilgrims also suffered; for in the case of shortages, the locals often were better placed to secure supplies. Similar problems occurred when the Beduins and their camels were decimated by droughts and epidemics. Not only were needed supplies held back in Jeddah or Yanbu', but desperate men were likely to attack caravans and thus contribute to the general insecurity. The whole set-up could only work if the Ottoman administration kept on channelling resources even from remote territories to the Hejaz and the Red Sea region.

At the same time this mechanism – an exchange of gifts and prestations linking not only Istanbul, but also settlements on the Rumelian frontier with Mecca and Medina – also served as a powerful integrating device. In pre-industrial societies it was usually difficult to set up a governing apparatus affordable by the as yet weakly developed productive forces of the society in question, and yet strong enough to hold together a large territory. Viewed from Istanbul, the state apparatus for the support of the pilgrimage had the great virtue of being flexible and multi-purpose. The Ottoman state protected the pilgrimage because this was an activity demanded by the Muslim religion, and because this protection legitimized the Sultan. At the same time, through the soldiers and foundation officials that were sent to the Hejaz to ensure the safety of pilgrims, the Ottoman state maintained a presence in some of its most remote border provinces. Often control was loose; sometimes it was almost symbolic. The Ottoman state nonetheless managed to maintain itself in the Hejaz with only one fairly brief interruption during the Wahabi wars of the early nineteenth century, and the mechanisms supporting the pilgrimage significantly contributed to this success.

A study dealing with the views and policies of the Ottoman central administration with respect to the hajj inevitably touches upon the images and representations then current in the upper reaches of Ottoman society, and from there diffused into the population at large. The Sultan, as a generous benefactor of the inhabitants of Mecca and Medina and as the organizer and protector of the pilgrimage, constituted a dominant image. This imparts a special colouring to even mundane matters such as the clogged water pipes leading from 'Arafat to Mecca, and a certain unity to the changing policies of Sultans and viziers. Large sums of money were spent upon the pilgrimage every year, and most of these expenditures yielded no economic return. This fact alone indicates that the Sultan's title 'Servant of the Holy Places' was more than a matter of rhetoric, and formed an important aspect of the Ottoman state's legitimation *vis à vis* the society it governed.

SOURCES

A discussion of these issues becomes possible because, by the middle of the sixteenth century, the Ottoman Empire possessed a developed bureaucratic structure and well-functioning state archives.[18] Everyday issues concerning food supplies, military security, public construction and many other matters were documented at length; and the Registers of Important Affairs (Mühimme Defterleri) in the Ottoman archives in Istanbul contain hundreds of sultanic commands concerned in one way or another with pilgrimage affairs. Some of these valuable sources have been used in specialized articles, often published in conference proceedings difficult to locate even for the specialist, but most of the Ottoman archival material concerning the pilgrimage has remained completely untouched so far.

From the beginning of the Registers of Important Affairs in the middle of the sixteenth century down to 1018/1609–10, more than fifty volumes were found to contain material on the hajj, on an average ten rescripts to each register. More often than might be expected, the rescripts preserved in the Mühimme Defterleri contain quantitative data, such as the sums of money spent on various repair and rebuilding projects in and around the Great Mosque of Mecca. Even more significant are the accounts of negotiations which preceded political action in the Hejaz, and which inform us of the manner in which the Ottoman administration bargained for political support in the Red Sea region.

Many pilgrimage-related activities were financed out of the resources of Egypt and Syria, and are thus documented in provincial financial accounts, of which we possess a few samples from late-sixteenth century Egypt and a larger number from seventeenth-century Syria. These documents contain information on the military expenditures connected with the caravan. Particular attention was paid to the soldiers' equipment, such as the cannons regarded as indispensable for any desert campaign. Moreover, the Ottoman administration's attempt to obtain a measure of control over the numerous endowments supporting the poor of Mecca and Medina resulted in the compilation of inventories which list all the relevant foundations existing at the end of the sixteenth century. These inventories mention the revenues each foundation was expected to send to the Hejaz, and thus allow us to assess the contribution of different regions to the hajj effort.

Among narrative accounts, our main source is the pilgrimage report of Ewliyā Čelebi.[19] Strangely enough, this text has all but escaped the attention of historians, although many other sections of his great travel narrative have been studied intensively. On the surface, Ewliyā's account is intended to help pilgrims fulfil their religious duties, and therefore occasionally mentions the prayers to recite at the various stations in a pilgrim's itinerary. Like the other sections of his narrative, however, Ewliyā's account of his pilgrimage concentrates upon a description of the larger cities and their inhabitants. Here are the experiences of a vibrant and adventurous Ottoman gentleman among Beduins, robbers and doughty pashas, and the serious purpose of the pilgrimage does not prevent him from describing humorous or satirical scenes.

A unique narrative account is that of Süheylī.[20] About his life nothing is known, except that he was a Damascene or Syrian living in the seventeenth century. He has left an account, in straightforward Ottoman, of the restoration of the Ka'aba under Sultan Murād IV, after the building had collapsed in a disastrous rainstorm in 1039/1630. Süheylī gives a stone-by-stone account of what happened on the site during the construction period, but also describes the manner in which the Egyptian official Riḍwān Beg, who headed the project, managed to short-circuit all opposition to his way of running the affair; if Süheylī's impression is correct, the Istanbul authorities avoided all direct involvement.

Another important narrative source is the life story of Meḥmed Agha, one of the two full-length biographies of Ottoman architects of the classical period.[21] This text has recently become available in English. The author is a certain Dja'fer Efendi, about whom we know almost nothing except that his father was named Shaykh Behrām and that he belonged to Meḥmed Agha's clientele. In Dja'fer Efendi's account, Meḥmed Agha is described in a style vaguely reminiscent of popular hagiography. For our purposes the biography is important because Meḥmed Agha was responsible for major restorations in Mecca, and Dja'fer Agha presents certain clues concerning the manner in which educated Ottomans regarded projects of this kind. A poem in praise of Medina, which concludes the chapter on Meḥmed Agha's activities in the Holy Cities, is also of interest in this context.

In the following chapter we will accompany some of the more famous pilgrims of the Middle Ages, particularly Ibn Djubayr, the twelfth-century Andalusian who has left a most detailed and lively description of his experiences in the Hejaz. This will give us the opportunity to discuss the major elements of the pilgrimage ritual and the localities which the pilgrims visited. This brief account of medieval pilgrimages is intended, however, as a mere backdrop for a discussion of the sixteenth and seventeenth centuries, in which pilgrims such as Ewliyā Čelebi and Meḥmed Edīb, provincial administrators such as the Egyptian Mamluk Riḍwān Beg, and rulers such as Süleymān the Lawgiver (1520–66) and Aḥmed I (1603–17) constitute the focus of our attention.[22]

1

The Pilgrimage to Mecca in Pre-Ottoman Times

With the expansion of the islamicate empire under the first four caliphs (632–61 CE) and the Ummayad dynasty (661–750 CE), an area reaching from Spain to Iran had come under Muslim sway.[1] The centre of this empire was first located in Medina, but soon moved to Damascus. The conquerors were all Muslims, and many members of the conquered people soon adopted their religion. Even though the islamization of the Iranian ruling class was not complete until the end of the eighth century, a multitude of pilgrims from a variety of linguistic and cultural backgrounds were already arriving in Mecca by the end of the seventh century CE. The area from which pilgrims travelled to Mecca expanded even further during the subsequent centuries: in the tenth century Maḥmūd of Ghazni, famed for the support which he gave to the poet Ferdosi, conquered part of northern India. The islamization of large numbers of Central Asian Turks also took place during this period. In the thirteenth century, the Mongol conquests at first resulted in a setback, as Chingiz Khan and his immediate successors did not adopt Islam, while favouring non-Muslims as a counterweight to entrenched Muslim elites. But, in the long run, the Mongols established in the Middle East did adopt Islam, while the Tatars, who dominated Russia for several centuries, also became Muslims. The islamicate world thus expanded impressively in the aftermath of the Mongol conquests. A fifteenth-century pilgrim crowd in Mecca would have included, apart from Arabs and Iranians, Turks from Anatolia and the Balkans, Tatars from what is today southern Russia, Central Asians, Indians and even the occasional African king.

A POET'S PILGRIMAGE HANDBOOK

For the history of the pilgrimage in the medieval period down to 1517, the accounts of travellers constitute the most important sources. These texts were written with a practical purpose in mind, namely to help a pilgrim find his way to the sanctuaries and perform the pilgrimage rites in a correct and dignified manner. Many of these accounts contain historical information, much of it referring to the major mosques. This historical and art historical detail was not considered in any way frivolous or futile. Events such as the activities of the Prophet and his companions were of major significance to the believer. Therefore the pilgrimage guides should be regarded both as pious works and as descriptions of actions and things located in time and space. Religious motivation and minute attention to mundane detail in no way excluded one another. Unfortunately, the pilgrimage accounts almost never contain information permitting us to estimate the number of people participating.

The poet Naṣīr-i Khosraw, who lived in the eleventh century CE, has left a detailed account of his pilgrimage.[2] Naṣīr-i Khosraw came from the town of Balkh in modern Afghanistan, and undertook the pilgrimage after a major religious experience, which induced him to transform his hitherto rather worldly style of life. While visiting Egypt, he was greatly impressed by the florescence this country experienced under the Fāṭimid caliphs. He converted to the Ismā'īlī version of Shi'ism which the Fāṭimids propounded, and ultimately achieved high rank in the spiritual hierarchy of this faith. Naṣīr-i Khosraw's first visit to Mecca fell in the year 1047, a time of drought and famine. Not only the Hejaz but Iraq was affected, so that outside support was not forthcoming, and no pilgrimage caravan could be sent. The Fāṭimid ruler dispatched an embassy, no more, to escort the covering for the Ka'aba, which even at this early period was sent every year from Cairo, and Naṣīr-i Khosraw formed part of this embassy. After crossing the Red Sea, the travellers visited the Prophet's mosque in Medina, then followed the pilgrimage route through the desert. They found the Holy City all but abandoned, but as the time for the hajj had just arrived, Naṣīr-i Khosraw was able to perform the rites of the pilgrimage. Yet the calamities of that year permitted no more than a short stay; the author admits to having spent but two days in Medina, and he probably remained no longer in Mecca than strictly necessary. He was able to return in later years, however, and his pilgrimage account refers to his second, more leisurely visit.

Naṣīr-i Khosraw's intention is to provide orientation to the pilgrim with no previous experience of the Holy City, and he therefore begins with an account of its geographical location. He then discusses the manner in which the city fits into the landscape. His description leads us to the walls which close off the wadis leading into Mecca and the very few trees growing within the city limits. He also evokes the hills of Ṣafā and Marwa, between which the pilgrims rush back and forth, thereby completing an essential part of the ritual – which is discussed in detail, so that the pilgrim knows where to go at different stages of his visit. Naṣīr's account also includes the hospices of Mecca and provides information about water supplies, presumably with practical purposes in mind. At the same time, he avoids any discussion of his personal religious experience.

After returning from the pilgrimage, Naṣīr-i Khosraw led an adventurous life in the service of the Fāṭimids and their particular variety of Shi'ism; in the end he was killed in the mountains of Badakhshan. But for many other scholars and literati, the pilgrimage was the beginning of a more conventional career. In Neyshapur, during the eleventh and twelfth centuries, scholars often visited Mecca before embarking on careers as teachers and judges. For these people, the pilgrimage was an occasion on which to visit centres of Islamic learning, and pursue their studies in Islamic law and the Prophet's words and deeds (*ḥadīth*). Some of them also taught for a while in the mosques and theological schools (*madrasa*) of the cities they visited, the caliphal city of Baghdad being especially popular in this respect. Upon their return to Neyshapur, these scholars, who were usually the scions of prominent families, had gained additional prestige due to their knowledge and piety, even though the hajj was not an indispensable precondition for an official career.[3] Unfortunately, we do not possess a pilgrimage account by a Neyshapuri traveller. All our information stems from brief notices in the biographical dictionaries of the time, whose aim was not to provide a record of pilgrimage and travel, but to document the reliability of individual scholars in the transfer of religious knowledge throughout the centuries. We therefore have no way of knowing what the Neyshapuri scholars brought home as their most important experiences.

ON THE ROAD TO MECCA

Matters are somewhat different when we turn to the pilgrimage account of Abū'l-Ḥusayn Muḥammad b. Djubayr, usually known as Ibn Djubayr.[4] He was a courtier and secretary in the service of the governor of Granada, and famed for his literary talents. But while participating in court life he had allowed himself to be persuaded to drink wine, and afterwards he much regretted this breach of Islamic law. His patron was moved by Ibn D̲jubayr's scruples, and not only gave him leave to undertake the pilgrimage, but also a generous allowance for his expenses.

Ibn D̲jubayr's pilgrimage was quite dramatic. In 1183 he travelled to the Moroccan city of Ceuta, where he embarked on a Genoese ship which took him to Alexandria in Egypt. He probably chose a Genoese ship because, during the period of the crusades, the Italian cities dominated Mediterranean trade and their ships were thus comparatively secure from pirate attacks. This use of European ships by Muslim pilgrims from the western Mediterranean was to persist throughout the centuries. Even in the seventeenth century, Algerians, Tunisians and Tripolitanians often travelled on English or French ships as far as Alexandria, and then joined the pilgrimage caravan in Cairo.[5] When Ibn D̲jubayr arrived in Egypt, the country was governed by Sultan Saladin (Ṣalāḥ al-Dīn Ayyūbī), who much impressed the author by his energetic rule and generous programme of public construction. Ibn D̲jubayr then journeyed to the Upper Egyptian port of Aydhāb, which at that time was still a major commercial centre, though it was to lose most of its importance by the fifteenth century.[6]

Ibn D̲jubayr's impressions of Aydhab and its inhabitants were mostly negative. An account of the pearl fisheries located near the city he concludes with the words: 'But indeed these folk are closer to wild beasts than they are to men.'[7] His bad impressions were probably prompted by the treatment meted out to pilgrims: the ships on which the latter were made to cross the Red Sea were always perilously overloaded, so that the passengers were squeezed together like chickens in a basket. In this fashion, the owners of the boats attempted to maximize their earnings without any regard for the safety of the passengers: some even said in so many words that the owner only provided the ship, responsibility for safe arrival resting with the passengers alone. Ibn D̲jubayr warns all pilgrims against the use of this route and suggests a long detour as an alternative. A pilgrim coming from the western Mediterranean region is advised to travel first to Baghdad by way of Syria, and continue his journey with the Baghdad pilgrimage caravan. 'And should he find this circling road to be too long, it will be easy in comparison with what he would meet in Aydhab and places like it.'[8] Ibn D̲jubayr also mentions a pilgrimage route near the coast, which led from Egypt to the Sinai and from there to Medina by way of 'Aqaba, and which probably corresponded to the route followed by seventeenth-century Egyptian pilgrims. In Ibn D̲jubayr's time, however, this route was impassable due to a Frankish crusader castle located nearby.

Ibn D̲jubayr's short voyage across the Red Sea was so troublesome that his negative reactions are easy to understand. (On his return journey, he did in fact travel by way of Baghdad, although we do not know whether this decision was motivated by security considerations alone.) Shortly before landing in Jeddah, his ship was caught in a severe storm and swept off its course, so that eight days were needed to cover the short distance between Aydhab and Jeddah. Nor were the pilgrims' troubles at an end once they reached the port of Mecca, which at that time was still a modest settlement with houses built mostly of reeds. Ibn Djubayr complains bitterly about the inhabitants of the Hejaz, who for the most part ruthlessly exploited the pilgrims and used all manner of stratagems to deprive them of their food and money. His worst experiences were with the amir of Mecca. Sultan Saladin at this time was trying to alleviate the difficulties of the pilgrims by assigning the amir grants of money and foodstuffs. In return, the amir was to forgo the customs duties he had hitherto demanded from pilgrims. The amir however viewed the pilgrims as no more than a source of revenue which he was legitimately entitled to exploit, and when Sultan Saladin's grant was slow to arrive, the wealthy traveller from Andalusia seemed as good a substitute as any. Ibn Djubayr was detained, and he and his companions were made to serve as hostages to guarantee the continuing prestation of Egyptian wheat and money. This experience caused Ibn Djubayr to pen a few harsh comments on the Shi'i beliefs of the Hejazis, whom he regarded as heretics. He wished that their lands might be conquered by the Spanish Sunni dynasty of the Muwahhidun/Almohads, and the inhabitants themselves be punished for their numerous sins and heretical practices. Yet even when expressing his anger, Ibn Djubayr uses moderation. Certainly the amir of Mecca acted unjustly and, as a ruler, was much inferior to Sultan Saladin of Egypt. Even so, he remained a descendant of the Prophet Muḥammad and, as such, was respected by the pious Ibn Djubayr.[9]

THE RITES OF THE PILGRIMAGE

On the short trip from Jeddah to Mecca, the company of pilgrims stopped to change into pilgrims' garb (*iḥrām*). This has remained more or less unchanged since the Prophet's time, and for men consists of two seamless pieces of white cloth. One of them covers the loins, reaching down to the knee; the other is worn on the shoulder.[10] The pilgrims wear sandals that leave the instep bare, or, if unavoidable, ordinary shoes. There are no special features to the women pilgrims' garb. The English traveller Richard Burton, who saw mid-nineteenth-century women pilgrims, remarks that the face covering should not touch the face and that the women therefore wore masks made out of palm leaves; but present-day photographs show that almost all pilgrims leave their faces uncovered.[11] Many theologians believe that this uniform garb symbolizes the equality of all believers in the sight of God.

Pilgrim behaviour is governed by a set of rules which emphasize the special status of the Mecca pilgrim. According to many theologians, these rules express the pilgrims' separation from wordly concerns and their complete dedication to God. The most important rule is the prohibition against killing living beings of any kind, apart from the ritual sacrifice at the end of the pilgrimage. Hunting is accordingly forbidden, and armed men through the centuries have expressed their peaceful intentions by entering the Holy City wearing the *iḥrām*. Marital relations and even the conclusion of marriage contracts are likewise prohibited, and the same applies to disputes and discussions. No perfumes are to be used, nor are pilgrims to cut their hair or their nails. Men are required to let their beards grow. Bathing is permitted, and the pilgrims take a bath before donning the *iḥrām*. At the end of the pilgrimage, when the pilgrim, now a hajji, reenters ordinary life, he cuts his hair, beard and nails.

For the rites of pilgrimage to be valid, pilgrims have to make a declaration of intent stating whether they wish to undertake the hajj or merely the lesser pilgrimage or *'umra*. The hajj, which includes a visit to the 'Arafat as mentioned above, can only be performed once a year; most pilgrims coming to Mecca from afar have this purpose in mind. The time for the pilgrimage is the ninth day of the twelfth month of the Islamic lunar year, known as D͟hū al-Ḥid͟jd͟ja. The *'umra* rites are limited to the perimeter of Mecca and can be undertaken at any time of the year.

Ibn D͟jubayr and his companions donned the *iḥrām* at a predetermined spot between Jeddah and Mecca. Pilgrims arriving from other directions also knew exactly where they were to change into pilgrims' clothing. The seventeenth-century Ottoman traveller Ewliyā Čelebi approached Mecca from the direction of Medina and stated that the pilgrims of his time put on the *iḥrām* in a place called Bi'r 'Alī, not very far from Medina.[12] Today, pilgrims who travel to Mecca from Medina change their clothing in D͟hū al-Ḥulayfa, sometimes called Ābār 'Alī, which is probably identical with Ewliyā Čelebi's Bi'r 'Alī. Pilgrims who wish to avoid the discomfort of travelling through the desert dressed only in an *iḥrām* can wear their ordinary clothes until they get to the locality known as Maḳām al-'Umra. They are, however, expected to compensate for this indulgence by a supplementary sacrifice. Pilgrimage guides, who showed the new arrivals the rites and sites as their successors do to the present day, came to Maḳām al-'Umra to meet their charges. In Ewliyā's time there was a pond at this place, which received water by means of a water wheel and was surrounded by rooms in which pilgrims could refresh themselves. This complex was still rather new, having been founded by a governor of Egypt in 1662–3, less than ten years before Ewliyā's visit. Pilgrims approaching the Holy City by sea donned the *iḥrām* in a place about the same distance away from Mecca as the locations in which this ceremony is performed today. Those who arrived from the south changed into the *ihrām* when they first saw Mount Yalamlam, which lies about 54 kilometres to the south of Mecca.

THE KA'ABA

Ibn Djubayr has left a most vivid account of the pious emotions of the pilgrims when they entered Mecca and saw the Ka'aba for the first time.[13] It was already night, and from all sides he heard prayers and invocations of God, particularly the 'here my God, here I am' which forms part of the ritual used on this occasion. After entering the mosque, the pilgrims circumambulated the Ka'aba seven times and touched its covering at a certain place, hoping for an answer to their prayers. If in spite of the crowd it was possible to approach the Black Stone, they kissed it. 'Alī b. Abī Bakr al-Ḥarawī, a contemporary of Ibn Djubayr, has left a matter-of-fact description of the Mecca and Medina sanctuaries.[14] He includes an account of the history of the building, which was a matter of interest to Muslim scholars and on which a considerable body of evidence had therefore been collected. His 'Inventory of Pilgrimage Sites' recounts that the original Ka'aba was built by the Prophet Ibrāhīm. This building remained more or less in its original state until one of the most important tribes of Mecca, namely the Ḳuraysh, rebuilt it in the seventh century, at the time of the Prophet Muḥammad. The latter was himself a member of the Ḳuraysh. It was assumed that he had intervened in person by solving a dispute over precedence which concerned the placing of the Black Stone, one of the most important elements of the structure.

During the civil wars of the early Ummayad period the Ka'aba was burned down. Ibn Zubayr, who for a time reigned as caliph in Mecca, rebuilt and enlarged it. The structure now could be entered by two doors; but when Ibn Zubayr had been deposed by the Ummayad governor al-Ḥadjdjādj, the latter tore down what his defeated rival had constructed and rebuilt the Ka'aba according to what was known of the building which had existed in the time of the Prophet Muḥammad. This new building was smaller than its predecessor, one of the doors had been walled up, and the floor was covered with stones taken from the previous building. The new structure thus was four cubits higher than ground level. This was the building seen by Ibn Djubayr and al-Ḥarawī. In later times, however, the Ka'aba was to undergo extensive repairs, which in one case amounted to a total reconstruction. With this aspect of the Ka'aba's history, which coincided with the reigns of the Ottoman Sultans Aḥmed I and Murād IV (1603–17 and 1623–40), we will deal in Chapter 5.

When Ibn Djubayr visited the Ka'aba, the building was richly decorated with the precious gifts of various Muslim rulers.[15] The door and its posts were made of silver gilt, while the lintel was of pure gold. The interior was decorated in coloured marble, and three teak columns supported the roof. A silver band surrounded the building on the outside. The flat and slightly inclined roof, as well as the walls, were covered with fine tissues of silk and cotton cloth. In Ibn Djubayr's time, the covering of the Ka'aba was green and set off with red bands, decorated with the name of the caliph then reigning, al-Nāṣir li-Dīn Allāh (1180–1225).[16] One of the last Abbasids to play an active political role, he attempted to reorganize the *fityān*, associations of pugnacious young men recruited from among the poorer city dwellers, as a base of his own power. Al-Nāṣir's name, mentioned in highly visible form as servitor of the Holy Places (*khadīm al-ḥaramayn*) was noted by pious visitors like Ibn Djubayr, and his symbolic presence at the Ka'aba considerably enhanced his political reputation. He did not, however, succeed in his attempt to establish himself as ruler of Mecca and Medina in a more concrete political sense.

Ibn Djubayr also visited the stone on which Ibrāhīm supposedly stood when building the Ka'aba. A small annexe had been specially built to accommodate it: Ibn Djubayr informs us that originally it had been kept in a separate wooden building, then transferred to this annexe for its better protection. The Andalusian pilgrim has also left a detailed description of the other buildings in the courtyard of the Great Mosque. Thus, even though his visit was not a part of obligatory pilgrimage ritual, he described the well Zamzam, whose water is highly esteemed and considered a cure for many diseases. After refreshing themselves at the well, Ibn Djubayr and his companions undertook the seven ritual courses between the hills of Ṣafā and Marwa, both located within the city proper. These courses serve as a commemoration of the plight of Hādjar/Hagar, after she had been cast out of the household of Ibrāhīm along with her infant son Ismā'īl, and reduced to a desperate search for water to keep her son and herself alive. With this rite, the *'umra* or lesser pilgrimage was at an end.

As the time of the hajj was as yet several months away, the pilgrims changed into their ordinary clothes, and began their lives as temporary residents of the Holy City. The pilgrims could repeat the *'umra* whenever they felt the desire to do so; in that case, they left the city and travelled to the spot where the regular inhabitants of Mecca donned the *iḥrām*. Being a wealthy man, Ibn D̲jubayr could afford to make himself comfortable while waiting for the month of the pilgrimage. He participated in local festivities and apparently liked the sweetmeats on sale in Mecca, as he confesses that he spent a lot of money in the confectioners' shops. His appartment was well-appointed, and offered a spectacular view of the Great Mosque and the Ka'aba. Ibn D̲jubayr probably used these months to collect the information on the buildings of Mecca which served to make his account into our principal source for the medieval pilgrimage.

THE HAJJ CEREMONIES

The Islamic calendar is lunar; the dates of religious festivals are determined on the basis of statements on the part of credible witnesses, who testify that they did in fact observe the new moon. In 1184, when Ibn D̲jubayr was in the Hejaz, the determination was more difficult than it normally is in the latitude of Mecca. At the time the new moon should have appeared, the sky was overcast and nothing was visible. On the other hand, many pilgrims ardently wished for the ritual 'station' on 'Arafat (*wakfa*), the plateau to the east of Mecca, to take place on a Friday. For a saying attributed to the Prophet Muḥammad promises that whenever this central ritual of the pilgrimage, which takes place on the ninth day of D̲h̲ū al-Ḥid̲jd̲ja, falls on a Friday, the pilgrims can expect much greater blessings than in an ordinary year. Therefore quite a few people came forward claiming to have seen the new moon, even though, physically speaking, this was an impossibility. The *ḳāḍī* of Mecca insisted on rejecting their testimonies, and was not exactly gentle with the over-zealous witnesses.[17] Apparently he commented that 'those Maghribis [several of the claimants were Maghribis] are deranged. A hair escapes from their eyelashes, they see something, and immediately they think it to be the new moon.' Ibn D̲jubayr approved of the *ḳāḍī*'s attitude, as he thought the pilgrimage was not amenable to what he felt to be frivolous manipulation. In his view, the pilgrims' devotion was bound to suffer if even minor details were not handled with the appropriate seriousness. In the end the *ḳāḍī* devised a compromise which satisfied both sides. He ordered the ritual station on the 'Arafat to begin on Friday afternoon and continue into Saturday.

Just before the day appointed for the *wakfa*, new groups of pilgrims entered the Holy City. Ibn D̲jubayr mentions the Yemenis and a former prince of Aden recently deposed.[18] On the 7 Dhū al-Ḥidjdja a messenger arrived from the Iraqi pilgrimage caravan which was still on its way. Thereupon the *ḳāḍī* preached a solemn sermon in front of the pilgrims assembled in the city, in which he explained the ritual of the hajj. He announced that on the next day the caravan would move to Mina, the first stop on the way to ʿArafat. On Thursday a large crowd set out; however the pilgrims hurried more than seemed desirable to Ibn Djubayr, as there was a constant danger of being attacked by Beduin marauders. As western Catholics of the fourteenth century felt few scruples when they enslaved Greek Christians, and many Beduins, even though they had been Muslims for centuries, did not hesitate to rob unwary pilgrims on their way to and from the sanctuary. Travellers who attempted to resist were often killed. Whoever claimed to rule the Hejaz, therefore, above everything else needed to protect the pilgrims from attack. According to Ibn Djubayr's testimony, the ruling amir of Mecca was quite successful in this task – which legitimized him in the eyes of the Andalusian traveller and, no doubt, in the view of a wider public.

The pilgrims spent their first night after leaving Mecca in an uninhabited locality called Muzdalifa where there was an abundant supply of water. This was due to the munificence of Hārūn al-Rashīd's wife Zubayda, who in the ninth century had built a number of water reservoirs in this place. The ʿArafat plateau was reached the next day. At this locality, surmounted by the 'Mount of Mercy' (Djabal al-Raḥmat), the pilgrims prayed in a number of mosques or at prayer niches in the open air. Here the assembly which constitutes the core of the pilgrimage took place. Ibn Djubayr says very little about this event, so that we have to supplement his story with other, much more recent information. According to the Ottoman traveller Ewliyā Čelebi, who participated in the 'station' at ʿArafat in 1672, the pilgrims prayed in the Mosque of Ibrāhīm and waited on the plateau for the *ḳāḍī* of Mecca to begin his solemn sermon.[19] In Ewliyā's time, the pilgrims assembled according to their region of origin; the Anatolians to the west, the Abyssinians, Yemenis, Iraqis and Hejazis at other prearranged places. This custom was already centuries old when Ewliyā Čelebi wrote, for Ibn Djubayr also noted that the Yemenis assembled by tribe, and that no tribe ever transgressed on the territory assigned to another.[20] Both Ibn Djubayr and Ewliyā were full of admiration for the large number of pilgrims who had assembled on ʿArafat. Ibn Djubayr particularly mentions the non-Arabs of high rank, both men and women. But unfortunately neither of these two writers, nor any other travellers from the time before the nineteenth century, have made an attempt to estimate the number of participants.

To ensure the validity of the *waḳfa* on 'Arafat, it was necessary to adhere to certain rules. The territory known as 'Arafat, where the pilgrims absolutely needed to sojourn, was set off from the outside world by a line of boundary stones. The time factor was also significant, as apparent from the dispute between the *ḳāḍī* of Mecca and the over-zealous Maghribis. It was essential that the pilgrims arrive at 'Arafat on time, that is while the preacher was still speaking. Ewliyā recounts how for that very reason his own caravan pressed forward in hurried marches, spending only the briefest possible time in Medina. That year, the Basra caravan was also in trouble; 1671–2 fell in a period of widespread political tension, and in such years Beduin tribes tended to be especially aggressive. The Basra pilgrimage caravan was set upon, but reinforcements sent from Mecca helped to repel the attackers. The unlucky caravan almost missed the meeting at 'Arafat. 'They [the Basra pilgrims] entered [the site of 'Arafat] at the boundary stones [marking off the site in the direction of] Iraq. They also brought along their dead to the *waḳfa*. Thank God, they were able to perform their pilgrimage: If they had arrived but a short time later, it would have been invalid.'[21]

At the beginning of the meeting, many people called out 'Here my God, here I am', and Ewliyā says that this continued for an hour. According to the same source, the *ḳāḍī*'s sermon concerned the further course of the pilgrimage. The pilgrims were instructed how to behave when sacrificing and throwing stones at the rocks of Mina, which in this context symbolize the devil. When the sermon ended, the pilgrims hurriedly left the site of the meeting. As it was already turning dark, this procedure gave rise to a certain amount of confusion. At Muzdalifa the pilgrims assembled for another ritual 'station', which this time took place by night and was particularly impressive due to the many candles lit by the Khorasanis. The pilgrims collected pebbles which they would need the next day for the stoning of the devil. Most pilgrims left Muzdalifa by night so as to perform the morning prayer in Mina and subsequently throw their seven stones against a specially designated rock. After that, those who could afford it sacrificed an animal, and thereby fulfilled their religious obligations for the day.

Ibn D̲j̲ubayr does not tell us how the pilgrims spent their free time in Mina.[22] Today it is customary for pilgrims to return to Mecca, which is close by, and to circle the Ka'aba seven times (*ṭawāf al-ifāḍa*) before taking off the pilgrim's garb.[23] The men shave, and everybody returns to Mina dressed in his or her best clothes. However, both Ibn D̲j̲ubayr and Ewliyā Čelebi are describing pilgrimages performed in unsettled times, in which people may have put off their visit to the Ka'aba to the time of their final return to the Holy City.

In Mina a large fair was held at this time. Ewliyā Čelebi, who calls this place 'Mine pazarı' ('the market of Mina'), records that many goods were on sale here, 'from precious pearls to the coarsest of glass'. Ewliyā's story is confirmed by an anonymous source from the sixteenth century. The Bahrain pearls, which Ibn Djubayr and Ewliyā both mention, were the most remarkable speciality of this fair. In addition a good many foods and beverages were on sale. The pilgrims, who during their stay in Mina were excused from most of the restrictions which they had imposed on themselves upon approaching the Holy City, now visited with one another and made merry. On the two following days the lapidations were repeated, most pilgrims throwing forty-nine stones in all. Ibn Djubayr explains that originally the pilgrims had spent an additional day in Mina, further extending the lapidations, but in his time the ritual had been abridged because of the unsafe conditions obtaining in the area.

When the pilgrims reentered the city after an absence of several days, they performed the concluding rite of their pilgrimage, namely the final circumambulation of the Ka'aba. For this occasion, Ibn Djubayr changes his perspective, thereby contributing to the liveliness of his tale. While up to this point he has recounted mainly his own experiences, he now concentrates upon the behaviour of his fellow pilgrims. He was particularly interested in the Khorasanis, who must have seemed most exotic both to him and to his readers, in all likelihood mainly educated Andalusians and North Africans. We learn that on this occasion the covering of the Ka'aba had to be pulled up, as otherwise it would certainly have been ruined by the pilgrims who threw themselves upon the covering and clung to it. This form of devotion was foreign to Ibn Djubayr, but he describes it with equanimity and tolerance. This is particularly obvious when he discusses the women pilgrims, who threw themselves into the crowd, hoping for a chance to visit the interior of the Ka'aba, and reemerged rather the worse for wear.[24] Ibn Djubayr also comments favourably on the Khorasani preachers, who could speak most impressively both in Arabic and Persian. He also approved of the Khorasanis' custom of soliciting questions from the congregation after their sermons; many of these question-and-answer sessions developed into an outright examination of the preacher by his listeners.

IBN DJUBAYR'S IDEAS CONCERNING THE PILGRIMAGE

In the course of his narrative, Ibn Djubayr quite frequently discusses his own reactions to different aspects of the pilgrimage. We already know that he had a strong sense of reality, and did not believe that manipulation for pious ends was a good thing. As a highly educated man, Ibn D̲j̲ubayr must have known very well that many religious scholars believed pilgrims derived greater blessings if they performed the *wak̲fa* on a Friday, yet he insists that God's mercy can be expected by any pilgrim. To put it differently, Ibn D̲j̲ubayr recommends that the pilgrims use the opportunity provided by the pilgrimage to reflect upon God's mercy, and avoid being overly anxious about the details of the ritual. He thus remarks that the Beduins of the Yemen lack even an elementary knowledge of the Islamic ritual, but possess an abundance of good intentions.[25] Ibn D̲j̲ubayr concludes his account of Beduin religious life, which includes an enumeration of the many mistakes these people make when saying their prayers, with a saying ascribed to the Prophet Muḥammad: 'Teach them ritual prayer, and they will teach you the prayer of the heart.'[26]

On a more personal level, Ibn D̲j̲ubayr also discusses his religious experiences in the course of the pilgrimage. He praises the night when his caravan first entered Mecca, and thanks his Creator for the grace of pilgrimage, for now he feels included in the community of those who may hope for the intercession of the Prophet Ibrāhīm. The humble invocations by which pilgrims acknowledged their being in God's presence are mentioned as an awesome experience, and the nightly prayers held in the Great Mosque during the fast of Ramadān made a profound impression on Ibn D̲j̲ubayr.

Concerning the Prophet's miracles, Ibn D̲j̲ubayr occasionally mentions them and does not express any doubts on that score. But it is obvious from his account of the Meccan sanctuaries outside the Great Mosque, often associated with the personal and family history of the Prophet, that miracles play a very subordinate role in his style of piety. As to assorted practices pilgrims engage in for the sake of obtaining blessings (*baraka*), Ibn D̲j̲ubayr is quite critical. Thus he describes pilgrims who try to pass through a narrow opening in a cave because the Prophet allegedly did the same, and remarks that they are likely to get themselves into trouble: apart from looking ridiculous, trying to wriggle out of the narrow opening is painful as well.[27]

At the core of the Meccan pilgrimage rituals there survive pre-Islamic practices which have interested both scholars of the early Islamic period and twentieth-century specialists in comparative religious studies. These rituals have been transformed by the Prophet Muḥammad and his immediate successors, however, and reinterpreted in a strictly monotheistic sense. Ibn D̲j̲ubayr's account permits us to see how a pious and learned person of the twelfth century who possessed a strong critical sense, viewed the rituals of the pilgrimage. Pilgrims of his calibre took the hajj as a way toward a more profound understanding of their monotheistic religion. Ibn D̲j̲ubayr stressed the importance of an interior life, and had no time for an overly ritualistic approach. Certainly the author, who was a courtier in addition to being a scholar, came from an elite milieu, and his understanding of the pilgrimage may well have been a minority phenomenon. But we are fortunate that at least one writer of the twelfth century has been so explicit about his thoughts and feelings.

THE PROPHET'S MOSQUE IN MEDINA

The Prophet Muḥammad died in Medina in 624 CE, in the year 10 according to the Muslim reckoning. He was buried in his former dwelling place, soon to be rebuilt as a mosque.[28] Later, other important personages of early Islamic history were buried there, including his first two successors Abū Bakr (reigned 632–4) and 'Umar (reigned 634–44). During the years immediately following the death of the Prophet, Medina was the capital of the Islamic empire which was then expanding rapidly. But with the reign of Mu'āwiya (661–80) the empire's political centre moved to Syria and Iraq, and Medina became a city inhabited by religious scholars, who developed and elaborated Islamic law. Throughout the history of Islam the city has held a particular attraction for pious people. Although a visit to Medina does not form part of the Islamic pilgrimage ritual, many visitors to the Hejaz use the opportunity to pray at the Prophet's grave, either when travelling to Mecca or else on the return trip.

Naṣīr-i Khosraw, when visiting the Hejaz in 1048, also paid a visit to the Prophet's mosque in Medina, and has left a brief description of the sanctuary.[29] In his time, the building consisted mainly of the following parts: a chamber with an adjacent court, an enclosed and partly roofed area in which the Prophet's grave was located, the preacher's chair and the hall named the 'Garden' (*Rawḍa*) which separates the preacher's chair from the Prophet's grave. Naṣīr-i Khosraw even mentions the net, which closed off the unroofed parts of the mosque, so birds could not get in. But we possess even older descriptions, one of the most remarkable being that of Ibn 'Abd Rabbih, written in the tenth century. Ibn 'Abd Rabbih relies almost completely on his own observations and seems to have paid but scant attention to the work of his predecessors. He came from the same region as Ibn Djubayr, namely Andalusia, and was a courtier like his successor, active in the entourage of the caliph 'Abd al-Raḥmān III; to his contemporaries he was mainly known as a poet and literary man.

Ibn 'Abd Rabbih's description is extremely careful and detailed, so that his text has often been used by modern scholars attempting to reconstruct the appearance of the Prophet's mosque in the early centuries of its existence.[30] The author gives an account of the columns carrying the roof of the gallery and of the windows, which he compares to those of the Great Mosque of Cordoba; he also cites the text of the inscription which decorated one of the mosque walls. In Ibn 'Abd Rabbih's time a mirror hung on the mosque wall, which purportedly had belonged to 'Aysha, the Prophet's favourite wife, who was very active in politics after her husband's death. The preacher's chair used by the Prophet struck the observer by its simplicity, lacking any adornment or special elegance. The platform used by the preacher had been closed off by a slab of wood, so that the seat of the Prophet was not used by the preachers of Ibn 'Abd Rabbih's time. The author did not doubt the authenticity of the chair, but with respect to the other mementoes preserved in the mosque, he merely comments 'and God knows best'.[31]

The most detailed description of the Prophet's mosque dates from the concluding years of the fifteenth century.[32] Its author is the Egyptian scholar al-Samhūdī, and it is a critical and carefully documented account. Al-Samhūdī has located a great many sources concerning the mosque and compares them so as to arrive at a realistic reconstruction. He also discusses the buildings originally located in the vicinity, which in the course of various building campaigns were included in the mosque itself. We find a moving description of the weeping and lamentations with which the pious people of Medina reacted to the decision of the caliph Walīd b. 'Abd al-Mālik (reigned 705–15) who had the modest habitations of the Prophet's wives torn down to make room for the enlarged mosque. Apparently many devout people felt that these dwellings should have been preserved to demonstrate the extreme modesty and lack of ostentation practised by the Prophet, at a time when all the treasures of this world were readily accessible to him.[33]

From al-Samhūdī's description we understand that in Ummayad times, the Great Mosque of Medina was built of hewn stone. The stones were held together by the application of plaster, and several loads of shells had been used in the decoration of the building. Only the roof was made of gilt palm wood. In the eighth century the mosque did not yet possess any minarets; the latter were added later and had to be rebuilt several times because of lightning damage. When al-Samhūdī wrote, however, little remained of the mosque of Ummayad times, as it had been struck by two devastating fires, in 1256 and 1481. After the first fire only casual repairs could be undertaken due to lack of means, for two years after this event, in 1258, the Mongols conquered Baghdad, killed the Abbasid caliph and destroyed the city. With no help forthcoming from that quarter, major repairs had to wait for the Mamluk Sultans of Egypt to stabilize their position. Repairs were finally undertaken by Sultan Ḳā'it Bāy (reigned 1468–96), who was also active as a builder in Mecca. In Medina, Ḳā'it Bāy twice sponsored the rebuilding of the Prophet's mosque, as the fire of 1481 destroyed most of what had been built a few years previously. This Sultan had the wooden dome over the Prophet's grave taken down and a cupola of stone erected in its place. Little trace remains of Ḳā'it Bāy's buildings today, as a further campaign of restoration, or indeed rebuilding, was undertaken in the time of the Ottoman Sultan 'Abd ül-Medjīd (reigned 1839–61). The medieval mosque therefore needs to be reconstructed from written sources.

Ibn 'Abd Rabbih had little to say on the grave of the Prophet proper, which in his time bore only modest decorations. This is in accordance with the views of certain Islamic schools of law, which recommend this simplicity even today. Ibn 'Abd Rabbih simply discussed the prayers to be performed at the Prophet's grave, and recommended that worshippers observe a certain decorum. Particularly, pilgrims should not cling to the grave, behaviour which in the author's view is characteristic of the ignorant. When visiting the Prophet's grave, the principal concern was to offer prayers to God, even though visitors were free to invoke the intercession of the Prophet as well.

THE HOLY CITIES IN THE LATER MIDDLE AGES

For the late Middle Ages, that is the period preceding the Ottoman conquest of Egypt in 1517, we possess a comprehensive history of Medina and a series of Meccan chronicles. These texts document the tensions between the Mamluk Sultans of Egypt, who exercised suzerainty over the Sherifs of Mecca (functioning as local rulers), and other important princes of the Islamic world. These rivalries sometimes had repercussions upon ceremonial life in the Holy Cities.[34] Thus, in 1424–34, the Egyptian Sultan Barsbāy refused the demands of Shāhrukh, son and successor of Timur Lenk, who repeatedly requested the privilege of being permitted to donate a covering for the Ka'aba. Meḥmed the Conqueror (reigned 1451–81) was likewise refused when he made a similar offer. Difficulties of this kind had a long tradition: a full century earlier, amir Čūbān (died 1327), one of the most powerful figures at the court of the Ilkhanid Abū Sa'īd, had undertaken to construct a waterpipe to alleviate the lack of water in Mecca, which had grown ever more serious with the passage of time.[35] Amir Čoban donated 50,000 gold coins for this purpose. Conditions of work on this line, which led from Ḥunayn over 'Arafat to the Holy City, were reputed highly satisfactory, and many Beduins, including their womenfolk, accepted employment on the construction site. Work was completed within four months, but the reaction of the Egyptian Sultan to a project initiated by a rival court was decidedly negative. Luckily a skilled negotiator, who previously had been in charge of the construction site, managed to make the whole affair palatable to the Egyptian Sultan. The latter contented himself with the construction of a second pipeline next to the one built by amir Čūbān, without taking revenge for the flouting of his authority.

In addition to the rulers of Egypt and Iran, the Sultan of Yemen occasionally claimed suzerainty over Mecca.[36] Thus the Sultan al-Mudjāhid performed the pilgrimage several times and built a major complex of pious foundations in Mecca. But while sojourning in the Holy City on his second pilgrimage in 1351, he was arrested because he insisted upon his rights as an independent sovereign, *vis à vis* both the Sherifs of Mecca and the envoy of the Egyptian Sultan. The next years were filled with extraordinary adventures. Due to his arrest, al-Mudjāhid was unable to complete the requirements for his second pilgrimage. Instead he was brought to Egypt, where the ruling Sultan treated him in a manner befitting his station and soon released him. Al-Mudjāhid was already on his way back to Yemen when the Egyptian authorities changed their minds and decided to hold the Yemeni ruler captive as a possible rival. This time he was held in a castle not far from the Dead Sea, but soon released when a former fellow prisoner, who had once again achieved a powerful position in Cairo, interceded for him. While in this region, al-Mudjāhid demonstrated his piety by visiting the Muslim sanctuaries of Jerusalem and Khalīl al-Raḥmān (Hebron) and ultimately managed to return to Yemen by way of the Red Sea (1352). The chronicler who reported all these events evidently felt some sympathy for al-Mudjāhid. He reports that the offended ruler took revenge by prohibiting all trade with Mecca, which must have increased the perennial supply problems of the Holy City. Unfortunately the account does not tell us whether al-Mudjāhid really had the intention of annexing Mecca, or whether these designs had merely been imputed to him by his opponents. Be that as it may, the Sultans of Yemen certainly attempted to establish a presence in Mecca; thirty years after the adventures of al-Mudjāhid, a new conflict ensued, when a Yemeni ruler sent a covering for the Ka'aba, a gesture which the Egyptian rulers apparently regarded as their own exclusive prerogative.

During the fifteenth century, the last hundred years of Mamluk domination over Mecca, several large-scale building projects were undertaken. A fire which had broken out in a hospice near the Great Mosque had spread to the northern and western galleries of the sanctuary, and 130 columns had collapsed.[37] This part of the Meccan Great Mosque was completely rebuilt – even the foundations were dug out and reinforced. The new columns consisted of several pieces of stone held together by iron rods and crowned by marble capitals. The latter carried a wooden roof, gilt and painted in bright colours. The lack of suitable timber in the Hejaz greatly retarded the completion of the project, however, as supplies had to be imported from India or Asia Minor.

In the third quarter of the fifteenth century the Egyptian Sultan Ḳā'it Bāy and his amirs sponsored further large construction projects, many of them quite controversial.[38] Thus Ibn al-Zamin, a close friend of the Sultan, built a hospice which created a serious obstruction on the way between Ṣafā and Marwa, which all pilgrims had to traverse many times in the course of their sojourn. A *ḳāḍī* of Mecca and other religious scholars protested in Cairo against the project, but Ibn al-Zamin had the ear of the Sultan, and the hospice was built anyway. The authorities were so worried about public disturbances, however, that construction could only go on by night.

Sultan Ḳā'it Bāy also built a theological school and a hospice in the immediate vicinity of the Great Mosque, and several private houses and hospices were torn down for that purpose.[39] The new complex, named As͟hrafiya, was built of multi-coloured marble and contained a library; due to the negligence of librarians and users, however, a few decades later the latter had lost many of its books. An Indian scholar named Ḳuṭb al-Dīn, who lived in Mecca in the sixteenth century, was in charge at that time and in his chronicle of the city of Mecca has left a graphic account of the desolate conditions he found at the beginning of his tenure of office. He also describes how he attempted to improve them, tracking down the people who had borrowed library books and in some cases securing their return. He also had many damaged volumes restored and rebound. To repair damage to the building fabric was apparently not within his power, however.[40] As we will see in the following chapters, the Ottoman Sultans of the sixteenth century were more concerned about establishing new foundations than restoring old ones. The only exceptions to this rule were the Great Mosques of Mecca and Medina.

Ḳuṭb al-Dīn has also left an account of the manner in which the Ottomans took over the Hejaz in 1517.[41] In the first stages of Ottoman rule, changes were limited in scope. At this time the Holy Cities were already totally dependent on Egyptian foodstuffs.[42] As a result, even short interruptions of the connection between the two regions, which occasionally occurred in the early sixteenth century owing to Portuguese incursions into the Red Sea, led to panics and uncontrolled price rises. Given this situation, the Sherif of Mecca sent his young son to Cairo to offer the Ottoman Sultan Selīm I (reigned 1512–20) suzerainty over the Hejaz. Selīm I accepted this proposition and, for the stretch of four centuries, Mecca and Medina became part of the Ottoman Empire. The following chapters will deal with the structures and networks which during the first two centuries of Ottoman rule ensured the survival of pilgrims and Hejazis. The interplay of long-term structures and *ad hoc* improvisation will constitute the dominant theme of our account.

2

Caravan Routes

With the Ottoman takeover of the Hejaz, the two Holy Cities came to depend on the protection of a Sultan whose capital and principal scenes of activity were much more remote, both geographically and in terms of language, than had been the case in Mamluk times. Ties between the Holy Cities on the one hand and Damascus and Cairo on the other continued to exist, but Cairo was now no more than a provincial centre. Major political decisions, such as the institution and occasionally deposition of the Sherifs of Mecca, were from now on made in Istanbul. Officials of the Sultan residing in the Ottoman capital also decided whether new buildings were to be erected in the Holy Cities, or whether the grain supply to the Hejaz should be increased by adding further Egyptian villages to the public foundations inherited from Mamluk times. However the caravan routes linking the Hejaz to Cairo and Damascus in no way lost their previous importance, for connections between the Holy Cities and Istanbul continued to pass through either one of these two provincial capitals. From Alexandria, the seaport of Cairo, a short and under normal circumstances reasonably comfortable voyage took the traveller to Rhodes, an Ottoman possession since Sultan Süleymān had conquered the island from the Knights of St John in 1522. From Damascus Istanbul was reached by way of a long but well-travelled caravan route, which passed through northern Syria and then entered Anatolia by a narrow defile between the mountains and the Mediterranean. Caravans stopped in Adana, then crossed the Taurus Mountains and the dry central Anatolian steppe before the next major staging post, Konya. Ultimately the Sea of Marmara was reached, and skirting it the caravans came to Üsküdar, which in the sixteenth century was still an independent town and not merely a suburb of Istanbul. If the extant pilgrimage accounts reflect the real preferences of travellers, most pilgrims coming from Anatolia and Rumelia journeyed by way of Damascus.

The present chapter deals with the two official pigrimage caravans, which every year left Cairo and Damascus for the Hejaz. In addition, a Yemeni pilgrimage caravan must have existed, but almost no information on this matter can be found in the Ottoman records. At certain times a separate caravan from Basra on the Persian Gulf crossed the Arabian peninsula from east to west, but political conflicts between Ottomans and Safawids often closed this route. Certain pilgrims doubtless reached Mecca on their own, without the protection of an officially sponsored caravan. The Maghribis, particularly, often travelled in this fashion, and the same probably applied to many pilgrims living on the Arabian peninsula.[1] Since these unofficial caravans have left few traces in Ottoman government records, however, very little is known about them.

The two main caravans, on the other hand, are abundantly documented. We can trace the history of the Cairo and Damascus caravans back to the time of the Abbasid caliphs: Hārūn al-Ras͟hīd (reigned 786–809), a contemporary of the Byzantine empress Irene (reigned 797–802) and Charlemagne (reigned 768–814), performed the pilgrimage nine times.[2] While most of his successors did not travel to Mecca personally, they regularly sent high-level officials to represent them at the pilgrimage. The pilgrimage caravans that we know from the Ottoman documentation of the sixteenth and seventeenth centuries, however, took shape under the Mamluk Sultans, between 1250 and 1517. Sixteenth- and seventeenth-century authors, dealing with the Ottoman Sultans in their role of protectors to the pilgrimage, have often measured Ottoman performance against the yardstick of what had been done, really or presumedly, by their Mamluk predecessors. This explains why Ottoman Sultans adhered as closely as they could to the practices connected with the names of Ḳā'it Bāy (reigned 1468–96) and Ḳānṣūh al-G͟hūrī (reigned 1501–16).

THE CAIRO PILGRIMAGE CARAVAN

The Cairo caravan has frequently been described. One of the most valuable accounts was written by the Egyptian 'Abd al-Ḳādir al-D͟jazarī in the middle of the sixteenth century.[3] This writer was able to draw upon extensive personal and family experience with respect to the administration of pilgrimage caravans, as both he and his father had worked in this line. As al-D̲j̲azarī's account has been published and extensively studied, a summary of its main points will be sufficient for our present purpose.

Down to 1406–7, there was no fixed order in the Cairo caravan, which resulted in a good deal of confusion when crossing narrow defiles. An order of precedence was then instituted, which in al-D̲j̲azarī's opinion had become unavoidable due to the large number of pilgrims. It had the disadvantage, however, that the better-off among them, who were able to afford faster mounts, secured places in the front or middle of the caravan, leaving the poorer pilgrims in the caravan's rear, the most vulnerable section. The caravan commander was in charge of assigning the pilgrims their places; he normally joined the caravan at ʿAd̲j̲rūd, five stops away from Cairo and not far from Suez. Apparently the officials who planned the trip back in Cairo believed that the really difficult part of the desert journey only began at this spot. Al-D̲j̲azarī describes the caravan as divided up into several subsections, which he calls *ḳaṭār*s. Their number varied with the size of the caravan; in a large one, there might be as many as nine.[4]

At the very head of the caravan travelled the 'desert pilots', who were often Beduins and thoroughly familiar with the stretch of desert to be traversed. They were followed by water carriers and notables. Next came the cash supplies carried by the caravan, namely donations to the inhabitants of Mecca and Medina provided by the public foundations instituted by different Mamluk Sultans, along with subsidies to be paid to Beduins providing various services to the pilgrims (see Chapters 3 and 4). The cash was guarded by soldiers, and the caravan's artillery travelled in the immediate vicinity. A troop of soldiers had special orders to march on that side of the caravan which faced not the Red Sea but the mountains, which on this route are often located close to the seashore. Since navigation on the Red Sea with its many coral reefs was highly dangerous, an attack from that direction was much less likely. The next section of the caravan consisted of another treasury, which belonged to the Mamluk Sultans and presumably was meant for the ordinary expenditures of the caravan. Sharpshooters armed with bows and arrows as well as torchbearers were responsible for the security of this section of the caravan. Merchants carrying valuable goods usually travelled close to the treasuries, while ordinary pilgrims made up the rear.

Among the numerous officials accompanying the Cairo caravan, the commander's secretary occupied a key position.[5] He had to be consulted whenever important decisions were taken, and he was responsible for the payment of subsidies to the Beduins who travelled with the caravan and thus ensured its safety. A *ḳāḍī* settled disputes among the pilgrims. Al-Djazarī liked to praise past times in contrast to a present which he regarded as much less brilliant; he claimed that the office of caravan *ḳāḍī* had lost much of its previous lustre and now was almost always filled by Turks. Quite possibly his opinion is coloured by his own disappointment with his career. After all, he was the descendant of a family well-established both in Cairo and Medina, yet had to content himself with a fairly modest position. The caravan *ḳāḍī* was accompanied by a number of subordinates. Pilgrims wishing to conclude contracts or make their wills needed men of irreproachable lifestyle to act as witnesses; moreover, these men had to be found readily if ever their testimony was needed. To ensure that they were available in such cases, al-Djazarī's father had begun to assign them stipends.

In addition to his secretary the caravan commander employed a second scribe, and this office was filled by al-Djazarī's father and later by the author himself. Al-Djazarī thought that the scribes had a most important role to play, since the Mamluks – in contrast to later Ottoman practice – never allowed an amir to act as caravan commander more than once; therefore his scribes were responsible for ensuring continuity. Other officials were in charge of supervising the camels and horses as well as the official stores of food, fodder and water. The pilgrimage caravan of the late Mamluk and early Ottoman periods thus should not be envisaged as a simple crowd of pilgrims and soldiers. It appears more reasonable to regard it as a well-organized enterprise, in some ways comparable to an army on the march, with its commander as a temporary ruler holding court, and accompanied by his treasuries, scribes, subordinate officers, soldiers and Beduin auxiliaries.

THE ORGANIZATION OF THE DAMASCENE CARAVAN

For the Syrian caravan we do not possess an account even remotely comparable to the work of al-Djazarī. However, a mass of official documents have survived, including a large number of sultanic rescripts from the second half of the sixteenth century, and a significant number of account books covering the years 1600 to 1683. The Damascus caravan resembled its Cairo counterpart in possessing a well-defined structure, which did not change much in the course of the period under investigation. Presumably the Ottomans also followed Mamluk models quite closely in this case.

Syrian provincial budgets of the seventeenth century routinely contain figures concerning expenditures on behalf of the officials forming part of the caravan.[6] A number of officials travelling with the pilgrimage were assigned camels for their journeys. The numbers of mounts varied according to the rank of the official involved. We thus gain an idea of the caravan hierarchy. As an example, we may study the records of 1636–7: the commander was granted the use of eight camels, while his substitute, the *ketkhüdā* had two at his disposal.[7] It was the latter's job to distribute the pilgrims among the different subsections of the caravan; if the Damascus caravan resembled its Egyptian counterpart, this task was not always an easy one. In addition there was an amir in charge of stopping points, also assigned two camels; this official probably coordinated the movements of the different subsections of the caravan whenever the latter settled down to rest or began a new stretch of the journey. This, too, was probably a difficult job: at the end of a long day, many people – all thirsty, tired and nervous, and for the most part armed – competed for scanty water supplies, and the amir had to ensure that disputes did not degenerate into violence. The Master of the Stables (*mirākhōr*) was in charge of the horses and camels of soldiers and officials; he also helped the *ketkhüdā* of the commander to keep the caravan in order. There was also an *emīn* in charge of finances; he had a scribe at his disposal, and thereby ranked lower than his colleague in charge of supplies, who was aided by two scribes. But possibly the difference in this case was not a matter of rank, but simply reflected the fact that supplies were more cumbersome to handle than cash. The Damascus caravan also possessed a *ḳāḍī* and a supervisor (*nāẓır*). The latter's duties remain unspecified; however, the supervisor was a high-ranking official with two camels at his disposal, and thereby comparable to the *ḳāḍī*. He also required the services of a scribe. There was also a supervisor in charge of 'the poor'. It was probably the supervisor's job to administer the alms to be distributed among poor pilgrims on the Sultan's behalf; but this official, along with prayer leaders and muezzins, only possessed a comparatively modest status. All these men were assigned a single camel per person. The same applied to the official who confiscated heirless estates for the Sultan's treasury, and also to musicians, messengers and other service personnel.

Seventeenth-century accounts permit us to identify yet other officials. The Damascene caravan was accompanied by several *poursuivants*, who as a group were granted five camels, an official who administered the gifts of the Sultan to the population of Mecca and Medina and a police officer (*ṣūbashı*). When the caravan was about to leave Istanbul, the official dealing with largesse to the Hejaz was received by the ruler in a private audience. But in the older account books his office does not even occur, possibly because his expenses were paid from Istanbul directly and therefore did not concern the finance department of Damascus. While most officials accompanying the caravan were chosen from among the notables of Syria, the official in charge of imperial largesse directly represented the Ottoman Sultan.

CEREMONIES ACCOMPANYING DEPARTURES AND RETURNS

In the Ottoman Empire, festivities connected with the pilgrimage served to emphasize the position of the ruler, his capacity to win victories and the continuing florescence of the dynasty in a form easily accessible to the subject population. These festivities were for the most part public, and thus comparable to the *joyeuses entrées* and other ceremonies of medieval and early Renaissance Europe.[8] From the sixteenth century onward, however, European festivities increasingly retreated into a non-public space, accessible to the ruler and his courtiers or to the patriciate of a city, while the public celebrations lost much of their previous lustre. A comparable development was less obvious in the Ottoman context, where public festivities remained important; and among the occasions celebrated on the streets of Istanbul, Damascus and particularly Cairo, the departure and return of the pilgrimage caravans constituted one of the most brilliant events.

These festivities have been recorded extensively by the Ottoman traveller Ewliyā Čelebi, who lived in Cairo for about a decade and therefore had the opportunity to observe them in minute detail. His testimony gains in significance because he was a product of the Ottoman Palace school and therefore intimately acquainted with imperial ceremonial. This latter qualification does not apply to European visitors, who have also left accounts of these festivities. Ewliyā's description, therefore, has been employed as the basis of our study.

The high point of the departure ceremony came when the caravan commander appeared on the square of Ḳara Meydān, which was normally used for military exercises and parades.[9] He was accompanied by a numerous suite of soldiers and officers, while the band played, and janissaries and other soldiers saluted their commander. The caravan commander then visited the governor of Egypt in his tent, which must have been put up in this place for the occasion. Now artillery was brought to the square, presumably the cannons which the commander was to take along with him on his desert journey. The flag of the Prophet, a major relic, was paraded about the grounds along with the palanquin symbolizing the Sultan's presence, which was to accompany the caravan to Mecca; the palanquin was carried by a camel. At the formal audience, with all the notables of Cairo present, the Pasha asked the caravan commander whether he had received the money he was going to need – subsidies for the Beduin shaykhs along the desert route and for the Sherif of Mecca, donations to people living in the Holy Cities, and ready cash for all the other needs of the caravan. The caravan commander formally acknowledged that everything had been handed over, 'down to the last grain and the last cloak', certain gifts taking the shape of clothing. The Pasha instructed a judge to record the matter in his register and then, with a ritual invocation of God, rose from his seat and walked up to the camel carrying the palanquin. After rubbing his face and hands against this symbol of the Sultan's presence, he once again invoked God and took the camel's silver chain to lead the animal around the Ḳara Meydān. Ewliyā states that by this gesture he proclaimed himself the Prophet's camel driver, or humble servant, and the author states that the audience was much moved when watching this gesture of humility. In the meantime, the soldiers in a loud voice invoked the intercession of the Prophet. Then the Pasha turned to the caravan commander, affirming that the Ottoman Sultan controlled Mecca and Medina, acting as servitor of the two Holy Places. He, as the Pasha, was at once the Sultan's representative and the ruler's slave. Acting in his official capacity, with the force and impressiveness required by his office, the Pasha now handed over the palanquin to the caravan commander and commended the pilgrims to the protection of God, wishing them a victorious and safe return. The Pasha then returned to his seat in the tent, and now it was the turn of the caravan commander to parade the palanquin. After that, the caravan set out on its way.

As to the ceremonies accompanying the return of the pilgrimage caravan, Ewliyā describes them so to say as a participant observer, as he presumably entered Cairo as a member of the suite of the caravan commander. After completing the pilgrimage in 1672, Ewliyā did not return to Damascus where he had spent time before, but took the opportunity of travelling to Cairo, where he seems to have resided for most of the remaining years of his life.[10] When the caravan had reached Birkat al-Ḥadjdj the last stop before Cairo, the commander stayed in this locality overnight, and gave a feast for the notables and officers of Cairo. The soldiers fired their muskets and cannons, and at the end there were fireworks which Ewliyā greatly admired. The next morning's principal event was the ceremonial entry into the city. The notables of Cairo and the palanquin preceded the commander, who stopped at the tents of various officers to salute them. At the entrance to the city, by the gate of Bāb Nāṣir, the governor's soldiers awaited the returning pilgrims. Leaving his suite behind, the Pasha galloped ahead to meet the arriving palanquin. He then dismounted, and for forty or fifty steps ran beside the camel carrying the symbol of the sultanic presence. Invoking the prayers of the Prophet, the governor kissed the palanquin's covering. The caravan commander now welcomed his illustrious visitor with military music, and dismounted to rub his face against the foot of the Pasha, who thereupon honoured the new arrival with a gown of honour lined with sable. In response, the caravan commander kissed the ground, then entered the city by the gate of Bāb Nāṣir. He spent the night as a visitor to the mosque of Djānbulāt, while the governor remained in 'Adiliya. At this time, the people of Cairo came to the mosque to pay their respects to the palanquin. At night religious scholars, pious people and derwish shaykhs assembled in the mosque and recited prayers in honour of the Prophet.

We observe certain obvious parallels between the two ceremonies; in both instances, the two principal actors were the caravan commander and the Pasha of Egypt. The initial ceremony of handing over the money to be spent on the pilgrimage had its parallel in an equally official encounter at the end, in which the caravan commander gave an account of how he had spent the money entrusted to him. These two ceremonies emphasized the delegation of power and responsibility from the Pasha to the caravan commander. But at the same time the ultimate sources of power and responsibility were made vividly apparent. When the Pasha led about the camel with the sacred palanquin, he declared that he was the Prophet's camel driver, and thereby established a close, albeit subordinate relationship to the founder of the Muslim religion. Since Ewliyā's contemporaries believed that the palanquin, a symbol of the sovereignty of Islamic rulers, was directly connected to the practice of the Prophet, the religious aura of this ceremony was reinforced.[11] According to Ewliyā, the palanquin originally had contained the most indispensable personal belongings of the Prophet, namely his gown, a toothbrush manufactured from the twig of a tree, wooden clogs and a ewer for religious ablutions (since clay apparently was not available, the latter consisted of basketware made impermeable by a coat of pitch). The Prophet's favourite spouse 'Aysha also supposedly had travelled in this palanquin. When the Pasha played the role of the Prophet's camel driver, literate contemporaries may have been reminded of another event, this time pertaining to Mamluk history. When Sultan Baybars (reigned 1260–71) wanted to perform this same gesture of humility and lead the camel around, a saint intervened and performed the office himself.[12] Given all these motifs from Islamic sacred history, the Ottoman ruler and his governor were firmly linked to the religious sphere and legitimized by this connection.

On the other hand, a major misunderstanding had to be avoided: since the Sultan was far away in Istanbul and the Pasha represented him with the appropriate pomp and circumstance, the spectator might easily assume that the governor was the successor of the Mamluk Sultans, particularly since the caravan commander continually emphasized his subordination to the Pasha. Given the long tradition of Mamluk independence, that particular misunderstanding had to be avoided at all costs. This was achieved by the Pasha's public proclamation that he derived his power from the Sultan. Not the governor of Egypt, but the Ottoman ruler was the servitor of the Holy Places. Moreover, the Pasha explicitly declared that he was the Sultan's *ḳul*, his servitor, who owed his position entirely to the ruler's pleasure and whose inheritance was to return to the latter's treasury at his death. Such was the normal status of a high-level Ottoman official.[13] Probably these very explicit declarations were meant to balance the impression generated by the ceremony, namely that the governor possessed an independent source of religious legitimation due to his role as protector of the pilgrimage.

The ceremonies at the departure and return of the caravan also emphasized the ties of the pilgrims to their respective regions of origin, from which they were absent for months or sometimes even years, and to which some of them would never return. The ceremonies accompanying the departure of the caravan diluted the traumatic moments of departure and return by dividing them up into a sequence of events. For both those who departed and those who stayed behind, the separation thus was made more bearable. The caravan was not like a ship which at a given moment has left port and sailed out onto the high seas. After leaving Damascus, the Syrian caravan spent considerable time at the stopping place of Muzayrib, where pilgrims did their shopping in preparation of the journey.[14] In the Egyptian case, part of the ceremonies of departure and arrival took place at Birkat al-Ha<u>djdj</u>, the first stop after Cairo. Of course, there were practical reasons for this arrangement, which was popular in other Ottoman commercial centres as well.[15] If the caravan did not travel very far on the first day, latecomers could join it at the last moment, while travellers could send for items which they had forgotten. On the other hand, during the last stages of the return journey, the pilgrims and their animals were exhausted, so that it was of vital importance that they should be met by supply caravans while still in the desert, and relatives and friends of the pilgrims often joined the merchants and officials making up these caravans. But beyond this utilitarian consideration, the 'slicing up' of departure and return also had a symbolic significance.

TRAVEL ROUTES

The travel routes between Cairo and Damascus on the one hand, and Mecca on the other, are well known from a variety of pilgrimage accounts, the handbook compiled by ʿAbd al-Ḳādir al-Djazarī, and a few Ottoman official documents. Apart from al-Djazarī's account, all these sources pertain to the seventeenth century (compare map).[16] Particularly interesting is a document from the year 1647, which permits us to view the pilgrimage roads in connection with the major courier routes traversing the eastern half of the Ottoman Empire.[17] Anatolia was crossed by three important routes, which Ottoman sources describe as 'right', 'left' and 'centre'.

The right-hand route (the designation assumes a traveller turning his back to Istanbul) led from the capital to Aleppo and Damascus, crossing Anatolia from northwest to southeast.[18] From Damascus to Mecca, the pilgrimage route and that used by official couriers were virtually identical, as the lack of water severely limited choices. As it was, couriers would often have had trouble procuring horses even on the pilgrimage route, for some of the stopping points, such as Tabūk according to Ewliyā Čelebi, only consisted of an open space where water was to be found, and fodder was probably scarce.[19] Even in some of the desert forts along the hajj route, garrisons were unable to maintain themselves, and it is hard to imagine how the officials responsible for the couriers' mounts protected the animals from thieves. Probably special arrangements were made whenever an official messenger was sent outside the pilgrimage season. Moreover, the 1647 document does not tell us how a courier travelled between Cairo and Mecca, although such couriers needed to be sent with reasonable frequency. We do, however, possess evidence for a courier route leading from Damascus to Cairo by way of Ramla, Ghazzah and Bilbays, and also for a connection between Damascus and the pilgrimage centres of Jerusalem and Khalīl al-Raḥmān (Hebron, al-Khalil).

The courier route from Istanbul by way of Damascus to Mecca constituted one of the three major routes of the eastern Ottoman Empire.[20] In the empire as a whole, the Istanbul–Mecca route was one of seven, for in the Rumelian part of the empire three major routes also radiated from Istanbul. One of them was the successor to the Via Egnatia of Roman times, linking the Ottoman capital to the Adriatic coast. The central route led to Hungary, which at this time was still an Ottoman province, while for an observer turning his back to the capital, the right-hand route led through Moldavia and Walachia into southern Poland. Moreover, due to the recently increased importance of Izmir as a trade centre frequented by

European merchants, a new courier route to this city had been instituted not long before. Unfortunately, we have no way of knowing whether the Istanbul–Damascus–Mecca road was more or less frequented than the other courier routes. But given the numerous sultanic rescripts to recipients in the Hejaz made out by the Ottoman chancery and recorded in the Registers of Important Affairs, this route, at least in peacetime, must have been among the most frequented courier routes. Apart from correspondence with the Sherif of Mecca, the central administration needed to maintain liaison with the *emīn* of Jeddah, who directly represented the Ottoman Sultan in the region, aided by the *ḳāḍī*s of the two Holy Cities and a host of lesser functionaries. Both *ḳāḍī*s, as high Ottoman officials, maintained their own correspondence with the central administration. Since the affairs of the pilgrimage were considered so important by the Ottoman government, Mecca and Medina were supervised much more closely than would otherwise have been true of two remote towns separated from the core of the empire by vast stretches of desert.

SERVICES TO PILGRIMS AND SOLDIERS

In principle, every pilgrim was responsible for his or her own supplies. Only pilgrims who had fallen on hard times were, at least to some extent, under the care of the staff of the caravan commander. But soldiers and officials who accompanied the caravan as part of their official duties had to be supplied with food and water out of public resources. A special bureau was in charge of this business, called 'The Sultan's Larder for the Noble Pilgrimage'. The servitors of this bureau made sure that water was carried along in skins whenever there was reason to assume that there would be a shortage at the next stopping point. From the 1636–7 accounts of the Damascus caravan we learn that a hundred camels had been set aside merely for this purpose.[21] Presumably this was a year of drought, but even in normal years the Damascus caravan took along at least fifty camels to ensure an adequate water supply.

The Egyptian caravan also often had trouble securing the water it required, even though occasionally pilgrims were assisted by foreign Muslim rulers. Thus in 1543–4 an Indian prince, Maḥmūd Shāh, sent a quantity of ivory with the proviso that it be sold to finance the digging of wells for the Egyptian pilgrimage caravan. The project proved difficult to execute, however, and al-Djazarī was not greatly impressed by the success of the enterprise.[22] This author also reports that, on one of his numerous trips to Mecca, he unsuccessfully tried to persuade the caravan commander to hand over some of the water meant for soldiers and officials to the poor. But the caravan commander apparently was worried about the possibility that the soldiers might run out of water themselves. A thoroughly organized caravan with a well-oiled bureaucratic machine no doubt made life easier for ordinary pilgrims. At the same time, the privileges of high-level officials and the high operating costs of the bureaucratic apparatus often made it impossible to give poor pilgrims help when they most needed it.

Food for the return journey was sometimes deposited in desert forts protecting the caravan's stopping points. If these supplies were not in the meantime plundered by Beduins, this was a convenient arrangement. Sometimes, however, more complicated transactions were needed. Thus Ewliyā reports that, in 1672, supplies belonging to the Sultan's Larder were entrusted in Muzayrib to Beduins who undertook to transport them to al-'Ulā.[23] Other Beduins, probably the allies of those encountered in Muzayrib, then returned the supplies to the caravan in the locality previously agreed upon. We do not know whether the grain was physically transported, or whether the Beduins of al-'Ulā owned stocks from which they supplied the caravan. Given the fact that in a year of unseasonable rains Beduins would have had almost as much trouble getting the grain to al-'Ulā as the caravan itself, the second possibility seems more likely. Because the caravan represented a formidable accumulation of military and political power by desert standards, such arrangements could be made without taking too great a risk.

For charitable services to poor pilgrims, 60 camels were set aside in the Damascus caravan of the late sixteenth century.[24] Twenty of them carried foodstuffs, particularly ship's biscuits, while the remaining camels were intended to mount pilgrims in cases of emergency. Whenever the caravan stopped, a special tent was set up for the poor, who also received a warm meal out of the Sultan's bounty. A rescript from the year 1576–7 shows that this kitchen did not always function in the manner intended: sometimes the meals were cooked so late that the poor had no chance to eat before the caravan set out again.[25] At times the poor also received alms in cash, or were issued new trousers and shoes. We also hear of indigent pilgrims being buried in shrouds which had been donated by pious persons. Some of the foundations disbursing alms to poor pilgrims went back to Mamluk times. Thus in 1580–1 a charity established by the last major Mamluk Sultan Ḳānṣūh al-Ghūrī (reigned 1501–17) was still operating. It regularly provided twelve loads of ship's biscuits to the poor.[26]

However the administration in Istanbul needed to supervise these foundations constantly to make sure that they did, in fact, serve the poor. As it was customary to allow various dignitaries (*wādjib al-re'āyet*) the use of officially financed mounts, abuse was especially easy with respect to camels. In 1579–80 the governor of Damascus was threatened by the central government that he would have to foot the bill out of his own pocket if he insisted on assigning camels to people not entitled to them.[27] These admonitions, however, were only moderately successful. An account book of the Damascus caravan from the year 1647 shows that various influential people were permitted the use of no less than 349 camels. In the seventeenth century, however, this merely meant the payment of a subsidy, as the finances of the state no longer permitted major largesse; and the dignitaries thus honoured had to foot a good part of the bill themselves. But in the sixteenth century, the cost of renting camels for a sizable number of influential people had been paid by the Ottoman treasury.

SUPPLYING CARAVANS ON THE RETURN TRIP

More effective than the provisions in favour of poor pilgrims were the auxiliary caravans which, on a commercial basis, supplied the travellers with food, fodder and mounts. When this seemed necessary, the caravan commander demanded supplies for the return journey. Thus in 1567–8 the commander reported that food and camels would urgently be required in al-'Ulā, for all supplies would be exhausted by the time the caravan reached this settlement.[28] In such cases the governors of provinces along the pilgrimage route were solicited for help. Moreover, the place where pilgrimage and supply caravans were to meet was advanced further into the desert, and the treasurer of Damascus province was given the right to contract a loan in order to supply the caravan. In particularly urgent cases, he had the right to spend extra money on the caravan without first obtaining the consent of the chief treasurer.[29]

The provincial administrators in Egypt and Syria were obviously not in a position to check the references of those people who volunteered to meet the pilgrimage caravan in al-'Ulā or Ḳal'at al-'Azlam. As a result, legitimate traders and camel drivers were accompanied by a number of less welcome visitors. Ewliyā Čelebi claimed that the pilgrims, exhausted after their long trek, were often unable to guard their possessions against the thieves of Cairo, who 'will steal one's eye from under the eye makeup'.[30] Apart from thieves there were also outright robbers, whom the disgusted traveller compares with the 'Black Scribe' (Ḳara Yazıdjı) and Djānbulādoghlu, some of the major robbers and rebels from the crisis years before and after 1600. Every now and then travellers were awakened by cries of 'Don't let him get away!' and 'Now he is gone!'[31] The streets and markets of Cairo, on the other hand, must have been unusually quiet during these last weeks of the pilgrimage season.

A PERMANENT SOURCE OF TROUBLE: THE ESTATES OF DECEASED PILGRIMS

To the average Ottoman pilgrim, protecting life and property from thieves was difficult enough. Things got worse if a companion died on the road. Great courage, skill and finesse were needed to protect the estate of the deceased from the depredations of the official in charge of securing heirless property on behalf of the Ottoman fisc, and hand it over to the legal heirs. The general rule was that heirless property accrued to the fisc. But in the context of the pilgrimage caravans this often was taken to mean that property could be confiscated if none of the heirs was present in the caravan. Heirs who had stayed at home must have complained about these abuses, for the central administtration issued not a few rescripts to bring the situation under control. Pilgrims were explicitly permitted to choose an executor who could take charge of the estate.[32] If a pilgrim died without appointing an executor, in the Egyptian caravan the fisc took over. In the Syrian caravan a more liberal rule applied, and fellow villagers or townsmen of the deceased could also take charge of the estate.[33] Only if such people could not be located either, did the deceased's property fall to the Ottoman fisc.

Yet these rulings were not always applied in practice, as the officials dealing with heirless property had paid appreciable sums for their appointments, and therefore tried to maximize profits during their limited tenure. Temptations were numerous, as many pilgrims carried sizable quantities of money or goods to defray travel expenses. Some officials made a terrible reputation for themselves: 'When a Muslim pilgrim dies, his tent companions are afraid of the fiscal official, the scribe and the *ḳāḍī*. In order to avoid harm to property and honour, they do not wash the dead person and do not wrap him/her into a shroud, nor do they pray the prayers for the dead', as prescribed by Islamic ritual.[34] Instead, the body was furtively buried in the deceased's tent. Repeated attempts to curb the misbehaviour of fiscal officials met with only modest success, and these people probably were among the most detested members of the caravan.

THE NUMBER OF PILGRIMS

Even though the Ottoman state of the sixteenth and seventeenth centuries possessed a well-organized financial bureaucracy and frequently counted its taxpayers, there was never any attempt to count the pilgrims to Mecca. So we are limited to a few more or less informed guesses. The detailed description of the Cairo pilgrimage caravan which we owe to al-Djazarī claims that, in 1279, 40,000 Egyptians and as many Syrians and Iraqis undertook the pilgrimage.[35] A Christian pilgrim from the fourteenth century, Jacobo of Verona, encountered a single hajj caravan in the desert and estimated it at 17,000 people. In an anonymous account from the year 1580, probably written by a Portuguese, we find the figure of 50,000 participants for the Egyptian caravan alone.[36]

We also possess some late medieval figures concerning the number of camels in pilgrimage caravans. These appear more reliable, as camels are easier to count than people. A major Syrian or Egyptian caravan might be made up of more than 11,000 camels, but a small Iraqi caravan consisted of no more than four to five hundred. The Italian traveller Ludovico di Varthéma, who converted to Islam and visited the Holy Cities in 1503 as a Mamluk, reports that his caravan carried 16,000 camel loads of water. Ludovico di Varthéma travelled with the Damascus pilgrims; the Cairo caravan arrived in Mecca just before he did and, according to his estimate, it consisted of 64,000 animals. The Portuguese anonymous author believes that the Cairo caravan in about 1580 was made up of at least 40,000 camels. Unfortunately, it is all but impossible to compute the number of human beings from the number of camels, for many of the wealthier pilgrims brought along several loads of supplies and trade goods.

Very few eye witnesses of the prayer meeting at 'Arafat have recorded numerical data. Ludovico di Varthéma states that, in 1503, wealthy people sacrificed a total of 30,000 sheep; however, quite a few of them offered more than one animal. Supposedly 30,000 poor people were assembled on this occasion, and they consumed the meat of the sacrificial animals. According to the anonymous Portuguese author, 200,000 people and 300,000 animals participated in a late sixteenth-century prayer meeting at 'Arafat.[37] The Spaniard 'Alī Beg, who visited Mecca in 1807, mentions 80,000 men, 2000 women and a thousand children.[38] Seven years later, John Lewis Burckhardt estimated that about 70,000 people participated in the prayer meeting at 'Arafat.[39] This total includes not only the pilgrims who had come with the Cairo and Damascus caravans, but also Africans, Indians and

Afghans who had travelled by a variety of land and sea routes. In addition, there were people from Medina present, while the Meccans themselves probably constituted the majority of all pilgrims. Obviously, these estimates are not based on counts and therefore should be treated with caution.

FINANCIAL ADMINISTRATORS IN THE PILGRIMAGE CARAVAN

In this section we will not deal with the resources, both official and private, which ultimately paid for the pilgrimage (see Chapter 4), but with the day-to-day business of the caravans' financial administrators. The activities of these modest but indispensable personages are recorded in the accounts of the Damascus caravan, particularly the so-called daybooks (*rūznāmdje*). A daybook from 1592–3 records, in the case of each expenditure, the function of the official who had ordered it.[40] Usually no cash changed hands in the office of the caravan administration itself. The head of the 'Sultan's Larder for the Noble Pilgrimage' or other officials gave the payees pieces of paper with their seals, which the latter then presented to the financial administration for payment. Some people who had delivered goods to the caravan brought along a document from the *kāḍī* attesting their claims.

In procuring supplies for the Damascus caravan, the governor of the province played a central role. At times his chief doorkeeper deputized for him, but the more important payments were made in the governor's presence. The Pasha also checked the accounts of the pilgrimage caravan if there was any suspicion of irregularities.[41] In case such a suspicion was confirmed, the official responsible was required to make good the damage; after the accounts had been settled, a note to that effect was included in the registers.

Most caravan expenses had been met before the pilgrims left Damascus; but occasionally additional purchases became necessary en route. Sometimes the caravan ran out of cash, and pilgrims and merchants were required to raise the money needed. This arrangement was familiar from merchant caravans, money being raised *ad hoc* when the caravan had to pay customs and tolls.[42] In other instances officials borrowed money from wealthy pilgrims and merchants who happened to be travelling with the pilgrimage caravan. Often these debts were only repaid after a long lapse of time, particularly when a member of the caravan administration had reason to think that his expenditures might be questioned. In 1578–9 a former official of the Damascus caravan made sure that he went on campaign when the day of reckoning approached, and 5600 gold pieces had to be returned to a creditor of the caravan.[43]

Many caravans owed considerable amounts of money. In 1656–7, debts amounted to 23,000 *esedī ghurush* (Dutch silver coins, a popular means of payment in the seventeenth-century Ottoman Empire). In this case, some of the creditors were tax collectors active in Tripoli (Syria) and Safed (Palestine).[44] Other creditors had something to do with the port town of Saydā (Sidon), but the document does not specify the nature of the relationship.[45] Since many French traders visited Saydā, it is possible that the creditors in question were long-distance merchants dealing on the one hand with the Hejaz, and on the other with their European opposite numbers. Even the head of a craft guild was listed among the creditors of the caravan administration.

There was a good deal of variation among the sums advanced by individual creditors. One of the tax collectors had lent 6066 *esedī ghurush*, and two of the presumed Saydā merchants 2000 each. But other creditors were owed only a few hundred *ghurush* each; probably, they had delivered goods for which they had not yet received payment.

CAMELS AMD CAMEL ENTREPRENEURS

Securing camels in the appropriate quantity and quality constituted one of the most difficult problems confronting the caravan administration. Soldiers and officials by themselves needed more than 600 animals. In addition, a large number of spare camels had to be taken along, as losses on the long route to Mecca were quite high. This was merely the official part of the caravan, and thousands of camels were procured privately by pilgrims and merchants.

In order to encourage Beduins to supply the caravan with camels, their elders were sometimes granted the right to exhibit the flag of the Sultan.[46] These honours occasionally turned out to be counterproductive, as they intensified rivalries between different groups, and if the latter degenerated into fights, the supply of camels was adversely affected. To be less dependent on such eventualities, the Ottoman administration purchased its own camels and sometimes even sent them to the greener pastures of Anatolia to keep them in good condition.[47] Moreover, Sultan Murād III's Grand Vizier in 1586–7 experimented with a new solution to the problem of camel supply.[48] Ibrāhīm Pasha established a pious foundation in favour of the Damascus pilgrimage caravan, and donated 600 camels to the new establishment. The animals were placed at the disposal of the caravan commander. The provincial treasury of Damascus was very much opposed to the whole project, however, claiming that the money needed for the upkeep of the animals constituted a needless long-term commitment of resources. As a result, the foundation did not continue long in operation.

This attitude of the Damascene finance administration may have had something to do with the fact that a number of established entrepreneurs in the city made a living by renting out camels. The document which recounts the sad fate of Ibrāhīm Pasha's foundation is quite explicit in this respect: camel entrepreneurs (*mukawwim*), fearing for their profits, made sure that the foundation's herd was soon dispersed. However, the *mukawwim*s probably made most of their money from pilgrims and merchants, while the service of the Sultan was not a very profitable venture. In 1578–9 pilgrims paid between 50 and 55 gold pieces to get from Damascus to Mecca, while the Ottoman administration disbursed no more than 28 gold pieces for the same service.[49] In the seventeenth century, prices remained at about the same level; ordinary animals cost the Ottoman administration 26 gold pieces each, while the more expensive camels ridden by dignitaries rated 30 gold pieces per trip.[50] Admittedly, the camel entrepreneurs may have received some money over and above the sums officially assigned to them. But private persons certainly were the more lucrative customers.

In the sixteenth century the Ottoman administration several times tried to secure the services of camel entrepreneurs without any cash disbursement at all. Instead the latter were offered military prebends (*timār, ze'āmet*) of the kind which supported Ottoman cavalry troops.[51] This novelty did not work out very well; in 1578–9 the governor and finance director of Damascus were asked to determine whether the Ottoman treasury could expect to save money by giving out such grants, or whether entrepreneurs would continue to demand cash from the Ottoman administration even after receiving *timār*s and *ze'āmet*s. Apparently the whole business was given up soon after, for in seventeenth-century accounts we find no further trace of it.

Before the Damascus hajj caravan left the fair of Muzayrib, located a few days' travel to the south of the city, camel entrepreneurs working for the state received an advance payment in cash. Further advances were often made in the course of the journey, and if the entrepreneurs were not able to obtain money from the caravan authorities, they took a leaf out of the caravan commander's book and put pressure on merchants accompanying the caravan in order to obtain a loan.[52] Accounts were settled upon return to Damascus. Other entrepreneurs managed to secure payment before even leaving for Mecca, but that in no way prevented them from demanding loans from the caravan treasury.[53] Even though this procedure was illegal, many camel entrepreneurs managed to obtain about the same amount in loans and advances as they had received as regular payments. A popular pretext was the need to purchase grain and other foodstuffs, even though assignments from the 'Sultan's Larder for the Noble Pilgrimage' had already been obtained.

Not all entrepreneurs managed to make a profit, however, as risks were considerable even in 'good' years. A camel entrepreneur returning to Damascus might discover that he owed the administration money, because the amount received as advances surpassed the total price the authorities were willing to pay.[54] Some entrepreneurs devised quite remarkable strategies when they found themselves in this plight. One man, who died deeply in debt, was found to have sold his possessions or turned them into a pious foundation; he must have hoped to avoid confiscation in that way. The case was submitted to the Council of State (*diwān-i humāyūn*), which decided that a person with debts to the Treasury had no right to constitute a pious foundation. Sale and foundation deeds were therefore declared invalid.[55] Other bankrupt entrepreneurs fled to remote provinces, such as Egypt or the Yemen.

One of the risks that camel entrepreneurs had to bear was the high mortality of their beasts, for presumably they had to provide substitutes whenever one of their customers lost his mount. At least, this was the rule in late nineteenth- and early twentieth-century Damascus, and although sixteenth-century documents say nothing explicit on this point, indirect evidence makes it seem likely that this rule existed in earlier times as well.[56] Camel entrepreneurs often complained of soldiers and officials mistreating the mounts entrusted to their care by overloading them with trade goods.[57] When the animals then collapsed, the entrepreneurs were asked to foot the bill. These complaints induced the Ottoman administration to issue a rescript setting maxima for camel loads. But rules of this kind were often broken, and the problem remained.

Certain entrepreneurs invested large sums of money in the camel business, while others were discouraged by the high risks and provided camels as a sideline only. In 1591–2 some of the larger entrepreneurs supplied 100–120 beasts.[58] We have little information about camel prices, but in 1578–9 an animal could be bought for 60–70 Ottoman gold pieces.[59] Between 1578–9 and 1591–2 the Ottoman gold coin remained stable; thus a large entrepreneur of the late sixteenth century invested between 6000 and 8500 gold pieces. But sums of this magnitude were the exception rather than the rule; in the account books we find payments to quite a few entrepreneurs who had provided no more than a few dozen animals.

INVOLUNTARY SERVICES

In some instances camel entrepreneurs did not willingly furnish their animals to Ottoman dignitaries on official business, but were forced to do so. In 1591–2 some Damascus notables managed to avoid this unwelcome responsibility by bribing the caravan commander, and that year there were not enough entrepreneurs with the requisite capital.[60] The following year a Damascene named Hekīmoghlu Aḥmed, whom rumour granted a fortune of five million *akče* (or 41,667 gold pieces according to the official exchange rate), was ordered to furnish the caravan with one hundred camels. If the rumour was correct, Hekīmoghlu was meant to invest about 15 per cent of his fortune. Whether he did so or not is impossible to determine, however, and documents from the seventeenth century make no further mention of entrepreneurs rendering forced services to the pilgrimage.

Even though this case seems to have been exceptional in the history of the Damascus caravan, it conformed to late sixteenth-century Ottoman administrative practice as documented for Anatolia and Rumelia.[61] To provide meat for the inhabitants of Istanbul, and particularly the court and janissaries, wealthy inhabitants of the Balkans were obliged to furnish a set number of sheep at officially determined prices. Some of the people involved (*djeleb*) possessed large flocks. But others drastically had to change their patterns of investment so as to comply with official demands.

If Ewliyā Čelebi's evaluation is at all realistic, some of the *djeleb* managed to make a profit out of their involuntary investment.[62] But sixteenth- and seventeenth-century archival materials show that many *djeleb* attempted to avoid service, so that new people constantly needed to be recruited; apparently, most *djeleb* worked at a loss. Even less popular was service as a butcher in Istanbul, at least during the second half of the sixteenth century, when wealthy provincials who had made themselves unpopular by usury were often drafted to perform this service. For political reasons, Istanbul meat prices during this period were set at so low a level that they did not cover costs, and many butchers sustained heavy losses or even went bankrupt. In the long run, however, the Ottoman government did not continue this policy, probably because it became more and more difficult to find people with the requisite fortunes who were not in the employ of the Sultan and thereby exempt from services of this kind. In the seventeenth century, Istanbul meat prices were allowed to find a level that permitted butchers to live off their trade. Only the forced deliveries of sheep continued.

In the case of Hekīmoghlu, there is no evidence that the camel hire to which he was entitled was fixed at a punitively low level. In fact there is no evidence at all that the Ottoman administration interfered in the formation of camel prices. However, such an interference probably did occur: between the sixteenth and eighteenth centuries, officially administered prices were very much part of Ottoman economic life.[63] Even in the nineteenth and early twentieth centuries, the governor of Damascus and the Sherif of Mecca promulgated the prices camel entrepreneurs could charge for the outgoing and return trips respectively.[64] Admittedly entrepreneurs could try to charge higher prices under a variety of pretexts. But these men did not possess a monopoly, as at least the wealthier pilgrims could and did buy their own camels. Camel suppliers could not pass on all their losses to the pilgrims, therefore, and bankruptcies were not a rare occurrence.

CONTINUITY AND LONG-TERM CHANGE

If we compare the information provided by 'Abd al-Ḳādir al-Djazarī concerning the late Mamluk and early Ottoman pilgrimage caravans with the data provided by late sixteenth- and early seventeenth-century archival material, elements of continuity strike the eye. Whatever change occurred from Mamluk to Ottoman times happened gradually, and the Ottoman administration's approach was strictly pragmatic. In the late sixteenth century, the Registers of Important Affairs every year contained rescripts concerned with concrete complaints. We learn of a caravan commander who refused to stop the caravan at prayer time, so that pilgrims neglected their daily worship for fear of being left behind.[65] Other pilgrims were given to the enjoyment of fireworks, which disturbed the pious concentration of their more restrained brethren. After their return to Damascus, Istanbul or Cairo, or even while still travelling, pilgrims probably made an official record of their complaints and deposited it with the relevant *ḳāḍī* or in the offices of the provincial governor. Moreover, secretaries of the caravan commander, who like al-Djazarī were concerned with the affairs of the pilgrimage on a full-time basis, probably collected, organized and passed on these complaints to Istanbul. Admittedly we have no proof that this is what occurred. But if this assumption were totally false, the authorities in Istanbul could not have been as well-informed as our records show them to have been. The experience accumulated in Istanbul constituted the base of new regulations and, in the long run, modified previous practice. But this was by no means a universal rule. As we have seen, the attempt to force rich men to furnish the caravan with camels ended in failure, and it would be a mistake to believe that every Sultan's command was automatically obeyed.

Other changes were caused more by the general political situation than by the specific needs of the caravan. In the eighteenth century, the Pasha of Damascus was normally appointed commander of the pilgrimage, while in the sixteenth and seventeenth centuries he had intervened only in urgent matters and otherwise limited himself to a supervisory role.[66] This change was due to a different distribution of power in the province. Before the fall of the Druze amir Fakhr al-Dīn Ma'ān in 1635, a number of families with power bases in rural Syria had played a significant role in provincial politics, and were integrated into the Ottoman system by receiving the honour of commanding the pilgrimage caravan. But when these families were marginalized in the later seventeenth century, a caravan commander chosen from among their midst did not benefit either the Ottoman central government or the pilgrims themselves. On the other hand, the early eighteenth century was a period of political reform, when the Ottoman administration tried to reassert control over the pilgrimage route, which had slipped away during the Habsburg–Ottoman war of 1683–99. Thus it must have seemed expedient to grant a single figure sweeping powers, and this happened to be the governor of Damascus. As a result, we should imagine the pilgrims moving through a political terrain where they had no control over the main actors, even though in day-to-day matters at least the wealthiest and best-connected among the pilgrims were not unable to influence events to their own advantage. This situation will become even clearer when we analyse the institutions concerned with the military protection of the pilgrimage caravan.

3

Caravan Security

It was one of the obligations of the Sultan as 'Servant of the Holy Places' to protect the pilgrims during their long journey through the Syrian and Arabian deserts. This was not an easy task, as the deserts were controlled by the Ottoman Sultan only to a limited extent. The Yemenis travelled through a vast region where even nominal control by the Pādishāh in Istanbul ended in the 1630s. Moreover, the pilgrims who arrived from Basra in a special caravan needed to traverse a desert over which Ottoman control was all but non-existent, even though Basra itself formed part of the Ottoman Empire. It was not possible to secure the safety of the pilgrims by stationing major bodies of troops in the area. Quite apart from the expenses involved, large garrisons would have used up much of the water urgently needed by the pilgrims and the Beduins who constituted the permanent inhabitants of the desert region.

The pilgrimage caravan was accompanied by a detachment of janissaries and, in the case of the Syrian caravan, by cavalrymen in receipt of a military tax assignment (*timār*). Only in case of disturbances in the desert or the Holy Cities was this detachment increased to a more impressive size. For the most part, the safety of the pilgrimage caravan was assured by official subsidies to the Beduins living along the hajj route (*ṣürre*). In Ottoman government circles, these payments were interpreted as a counterpart to the food and water which the Beduins delivered to the caravan. But when the payments in question were not made on time or did not satisfy the recipients in terms of quantity or quality, the Beduins felt justified in attacking the pilgrims and thus securing their subsidies *manu militari*. Therefore the *ṣürre* should be regarded not as a mere payment for services rendered, but as a means of protecting the caravan from Beduin attack.

BEDUIN SUBSIDIES

For the late sixteenth and early seventeenth centuries we possess accounts of the Syrian and Egyptian provincial finance administrations, which record official expenses related to the caravan (see Chapter 2). In the secondary literature it has become customary to call these accounts 'budgets' even though they record past expenses, and do not constitute a guide for future behaviour as is true of regular budgets.[1] Some of these provincial accounts have even been published. But they were intended to serve strictly practical purposes and in no way to stand as scientific statistics. Therefore the headings under which expenditures were recorded differ from one account to the next without formal redefinition of the relevant categories. Officials of the time knew exactly what they were documenting, but very often we do not, and therefore accounts a few years or decades apart are often difficult to compare. Minor differences between years, therefore, should not be made to carry the weight of too much interpretation. But, even so, the provincial accounts are of great significance because they allow us to establish an order of magnitude with respect to the expenses of the pilgrimage caravan's official section.

A further difficulty stems from the fact that Ottoman accounts of the sixteenth and seventeenth centuries use a variety of coins, which exchanged at different rates in different parts of the country. Only for some of the major cities do we possess lists of the relevant exchange rates, and even these lists are often incomplete.[2] Extrapolations are therefore unavoidable, which increases the possibility of mistakes. But similar problems are quite familiar to the historian of the European Middle Ages or the Early Modern period. We thus have no alternative but to use the accounts with a degree of scepticism and to assume that even dubious statistics are better than none at all.

The Egyptian budget of 1596–7 contains the names of individuals and tribal units receiving subsidies.[3] Presumably the individuals recorded did not receive grants for their own exclusive use, but also represented groups of Beduins. Sometimes the provincial accounts inform us of the stretch of road for which the recipients were responsible. In Table 1 we have attempted to separate subsidies in the narrow sense of the word from the recompense for goods and services furnished. Payments for the provision of camels have been eliminated

Table 1 *Payments to Beduins from Egyptian Provincial Budgets, to Facilitate Hajj Travel*

Year	*Recipients*	*Payment in* pāra	*Payment in gold* (sikke-i hasene)
1005–6/ 1596–7[1]	Beduins, unspecified[2]	211,451	5286
1009/ 1600	Beduins, unspecified	206,170	5154
1010–11/ 1601–2	Beduins, unspecified (only payments not in compensation for specific services)	208,455	5211
1020/ 1611–12	Beduins, unspecified	222,945	5574
1023–4/ 1614–15	as in 1020/ 1611–12	222,945	5574

1 Shaw (1968), p. 158 ff.

2 The Banū Ḥusayn, descendants of the Prophet, were for the most part townsmen and not desert dwellers. But the accounts do not always permit us to distinguish subsidies to the Banū Ḥusayn, so they have been included in the total.

whenever recognizable as such. But often a tidy separation was impossible, because the accounts contain nothing but global figures. As far as Ottoman treasury officials were concerned, the difference between payment for services rendered and subsidies was quite irrelevant. In both cases, the ultimate aim was identical, namely to provide for the safe transit of the pilgrimage caravan. In the relationship of Ottoman administrators and pilgrims on the one hand, and Beduins on the other, political and economic factors were so closely intertwined as to be inextricable. The Ottoman administration obliged the Beduins to provide goods and services, but payments were especially generous so as to cement political loyalties.

Between 1596–7 and 1614–15, 5100–5800 Ottoman gold coins were assigned every year from Egyptian provincial revenues as *ṣürre* payments to Beduins. Oscillations are moderate and must have had local reasons which we cannot now determine. In the Syrian case, changes from year to year are much more dramatic (see Table 2).[4] Payments to tribes whose names appear in the table, such as the ʿAnaza or Wahīdāt probably constituted only a share of total subsidy

Table 2 *Payments to Beduins from Syrian Provincial Budgets, to Facilitate Hajj Travel*

Year	*Recipients*	*Payment in* pāra	*Payment in gold* (sikke-i hasene)	*Payment in* esedī ghurush
1005/ 1596–7	Rashīd, Nu'aym, Salāma (Beduins)	101,280	2532	
1018/ 1609–10	Beduins, unspecified		9057	
1019/ 1610–11	Beduins, unspecified		9268	
1020/ 1611–12	Beduins, unspecified		11,678	
1085/ 1674–5	Beduins: Banū Ṣakhr,[1] 'Urbān-i-Karak, 'Anaza, Waḥīdāt, al-'Umr		4271	9076
	Payment to Salāma, for transportation		2220	4718
	Total (1674–5)		6491[2]	13,794

1 On the Banū Ṣakhr, see Hütteroth and Abdulfattah (1977), p. 169 f. Evliya Çelibi (1896–1938), vol. 9, p. 571, gives a list of Beduin groups in receipt of subsidies in the late seventeenth century. On the 'Anaza, see Rafeq (1970), *passim*.
2 This is no longer the *sikke-i ḥasene*, but a later and less valuable gold coin known as *sherīfī*. Since our data are insufficient, conversion is approximate.

payments, albeit an important one. For although the Rashīd, Nu'aym and Salāma were influential tribes frequently mentioned in the context of the pilgrimage, the provincial accounts do not mention them as *ṣürre* recipients. It is probable, however, that the increase in *ṣürre* payments by the beginning of the seventeenth century (see Table 2) is more than a mere optical illusion due to the dubious character of the older data. For during those years the Kurdish Pasha Djānbulādoghlu 'Alī and the Druze prince Fakhr al-Dīn 'Alī II were both trying to seize power in the Syrian provinces.[5] As a result of the ensuing unrest, the Beduins living along the hajj route were able to demand higher *sürre* payments than was customary. The Ottoman administration having entrusted the Beduin notable Aḥmad b. Ṭurabāy with the task of breaking Fakhr al-Dīn's resistance, many tribal units were induced to abandon their normal routes of migration, and needed to be compensated by increased subsidies.[6] Nor were the 1670s a particularly calm period; but if the accounts of 1674–5 reflect reality to some extent, disturbances were less dramatic and *ṣürre* increases accordingly less marked than at the beginning of the century.

For 1681–3 we possess a further group of Syrian provincial accounts, which unfortunately contain only lump sums for all expenses connected with the Damascus pilgrimage caravan, so that the height of Beduin subsidies cannot be determined.[7] But in spite of all these gaps in our information we can conclude that payments from Syrian revenue sources were usually higher than those derived from Egypt.

Given the much more limited Syrian revenues, subsidies to the Beduins supplying and protecting the hajj caravan constituted a major item in the provincial 'budget'. At the beginning of the seventeenth century, the Ottoman administration paid out between 15,000 and 17,000 gold pieces to the Beduins residing in the vicinity of the caravan route; a sizable share, however, was handed over in the shape of silver coins. Thus the Beduins were able to purchase certain goods in urban markets, such as arms and textiles, and thereby were integrated into the Ottoman economic structure.

THE COMMANDER OF THE PILGRIMAGE CARAVAN

In the long run, the political situation in the desert, but also in the cultivated regions of Egypt and Syria, determined the height of *ṣürre* payments. In the short run, however, the amount of money to be paid over was determined in annual negotiations.[8] On the Ottoman side, the negotiators were the commanders of the Syrian and Egyptian pilgrimage caravans, supported by the central administration in Istanbul. The Beduins were represented by their tribal leaders, often allied to the Sherifs of Mecca by ties which were more or less solid according to circumstances. Since Beduin leaders did not put down their impressions in writing, documentation concerning the negotiation process is one-sided. There are not even any neutral observers, for Ottoman writers not in an official position at the time of their pilgrimage, such as Ewliyā Čelebi or 'Abd al-Raḥmān Ḥibrī, were close enough to the bureaucracy to reflect the official point of view.[9] Ewliyā and other authors have drawn heroic images of caravan commanders and military governors; but these accounts should be taken as part of the self-image of the Ottoman bureaucracy and not necessarily as a faithful depiction of reality.

Particularly the Egyptian records show us the caravan commander as responsible for the purchasing of supplies.[10] In addition he was in charge of distributing subsidies to the Beduins and commander of the detachment accompanying the caravan. He decided how long the caravan was to remain at different resting places. In case of danger he could order a detour or withdrawal to a fortified town or camp. Finally it was his responsibility to bring the Sultan's pious donations safely to Mecca and Medina. These basic responsibilities of the caravan commander had been determined in Mamluk times and did not change during the sixteenth and seventeenth centuries; this continuity becomes obvious when we study the sequence of appointment documents contained in the Mühimme Defterleri. In 1591–2, when Aḥmed Beg, governor of the sub-province of Gaza, was appointed commander of the pilgrimage, the importance of continuity was specifically invoked, and a major reason for the appointment was the fact that Aḥmed Beg had successfully commanded pilgrimage caravans in the past.[11] The appointment document particularly recognized his merits in procuring supplies for the caravan and having them transported to diverse stopping points. According to al-D̲j̲azarī's account of the caravan in late Mamluk times, similar administrative and political skills had been demanded of earlier caravan commanders.[12]

In the appointment document concerning the provincial governor of Gaza, only one of the customary duties of the caravan commander is not mentioned, namely the safe delivery of the Sultan's gifts to Mecca and Medina. In practical life, however, some caravan commanders considered this their principal responsibility. When Ewliyā Čelebi travelled to the Hejaz in 1671–2, the Syrian caravan was caught in a rainstorm only a few miles south of Damascus. Soon the desert was transformed into a sea of mud, in which the camels were unable to move.[13] A delegation of pilgrims visited the caravan commander, who in that particular year happened to be the governor of Damascus, to discuss what should be done next. The governor received them most ungraciously, and declared that if need be he would abandon the pilgrims to their fate in the middle of the desert. His own responsibility, he declared, was limited to the safe transport of the Sultan's gifts to Mecca and Medina, and of the state palanquin symbolizing the Sultan's presence to 'Arafat.[14] Now this was an unusual situation, as the governor had been charged with a punitive expedition against the rebellious Sherif of Mecca. In this particular year, therefore, political and military considerations must have been more important than in normal years. But this incident demonstrates that individual caravan commanders possessed, or thought they possessed, some leeway in determining the relative weight of their different responsibilities.

In the first half of the sixteenth century, when Ottoman rule over Egypt was still being established, the authorities in Istanbul were careful not to appoint a Mamluk to the office of caravan commander. This fact is worth noting, as at the time local administration remained solidly in Mamluk hands; the central government was anxious to avoid anything that might endanger the regular collection of revenues.[15] But the caravan commander was not concerned with tax collection, and it was considered necessary to establish a balance between Mamluk and non-Mamluk officials. These conditions were of special significance as the governor of the pilgrimage caravan had reasonable expectations of being appointed governor of Egypt in the future.

Beyond general considerations of this type, the factors which had a role to play in the appointment of a caravan commander are recognizable only from documentation pertaining to the second half of the sixteenth century. Candidates willing to subsidize the caravan out of their own fortunes apparently had an advantage over their competitors. Thus in 1560–1 Ḳara Sh̲āhīn Muṣṭafā Pasha, who as a governor of Yemen had been severely criticized for his avarice, declared himself willing to conduct the caravan with an official budget of only 14 'purses' of *aḳče*.[16] Possibly Muṣṭafā Pasha was trying to counterbalance the impact of the complaints levied against him by a show of generosity. At the same time officials in Istanbul commented that the Pasha's family lived in Cairo and that he was willing to pay in hard cash for the privilege of being reunited with them. All these special circumstances obviously did not apply to Muṣṭafā Pasha's successor. But the responsible authorities in the capital pretended to believe that future caravan commanders would also be willing to run the caravan on a budget of 14 'purses', even though before Muṣṭafā Pasha's tenure of office, 18 'purses' had been the going rate.[17] The document we possess concerns the negotiations which preceded the appointment of Muṣṭafā Pasha's successor. The governor of Egypt pleaded that 16 'purses' constituted the minimum sum on which the caravan could be conducted. If the sum offered lay below this limit, Özdemirog̲h̲lu 'Oth̲mān Pasha, known as a most successful military commander, would be unable to accept the appointment.[18] This argument induced the authorities in Istanbul to increase their offer to 16 'purses', but the governor was emphatically informed that a higher offer was totally out of the question. Other considerations which might determine an appointment involved relations between the two caravan commanders, at times a thorny issue. In the second half of the sixteenth century, disputes between soldiers of the Syrian and

Egyptian caravans occurred frequently, particularly when the two groups escorted the Sultan's palanquin (*maḥmal*). The subject of these disputes were mainly questions of precedence at 'Arafat, and usually occurred at the time when the prayer meeting which constitutes the high point of the pilgrimage had been completed and the pilgrims hurriedly left the site.[19] In Mamluk times, the Cairo *maḥmal* had enjoyed precedence, but toward the end of the sixteenth century the Ottoman central administration decided that the two *maḥmal*s should leave 'Arafat at the same time. This rule if anything exacerbated disputes. In 1570–1 the quarrel even degenerated into a brawl in which the Egyptian caravan commander was wounded in the head.

Given this situation, the responsible officials in Istanbul attempted to defuse matters by appointing caravan commanders who were on good terms with their opposite numbers. In 1580–1 Ḳānṣūh Beg, long-time commander of the Damascene pilgrimage caravan, had nothing but praise for his colleague 'Alī Beg, former governor of Jerusalem, who had just brought the caravan safely back under very difficult conditions.[20] 'Alī Beg therefore was reappointed commander of the Cairo caravan, and only his death shortly before the pilgrims were due to leave Egypt prevented him from actually filling the office.

Occasionally the authorities in Istanbul appointed two men to command the Damascus pilgrimage in one and the same year. These appointments may reflect disputes between Syrian amirs, in which the central government preferred not to take sides. By appointing the representative first of one faction and then of the other, the central power probably intended to play off the two sides against one another and thereby retain control of the situation. In certain instances, however, such a policy severely inconvenienced the pilgrims, for they risked attack by the partisans of the man disappointed in his hopes for preferment and more than ready to prove his rival's ineffectiveness. In other instances, Istanbul might appoint two candidates when the central administration's officials did not feel well enough informed about the distribution of power in the Syrian desert to make a choice. In that case, the decision was left to the governor of Damascus, who was in a better position to judge the situation even though he generally held office for a short time only. Thus we possess a rescript from the Ottoman Sultan dated 1570–1, in which the governor of Damascus is asked to choose between the governor of Gaza, Riḍwān Beg, and his own finance director, 'Alī Beg.[21]

Somewhat more complicated was the case recorded in 1585–6. Once more a governor of Gaza had been appointed commander of the Syrian pilgrimage caravan, this office in the sixteenth century being much more important than the location of Gaza would seem to warrant.[22] Quite frequently, this particular governorship was a stepping stone to more important positions, for instance the *pas̲h̲alık* of Yemen.[23] Yet when the candidate realized he was competing against Ḳānṣūh Beg, an old but very powerful man and for most of his life governor of the fortress of ʿAd̲j̲lun on the edge of the Syrian desert, he withdrew his candidacy. It must be admitted that Ḳānṣūh Beg's candidacy was merely symbolic, as at the time he was in Istanbul, after having been called there to give an account of his manifold and, from the administration's point of view, problematic activities. He thus had been appointed caravan commander as a mark of the Sultan's favour after having cleared himself, and not as a practical proposition.[24] As a result the Damascus caravan was left without any commander at all, a situation which much impeded travel preparations. The rescript we possess was meant to clarify this situation; the governor of Gaza was told that the appointment of his competitor was a mere formality and that he was to make sure preparations were completed on time. In this case, the governor of Damascus was not asked for his opinion; the officials in Istanbul felt sufficiently in control to make the decision on their own.

FROM THE BIOGRAPHY OF A CARAVAN COMMANDER

In order to understand why the governor of Gaza did not believe that he stood a realistic chance of becoming caravan commander in competition against Ḳānṣuh Beg of ʿAd̲j̲lun, we need to take a closer look at the latter's biography.[25] Ḳānṣūh Beg came from an old family, but although throughout his life he maintained close connections to the Beduins, his own relatives were village dwellers. In sixteenth- and seventeenth-century Syria it was common enough for influential families to maintain rural seats which under propitious circumstances might be passed on for a few generations within the same family. The fortress of ʿAd̲j̲lun, which still stands today, was just such a family seat.[26] Well known in the Crusader period and destroyed during the Mongol wars, it was rebuilt and entered the hands of Ibn Sāʿid's family in the later Mamluk period.

Ḳānṣūh's ancestor Ibn Sāʿīd had even, at times when he was fighting it out with the Mamluk governor of Syria, used ʿAd̲j̲lun's strategic location to deny passage to the pilgrimage caravans. However, the family had trouble adapting to the changed situation after the Ottoman conquest of Syria, and one of Ibn Sāʿīd's sons as well as one of his grandsons were executed. In later life Ibn Sāʿīd seems to have lost all his power, and the chroniclers do not even report how he met his end. The family survived this temporary fall from favour, however, and in the second half of the sixteenth century we find its members again established in and around 'Adjlun – it seems the family never lost its main seat, or at least managed to regain it in fairly short order.

We do not know for certain whether Ḳānṣūh Beg was a son, grandson or other relative of Ibn Sā'īd's. In a document dating from the year 1581 he is said to be eighty years old.[27] Allowing for the fact that the Islamic year is a lunar year, Ḳānṣūh would have been born about 1504–5, so that he may perfectly well be a son of Ibn Sā'īd's. But his political activity only began about 1551, so that either he must have been occupied with affairs of purely local importance during the first half of his life, or else he was born later than suggested by the aforementioned document.

We know that Ḳānṣūh Beg paid substantial sums to the Ottoman central administration to secure his various appointments, even though he never held office in agriculturally productive regions. When at one point he fell into disfavour and wished to reestablish himself and obtain an appointment, he offered the government a hundred thousand gold pieces.[28] This was certainly an unusual situation, and the offer does not sound like a realistic proposition. But even when, under much more 'normal' circumstances, he was appointed governor of 'Adjlun and Karak-Shaubak, and commander of the pilgrimage caravan, Ḳānṣūh Beg paid 5000 gold pieces directly to the Ottoman central administration; moreover, he promised to contribute 9000 gold pieces to the expenses of the caravan.[29] Thus the sale of offices, familiar to the historian of early modern Europe, was practised in the Ottoman Empire as well. The reasons in both cases were no doubt similar; governments were permanently short of cash and a bureaucracy regularly paid and remunerated according to performance criteria would have been much too expensive. In both cases, the taxpayer was the ultimate loser, as tax farmers and governors changed frequently and thus did not show much interest in preserving the population's ability to pay. In the regions close to the edge of the Syrian desert, the appointment of governors from locally prominent families somewhat mitigated these consequences.[30] In the sixteenth century, when the Ottomans were still in the process of consolidating their hold on the Syrian provinces, the appointment of governors with no local bases would have alienated a good many people and in most cases was therefore avoided.

Ḳānṣūh Beg's power in Syria thus rested upon his positions as governor, tax farmer and commander of the pilgrimage, all of which he owed to the Ottoman government. At the same time, however, he maintained close relations with the Beduins. Ḳānṣūh Beg belonged to the large faction of the Ḳızıllu (Reds), which was opposed to the faction of the Aḳlu or Aḳili (Whites).[31] Some modern historians have surmised that the two terms, Turkish in origin, hide two much more ancient groupings, namely the Kays and Yaman of early Islamic history. Be that as it may, the conflict had practical repercussions as far as the pilgrims were concerned. If Ḳānṣūh Beg, as a Ḳızıllu, commanded the caravan, the danger that pilgrims might be attacked at the stopping points under the control of the Aḳlu was not to be denied. One of Ḳānṣūh Beg's opponents did, in fact, try to prevent the appointment by declaring that 35 stopping points were controlled by the Aḳlu, and only three by Ḳānṣūh Beg's own group. Needless to say, the petitioner, a certain Salāma, belonged to the Aḳlu faction himself. Ever cautious, the Ottoman administration appointed neither of the two competitors. But the same year, Ḳānṣūh Beg was made a governor of the province of Karak-S͟hawbak, located directly on the pilgrimage road. The newly appointed official was enjoined to protect the pilgrims, and, as an additional safeguard, the governor of Damascus was ordered to reconcile Ḳānṣūh Beg and Salāma.

Among the documents, quite considerable in number, which deal with Ḳānṣūh Beg's tenure of office, a text from the year 1570–1 is particularly remarkable.[32] It constitutes an abridged version of an account of Ḳānṣūh's political career, which the governor himself must have presented to the central administration. Ḳānṣūh Beg declared that for a considerable time there had existed a state of enmity between himself and the Nu'aymog͟hulları, shaykhs of the Mafārid͟ja Beduins.[33] There may have been many reasons for this hostility, but Ḳānṣūh Beg chose to stress the fact that, in his 35 years' service to the pilgrims, he had always tried to keep camel rents low. We may thus conclude that the Nu'aymog͟hulları hired out camels and therefore were alienated by Ḳānṣūh's policy. The governor claimed that camel rents had gone down by half, because he had managed to increase the number of animals offered. This he had achieved by inviting Beduin groups that had not furnished any animals in the past to begin supplying the pilgrimage caravans. But when the news spread that Ḳānṣūh would not be commanding the next pilgrimage caravan, the suppliers who had recently entered the market rapidly withdrew. Presumably these were small and weak groupings, who feared the wrath of their competitors once Ḳānṣūh Beg was no longer there to shield them. As a result, camel rents once again increased, and the long-time commander apparently felt that the Ottoman authorities would draw the consequences from this situation.

Ḳānṣūh Beg's career only ended with his death in Istanbul in 1591, where he had gone to protest his recent deposition.[34] This event probably had been occasioned by a major Beduin rebellion. A governor of Damascus had attacked two groups of Beduins when they presumed themselves in a safe place, and it was claimed that Ḳānṣūh Beg was behind this attack. The result was a minor civil war, and 70 to 80 villages in the vicinity of Ḳānṣūh Beg's fortress of 'Adjlun were burnt down. The old governor did not succeed in regaining control of the fortress which had been in his family's hands for so many years, and this effectively ended his political career. His successors temporarily regained control of 'Adjlun; but rivalries among the sons, nephews and grandsons of Ḳānṣūh Beg permitted the Druze prince Fakhr al-Dīn II to extend his control over the region previously dominated by Ḳānṣūh's family. After about 1624, the descendants of Ibn Sā'id were not even locally prominent any more.

NEGOTIATIONS AND CONFLICTS WITH THE BEDUINS

Negotiations to secure the safety of the pilgrims began in Damascus, shortly before the previous year's caravan had returned to the city. It was important to appoint the caravan commander as soon as possible, for many arrangements with the Beduins were made by the commander as an individual and ceased to be binding if another person came to command the caravan. The designated caravan commander in addition conferred with respected inhabitants of Damascus, among whom the merchants accompanying every caravan certainly played an important role.

Further negotiation became necessary after the caravan had started on its way. In order to influence the behaviour of the Beduins the commander might manipulate the amount of *ṣürre* paid to particular groups. In extreme cases, when the commander was particularly dissatisfied, he might refuse payment altogether, but then an armed conflict became likely.[35] Sometimes payments for services rendered to the caravan were changed at the last minute. At other times the commander took hostages from certain Beduin families, and, in the case of open conflict, might order the murder or execution of a Beduin leader. Attacks on the pilgrimage caravan were a frequent occurrence, and as long as the number of dead and wounded remained within limits, these events were not considered particularly remarkable. Only when relations broke down completely were there major attacks on the caravan which the chroniclers of the time found worth reporting. Ewliyā Čelebi mentions an attack which occurred in the early 1670s.[36] Even more serious, but outside the period treated in this volume, was the attack on the Damascus caravan returning from Mecca in 1757, in which a large number of pilgrims perished. In some cases Ottoman government officials engaged in bloody reprisals against the Beduins, which might be legitimized in religious terms because of the threat the latter posed to the pilgrimage caravan.[37]

Some of the negotiations between Ottoman governors and Beduins living close to the pilgrimage route have been documented in the Registers of Important Affairs. We will discuss them here as examples of negotiations that took a normal course. In one case we again encounter Nu'aymoghlu, the Mafāridja shaykh, whom we already know as the opponent of Ḳānṣūh Beg.[38] The latter had offered to accompany the Damascus caravan for a stretch of the road, which meant that he also intended to guarantee its safety. But his Beduin allies, for reasons that remain unclear, withdrew from the agreement, and now Nu'aymoghlu refused to take the risk upon himself. It also happened that the Beduins who had offered to guarantee the safety of the caravan went back on their commitments, particularly if their *ṣürre* was not paid out on time. Such events might result in a sharp reprimand of the caravan commander by the Istanbul authorities.[39]

Some Beduin leaders received Ottoman titles and other marks of honour in addition to their *ṣürre* and food subsidies. In the Ottoman realm, as in the medieval Middle East, the grant of robes as marks of honour, comparable to modern decorations, was common.[40] Provincial governors, and particularly the Sherifs of Mecca, often received such honours, so that the grant of a robe integrated Beduin leaders into the Ottoman *cursus honorum*. Mamluk titles such as the amir al-'Arab were also awarded, probably with the same aim in mind.[41] Thus a document dated 1576–7 reports that an assembly of Damascene notables had testified that the personage to be awarded the title of amir al-'Arab had supplied the caravan in a satisfactory manner and therefore was worthy of the honour about to be conferred on him.

Conflictual situations also tell us a good deal about the relationship of the Beduins and the Ottoman central power. The scholar 'Abd al-Raḥmān Ḥibrī, who lived in Edirne and wrote a history of his town still used as a primary source, undertook the pilgrimage in 1632, a year in which there was a good bit of unrest on the Arabian peninsula.[42] At this time a local dynasty had reestablished itself in Yemen after several decades of Ottoman rule, and attempts to reconquer the rebellious province failed.[43] Ottoman soldiers obliged to leave the country settled in Mecca and caused so much trouble that the central government entrusted the powerful Mamluk Riḍwān Beg with the task of dislodging the soldiers from the Holy City.[44] One effect of Riḍwān Beg's campaign, however, was to make the pilgrimage routes insecure. According to Ḥibrī, things were made worse by the fact that Ibn Farrukh, long-time commander of the Syrian pilgrimage caravan, happened to be out of office in 1632: fear of Ibn Farrukh supposedly had restrained many tribesmen up to this time.[45] It does appear, however, as if the excesses committed by the soldiers returning from the Yemen, and the loss of Ottoman authority which these events entailed, played the key role in triggering Beduin attacks. There was fighting at almost every major stopping point that year, and near the settlement of al-'Ulā, where the Syrian desert becomes the Arabian, the caravan very narrowly escaped catastrophe. The Beduins attacked with muskets, and could only be kept under control by the firing of cannon. Four pilgrims were killed that very night, and Ḥibrī calculated that the caravan had lost 125 loaded camels along a stretch of road that measured less than half the distance from Damascus to Mecca.[46] But, in spite of everything, the caravan reached the Hejaz and returned in good order. This success must have strengthened the Ottoman position at a critical time, when the young Sultan Murād IV was taking the reins of government into his own hands and the Ottoman court was shaken by factional strife.[47]

The second example of a well-documented open conflict between pilgrims and Beduins occurred during the Ottoman–Habsburg war of 1683–99, when the central administration concentrated its attention upon events in the Balkan peninsula and pilgrims, Sherifs and Beduins were little protected or supervised. In this case, events were recorded by the Palestinian scholar and mystic 'Abd al-G̲h̲ānī al-Nābulusī, who travelled to Mecca as a pilgrim in 1693–5.[48] Before his pilgrimage to Mecca, al-Nābulusī had intended to visit the grave of the Prophet in Medina. But the Sherif Sa'd b. Zayd declared that the Ḥarb Beduins had closed the road from Yanbu' to Medina, and that it was impossible to get through. The Palestinian scholar thus had the opportunity to watch Sherif Sa'd's manner of conducting a war, and the behaviour of his Beduin troops. One village was found to be empty, because the inhabitants had joined the war on the side of the Ḥarb. Sherif Sa'd not only burnt the houses down, but even destroyed the date palms, a measure of unusual severity in desert warfare.[49] But Sherif Sa'd, who according to Ewliyā Čelebi had tried to cut off the water supply of Mecca during a previous dispute with the Ottoman administration, had no doubt that his actions were justified.[50] After all, so he argued, the Prophet Muḥammad had not treated the unbelievers any differently. The assumption that Beduins troubling the hajj caravan were to be treated as if they were unbelievers is found in other seventeenth-century Ottoman sources as well. Thus Ewliyā occasionally makes remarks pointing in the same direction. Sherif Sa'd's violent measures were successful; after a short while, the caravan was able to continue on its way toward Mecca.

Further evidence concerning violent repression of Beduins can be found in an unexpected place, namely the biography of Mi'mār Meḥmed Ag̲h̲a, the architect of the Blue Mosque in Istanbul.[51]

Mi'mār Meḥmed Agha was one of the few Ottoman artists to be honoured by a full-scale biography during his lifetime; it was composed by his admirer Dja'fer Efendi, son of Shaykh Behrām. In his varied career, Mi'mār Meḥmed Agha had also been sent to Syria as second-in-command to the governor of Damascus, Khusrew Pasha.[52] Later he was posted to the Hawran as a local administrator. This was a difficult assignment for, as we have seen in the biography of Ḳānṣūh Beg, this area was quite rebellion-prone, and unrest in the Hawran was likely to affect the security of the Damascus pilgrimage caravan. Mi'mār Meḥmed Agha, on the other hand, as a product of the levy of boys (*dewshirme*), who had seen service mostly in the Balkans, lacked the local contacts which constituted the strength, and occasionally the weakness, of Ḳānṣūh Beg and other inhabitants of the desert edge.[53]

At the time when Meḥmed Agha served the governor of Damascus, the pilgrimage caravan was attacked by Beduins, and Khusrew Pasha undertook a punitive expedition. But after a one-month campaign he was obliged to withdraw without having achieved anything. Meḥmed Agha was left behind with a small force and implored the help of the saint Seyyid Shaykh Ibrāhīm, to whose mausoleum he paid a pious visit. There the shaykh appeared to him in a dream, announcing that he would find the robbers in their camp, fast asleep, and commanded Meḥmed Agha to kill them all.[54] Meḥmed Agha's soldiers did, in fact, encounter a camp of sleeping Beduins, but they were afraid since the number of people was quite large, and did not dare to attack. Meḥmed Agha then told them about his dream and promised them the aid of Seyyid Ibrāhīm. But at least as effective as this assurance of saintly support was probably the threat that he, Meḥmed Agha, would kill any soldier who attempted to escape. Most of the Beduins were destroyed in the following battle; only the commander, a man named Djum'a Kāsib, was taken prisoner with his immediate associates. When the prisoners proceeded to offer a weighty ransom, Meḥmed Agha decided that, if they were let go, they would soon be molesting pilgrim caravans again: he therefore had his prisoners slain. At first his deeds were celebrated in Damascus as a great victory. Later, however, Khusrew Pasha seems to have had doubts concerning the political wisdom of his second-in-command, and Meḥmed was transferred to another post.[55]

In Dja'fer Efendi's account, a remarkable religious aura surrounds this minor episode of desert warfare. The author aims at creating an image of Meḥmed Agha as a hero of the Holy War and a person directly inspired by God, and this story is but one of many episodes marshalled for the purpose. That the Beduins were themselves Muslims is quite secondary to Dja'fer Efendi, who presents the event as an example of an authentic Holy War, in which the Ottoman soldiers are supported not merely by a saint, but by God himself. This is all the more remarkable as a pious medieval writer, namely Ibn D̲jubayr, had been favourably impressed by the religious attitudes of the Beduins.[56] By the seventeenth century things had completely changed; now we find an Ottomanized upper stratum in Syria and occasionally even in the Hejaz, who often spoke Arabic as their native language but were complete strangers to the world of the Beduins. In this context, it may be of some importance that Sherif Sa′d had had a career in the Ottoman core lands, officiating in the Thracian subprovinces of Ḳırḳkilīse and Vize, and therefore belonged to this Ottomanized milieu.[57] Beduins attacking the pilgrimage caravan were easily placed on the same level as unbelievers because, from a cultural point of view, they were regarded as total strangers by the ruling elite.

WEAPONS AND SOLDIERS

Ḥibrī's caravan of 1632 was able to get through the desert without major disasters because it carried cannons. Every one of these valuable weapons was accompanied by a cannonier and transported by horses or occasionally camels.[58] The anonymous writer of the 1580s, who wrote about the Cairo caravan, reports that six cannons were transported by twelve camels.[59]

In the late sixteenth and early seventeenth centuries many Beduins owned firearms, mainly muskets. We know that there was a tax farmer in the Palestinian town of Zefat (Safed) who sold grain to European unbelievers, which at that time was strictly forbidden.[60] His illegal gains he invested in muskets, which he smuggled to the Beduins. Artillery, on the other hand, was the exclusive privilege of the Ottoman authorities. Thus the twelve cannons which the Syrian caravan usually carried were a reasonably effective deterrent.

During the last years of Süleymān the Lawgiver's reign, approximately in 1558–9, the Damascus caravan was accompanied by 150 janissaries and garrison soldiers and 100 cavalrymen[61]. Even though the janissaries were normally infantrymen, they could not traverse the long distance from Damascus to Mecca without mounts. When spies, whom the caravan commander regularly sent out to gather information on Beduin plans, reported suspicious movements, the number of accompanying janissaries was increased. In 1571–2, a detachment of 300 soldiers was considered indispensable even in 'normal' times.

Even under the Mamluk Sultans, camels, foodstuffs and

implements needed by the soldiers had to be paid for by the fisc.[62] A special bureau took care of these matters. Its mode of operation is known to us from the careful account of 'Abd al-Ḳādir al-D̲j̲azarī, who had worked in this office for many years, as had his father (see Chapter 2). After Syria and Egypt had been conquered by the Ottomans, the office continued to operate in the accustomed manner. But after the death of Süleymān the Lawgiver in 1566, his successor Selīm II (reigned 1566–75) attempted to save money.[63] The new Sultan ordered that all the holders of *timār*s (tax assignments) accompanying the pilgrimage caravan would have to take care of their own equipment, as there was no reason to grant them advantages not accorded to other *timār*-holders, who all needed to spend considerable sums of money on their horses and outfits. But this order proved to be unworkable in practice. The vizier Muṣṭafā Pasha objected that the Syrian cavalrymen's revenues were so insecure that he could not recommend burdening them with supplementary expenditures. Selīm II gave in, and the cavalrymen were assigned 25 gold pieces per person for their equipment (1567–8).

Even so, it proved to be difficult to find military men suitable for the protection of the pilgrimage caravan. In a sultanic rescript from the years 1571–2 the governor and finance director of Damascus were warned that many cavalrymen turned the money they had been assigned over to prospective pilgrims.[64] The men accepting the money agreed to shoulder the obligation to protect the caravan, but often they were quite old and no longer suitable for military service. This practice was sternly prohibited by the Sultan's council, but to enforce the prohibition was quite a different matter. In 1587–8 there were renewed complaints that older janissaries who sought to combine the protection of the caravan with a pilgrimage were unable to support the rigours of military service in the desert.[65] On the other hand, caravan commanders probably viewed the participation of elderly and sober soldiers with some favour; for on the long desert stretches inhabited only by Beduins, disciplinary problems were widespread.

Certain cavalrymen and janissaries sought to avoid service in the caravan because, in a time of rising prices, they were unable to support themselves on their tax assignments or soldiers' pay, and needed to work in a secondary civilian occupation as well. Those soldiers possessing a small amount of capital often farmed the collection of taxes. Thus Turkmen *timār*-holders from the province of Aleppo farmed taxes due from the nomads and semi-nomads in this province, and were unavailable when their services were needed by the caravan.[66] The Sultan's Council threatened to take away the *timār*s of those cavalrymen who neglected their official duties. But the authorities could not make up their minds to increase the soldiers' tax assignments.

Military men in the service of the caravan commander were frequently caught trying to increase their incomes in more or less illicit ways. Deliveries of foodstuffs to the caravan offered certain possibilities in this respect.[67] Beduins in receipt of *ṣürre* were obligated to deposit foodstuffs at prearranged stopping points, and pilgrims unable to transport large quantities of supplies depended on the possibility of purchasing them en route. Certain janissaries, however, met the Beduins in the desert and either robbed or purchased below market value the foodstuffs the latter had been carrying, which they then proceeded to resell at a hefty profit to the pilgrims. This kind of profiteering hurt the pilgrims in two different ways: not only did they have to pay high prices for necessities, but the Beduins in question were likely to make good their losses by stealing from the caravan.

Apart from the conflicts caused by the soldiers' insufficient pay, the rivalries between Syrian and Egyptian military men occasioned quite a few disturbances. The sixteenth-century historian and littérateur Muṣṭafā 'Ālī recounts an anecdote about a Cairo soldier who is congratulated by his friends upon his safe return from the pilgrimage.[68] The man does not feel that there is any need for special felicitation; after all, he had gone to Mecca mainly to have a good fight with his Syrian rivals. Ewliyā also recounts a dispute between the soldiers of the Syrian and Egyptian caravans, when they encountered one another on a narrow stretch of road not far from Medina.[69] This rivalry was well known to the Ottoman central government, which had arranged the travelling schedules of the two caravans in such a way as to minimize contact. Apart from the fact that the market of Medina could not supply two large caravans at the same time, concern about brawls and fights determined route arrangements.

DESERT FORTIFICATIONS

Many stopping points in the desert were defended by small garrisons in charge of guarding the wells or reservoirs which contained the caravans' water supplies. In years of drought this was a major task, for Beduins in need of water for themselves and their animals were liable to take by force whatever was available.[70] Moreover, during desert fighting it was common practice to fill up or defile wells so as to render them unusable to the opponent. Pilgrim caravans might also be affected by this kind of warfare. According to Ewliyā Čelebi, the Damascus governor Ḥüseyin Pasha, who led the Syrian caravan to

Mecca in 1672, refused subsidies to rebellious Beduins whom he accused of having filled up wells, and had those who protested imprisoned and in some cases killed.[71]

New desert fortresses could not be built without the consent of the Ottoman central administration. Since the protection of the pilgrims was a major concern in Istanbul, provincial governors desiring to fortify this or that place usually adduced the needs of the pilgrimage as a motivation. When the governor of Egypt wished to build a fort in al-ʿArish, at the provincial border between Egypt and Syria, he declared that this place was frequently visited by pilgrims and merchants, who often suffered from Beduin attacks.[72] If a fortress were to be erected in this place, these attacks would become much less frequent, and the state would save money on the pay of the soldiers now needed to protect the caravans. Pilgrims visiting the sanctuary of Ibrāhīm in Hebron and Jerusalem were to be protected by a fortress at the often unsafe stopping point of ʿUyūn al-Tudjdjār.[73]

Yet Ewliyā's account makes it clear that the security problem was not solved by the construction of a desert fort alone.[74] Frequently enough, these isolated fortresses were attacked by Beduins and ultimately given up by a discouraged garrison. Ewliyā has a good deal to say on the tricks and feints which reputedly formed part of desert warfare. In 1625–6 Beduins attacked the fort of Muʿaẓẓama after having drugged the garrison with a sweetmeat into which a sleeping drug had been mixed. The garrison soldiers had been deceived by the blandishments of young Beduin maidens, who distributed the sweets as an offering in the name of a deceased person, to be accepted out of charity. Shortly after the lively and imaginative Ewliyā, the sober pilgrim Meḥmed Edīb enumerated all the desert forts he had encountered, but also described the elaborate precautions taken to protect the caravan while on the road.[75] Obviously Meḥmed Edīb also did not believe that the fortresses in the desert really guaranteed the pilgrims a safe trip.

IN SPITE OF EVERYTHING: AN ACCEPTABLE DEGREE OF SECURITY

But even though the pilgrim of the sixteenth and seventeenth centuries had to expect a good deal of trouble and even danger, major attacks upon the pilgrimage caravan were not all that frequent during this period. Ottoman officials, historians and travellers have written a good deal about the disasters of 1670–1 and 1757; therefore, they would presumably have written about other catastrophes of this kind had they occurred.[76] Other indirect evidence points in the same direction: narrative as well as documentary sources of the time frequently mention merchants accompanying the caravans, who used the time that pilgrims spent in Mecca after the pilgrimage ceremonies to conduct a profitable trade. If the pilgrimage routes had been as insecure as some historians of the twentieth century would have us believe, traders would not have taken their valuable wares through the desert.[77] Admittedly, the alternative route through the Red Sea was difficult from a navigational point of view, and shipping scarce and of poor quality. But Egyptian and Syrian traders could have invested in better ships, and if they failed to do so it was probably because the desert routes remained reasonably safe.

Ottoman administrators considered it necessary to secure the route to Mecca by means of negotiation and if necessary by violent repression because, by so doing, they legitimized the domination of the Ottoman Sultan. Every unavenged attack on the pilgrimage caravan jeopardized the claim of the ruler to be the supreme protector of the pilgrims. This situation also explains why Ottoman commentators like Ewliyā Čelebi and D̲ja'fer Efendi made no attempt to understand the Beduins' point of view. In the eyes of Ottoman officialdom, the Sultan's control over the pilgrimage routes constituted a major aspect of his legitimacy as a ruler. When Beduins challenged this control, members of the Ottoman ruling stratum might easily assume that the rebels had lost even their claim to the status of Muslims.

4

The Finances of the Holy Cities

After the rapid collapse of Mamluk domination in Egypt, pilgrims and inhabitants of the Holy Cities, or at least those among them with a certain political standing, needed to determine their attitude toward the rule of the Ottoman Sultan. Ever since the times of the Ayyubids (1175–1250) and, especially, the Mamluks (1250–1517), the Hejaz had been tied to Egypt politically – the Abbasid caliphate having been eliminated by the Mongol conquest in 1258. To those inhabitants of Syria, Egypt or the Hejaz familiar with the international situation, the Ottomans were by no means unknown: in the fifteenth century, both Meḥmed the Conqueror and Bāyezīd II had waged wars against Mamluk Sultans. Those wars had not led to major Ottoman gains of territory, however, so that the rapid and total Ottoman victory in 1515–17 necessitated a complete reorientation of the Egyptian, Syrian and Meccan upper classes. This reorientation was made more troublesome by the fact that sixteenth-century Islamic writers on political questions had some difficulty legitimizing Ottoman rule in general.[1] Contrary to the Safawids ruling sixteenth-century Iran, the Ottomans never claimed descent from the Prophet Muḥammad, and therefore lacked an important element of religious legitimation. Moreover, down to 1517 these Sultans did not control the Islamic heartlands. Instead they ruled an extensive area which for the most part had been Christian territory before the conquest, namely the Balkans as far as Belgrade in addition to western and central Anatolia. The Ottoman Sultans thus abruptly relocated themselves from the periphery to the centre of the Islamic world.

Given these circumstances, the Ottoman administration must have considered it expedient to change as little as possible in the established manner of supplying the Holy Cities. This conformed to Ottoman practice in other newly conquered territories as well; financial arrangements, particularly, were often allowed to subsist for decades before being adjusted to Ottoman practice, and, in some cases, taxes from pre-Ottoman times were even retained on a permanent basis.[2] But in the Hejaz the reasons for continuing Mamluk supply policies were more compelling than anywhere else; after all, the Ottoman Sultans sought legitimation not through descent, but through contemporary immediate political success. A policy of generosity toward pilgrims and inhabitants of the Holy Cities, which equalled and if possible surpassed the performance of the most brilliant Mamluk Sultans, constituted an effective source of legitimacy. Comparison with the Mamluks was facilitated if overall arrangements in favour of pilgrims and residents of the Hejaz were retained. However, as Ottoman administrators were to discover to their cost, certain Hejaz dignitaries were to continue regarding Mamluk Sultans such as Ḳā'it Bāy as the apogee of pious rule, to whom even Süleymān the Lawgiver came but a poor second.

SUBSIDIES AND THEIR RECIPIENTS

Since Mecca possesses almost no agricultural hinterland, it would have been impossible even in Abbasid times (750–1258) to feed a large number of pilgrims without subsidies from foreign rulers. In and around Medina, water resources were somewhat more abundant and agricultural production larger, but, on the other hand, demand was not insignificant either. Even before the Ummayads took power in 661, this city had developed into a centre for the study of all information concerning the Prophet's life and deeds, which was collected, subjected to critical study and taken down in writing.[3] It was the purpose of this activity to put together an image of the ideal Islamic community and present it to all Muslims as a model to be followed. This intimate concern with the life of the Prophet gave the city a special prestige, so that even in Abbasid times it was considered meritorious to settle there permanently. Moreover, wealthy Muslims who were not themselves in a position to retire to Medina, increasingly developed the inclination to support the inhabitants by donations, which would permit the latter a life of pious meditation. By the fifteenth century, donations for the poor of Medina were a popular form of charity throughout the Islamic world.

Support for the Sherifs of Mecca, who as a semi-independent local dynasty governed the Hejaz under Abbasid, Mamluk and ultimately Ottoman suzerainty, had more mundane reasons.[4] While the Sherifs were too poor to operate as fully independent princes, a ruler based in Baghdad, Cairo or Istanbul could not possibly control the Hejaz without the cooperation of the Sherifs. A member of this family who had fallen foul of his remote suzerain only needed to seek refuge with his Beduin allies in the desert, and from this all but impregnable position could make life very difficult for the pilgrims. Even in Ayyubid times it therefore had become customary to bind the Sherifs, and other Hejazi notables as well, to the Mamluk Sultans by means of gifts. As we have seen from Ibn Djubayr's account (see Chapter 1), in the twelfth century these gifts had not become institutionalized to any great extent, however.[5] Thus Ibn Djubayr does not mention pious foundations benefiting the inhabitants of the Holy Cities; these were not instituted on a large scale until the time of the Mamluk Sultans.

FOUNDATIONS AND GIFTS

By the fifteenth century, foundations benefiting the Holy Cities were not limited to Egypt, though that was where the most extensive foundations of this type were located. In the sparsely settled and politically fragmented Anatolia of that time, the Karamanid dynasty of Konya, at one point the ally of Venice against the Ottomans, established such foundations around the steppe town of Ereğli.[6] In the Balkans, newly conquered by the Ottomans, such foundations also began to operate quite early on, the oldest known Rumelian foundation dating from 1460–1.[7] High officials at the court of Sultan Meḥmed the Conqueror appear to have been among the founders, and, by the sixteenth century, foundations benefiting the Holy Cities could be found in the Balkan borderlands of the rapidly expanding empire.

These foundations were supported by peasant taxes from villages originally owned by the founder and assigned to this purpose in perpetuity. In addition, the Holy Cities received grants from the Ottoman Sultans which appear in the yearly budgets (see Chapter 2) and which were financed by ordinary revenues; but, in this case, the Sultan could decide every year how much money he was going to send. We possess a list of gifts made by Sultan Bāyezīd II (reigned 1481–1512) to various recipients in the Hejaz: the poor of Medina received 14,442 gold pieces.[8] Apparently Mouradjea d'Ohsson, eighteenth-century dragoman to the Swedish embassy in Istanbul and author of a comprehensive work on the Ottoman Empire of his own time, must have seen either this document or else another one very much like it; for he reports that Bāyezīd II annually donated 14,000 gold pieces to the poor of Medina.[9] Table 3 lists the donations which

Table 3 *Bāyezīd II's Gifts to the Hejazis*

Recipients	akče	*Ottoman gold coins*
Pilgrims, in general	21,500	
Individual inhabitants of Mecca and Medina	3300	
'Beduins from Mecca'	10,400	
Messengers bringing gifts to the Holy Cities	25,500	
Inhabitants of Mecca		735
Inhabitants of Medina		1210
The poor of Mecca and Medina		831 14,422
Miscellaneous	5000	
Total	65,700	17,198

Since there existed different types of gold coins, the rate of exchange is approximate. A gold coin was worth about 50 *aḳče*, see Artuk and Artuk (1971, 1974), vol. 2, p. 494. This table does not include certain gifts to individuals identified as Meccans or inhabitants of Medina, as it is not clear whether they benefited as individuals or as inhabitants of the Holy Cities. Certain Arabs or Beduins from Mecca also mentioned in the register probably had come to the court as messengers; the largesse they received has therefore been included.

this Sultan, whom some chroniclers regarded as a saint, sent to Mecca and Medina in 1503–4. Among the recipients, we find the Ḥanefī *ḳāḍī*s of both the Holy Cities, a son of the amir of Yanbu', a teacher in a theological college and the descendants of certain well-known derwish shaykhs.[10] The mosque of the Prophet in Medina formed the subject of the Sultan's special solicitude; its employees received donations which were far more generous than those assigned to their counterparts in Mecca.

The gifts of 1503–4 probably did not constitute a unique case, but were repeated with slight variation from year to year. As an indicator of institutionalization, we may cite the fact that an envoy of the people of Medina appeared in Istanbul to collect the gifts on behalf of his fellow citizens. When regular recipients of the Sultan's bounty died, the ruler was informed of the fact by letter from the *ḳāḍī* of Mecca; then the place of the deceased was normally filled by a new beneficiary. Thus certain features of the Ottoman Sultans' gift-giving were established well in advance of the conquest of Cairo.

Table 4 *Expenditure for Pilgrims and the Holy Cities from the Central Administration's Budget*

Year	*Expenditures in* akče *(a)*	*Total budget (b)*	*a/b as %*
1527–8	4,286,475	403,388,322	1.1–1.2
1653	7,142,298	676,106,387	1.1
1660–1	10,898,778	593,604,361	1.8
1690–1	16,567,320	812,838,365	2

DONATIONS ON THE PART OF THE OTTOMAN CENTRAL GOVERNMENT

In the Ottoman financial accounts, which most historians are in the habit of calling budgets (see Chapter 2), we not infrequently find information concerning expenditure on the pilgrimage and the Holy Cities.[11] It is difficult, however, to determine to what extent the disbursements listed in Table 4 can be compared with one another, since a heading which remained more or less unchanged over the years might group expenditures which varied in nature in the course of time. For Ottoman finance officials, concerned with an overview of the past year's finances and not with long-term comparisons, this was irrelevant; for us, unfortunately, it is not. Moreover, the budgets did not record expenditures in an exhaustive manner, so that certain donations to the inhabitants of the Hejaz may have gone unrecorded. The figures we possess, therefore, should be regarded as minimal values. It is also often impossible to separate expenditures for the pilgrimage from those destined for the year-round inhabitants of the Holy Cities. In the present chapter, we will concern ourselves mainly with the latter. Under the circumstances it seems best to compare the percentages of pilgrimage and Hejaz-related expenditures with respect to the relevant totals, without according too much importance to minor discrepancies from one budget to the next.

Table 4 shows an increase in absolute terms which is largely due to the devaluation of the currency which occurred in the 1580s and thereafter.[12] There is also a notable increase in the percentage value of hajj- and Hejaz-related expenditures toward the end of the seventeenth century. This may be due to the fact that the central administration needed to make up the deficit which ensued when the Mamluks retained more and more Egyptian revenue sources for their own use.[13] Since the safe travel of the pilgrims was such a vital affair, payments were not interrupted even during the turmoil of the

Table 5 *Expenditure on Behalf of the Holy Cities According to the Egyptian Budget of 1596–7 (in* pāra*)*

For the caravan commander	400,000
Subsidies for the Holy Cities	1,327,040
Other	2,630,985
Total	4,358,025

Ottoman–Habsburg war (1683–99), a time when many other concerns were neglected.

PAYMENTS FROM EGYPTIAN BUDGETS

Even though Ottoman domination in the Hejaz became more costly to maintain with time, the load on the central administration's budget was not too great. Before the increasing political strength of the Mamluks allowed them to curtail the Egyptian contributions, and to some extent even beyond, Egypt was the main source of grain and funds for the pilgrimage. Grain prices in Mecca being always much higher than those in Egypt, an increased remittance of money at the expense of grain was always to the disadvantage of recipients in the Hejaz. According to the budget of 1596–7, subsidies sent to Mecca and Medina out of official Egyptian revenues amounted to at least 903,892 *pāra* or 22,597 gold pieces, and this total does not include the Beduin *ṣürre*s, some of which also went to the Hejaz.[14] Almost 10 per cent of the Egyptian budget of those years was spent on the support of the Hejaz, even though the revenues secured from the Egyptian public foundations almost certainly were not included in the totals.

From the money assigned to him the caravan commander had to purchase a variety of goods, on which in many cases he must have made a substantial profit. The same probably applied to other members of the provincial administration, for complaints on this score are routinely repeated in administrative records of the time, to say nothing of the bitter denunciations of the contemporary historian Muṣṭafā 'Ālī.[15] Some of these profits may have been hidden under a vaguely phrased heading which for the most part covered administrative and transportation expenditures. Admittedly, both grains and coin, the principal goods carried to the Hejaz, were both expensive to store and transport. Even so, the share of insufficiently identified and therefore possibly illicit expenses appears suspiciously high.

Even if the caravan commanders and their servitors made more or less illicit profits, genuine transport expenditures cannot be neglected.

Many camels died on the long march through the desert and needed to be replaced. Shipwrecks were common, and the construction of ships in an all but treeless environment was very expensive. In many cases, the Egyptian provincial administration must have subsidized transportation to the Hejaz of grain from the Egyptian foundations, whose budgets were notoriously insufficient.

Certain tendencies of the 1596–7 budget equally recur in seventeenth-century financial accounts, even though there was some variation from year to year which we can explain only in certain instances, while others remain somewhat opaque.[16] In 1601–2 there was probably a harvest failure, as remittances to the Hejaz were surprisingly low. On the other hand, in 1612–13 expenditures were much higher than in previous years, because the major costs of the extensive rebuilding projects of Sultan Aḥmed I (reigned 1603–17, see Chapter 5) were paid out of Egyptian revenues.[17] But the high costs of administration and transport and the amalgamation of genuine transportation expenditures with Beduin subsidies were permanent traits of the Egyptian Hejaz-related budget. For that reason the seventeenth-century budgets provide no better opportunity for checking official probity than the budget of 1596–7.

EGYPTIAN FOUNDATIONS BENEFITING THE HOLY CITIES

When Sultan Selīm I conquered the Hejaz in 1517, quite a few foundations providing grain to the Holy Cities and instituted by Mamluk Sultans and amirs were still in operation.[18] The latter were ultimately reformed and subsumed under the overall heading of the Greater De<u>sh</u>ī<u>sh</u>e foundation, whose core was made up of the foundations of Sultans Ḳā'it Bāy and Čaḳmaḳ.[19] Sultan Süleymān the Magnificent and his successor Selīm II expanded these foundations by their own additions. Moreover, Murād III (reigned 1574–95) established the so-called Lesser De<u>sh</u>ī<u>sh</u>e foundation, which mainly remitted money. There were also two soup kitchens founded in Mecca and Medina by Sultan Süleymān in the name of his consort <u>Kh</u>urrem Sultan, better known in Europe under the name of Roxolana; these were also funded out of Egyptian tax revenues.

All Egyptian foundations had been assigned villages whose taxes constituted their yearly revenues. In the sixteenth century, these foundations were frequently enlarged by the addition of new villages. In some cases, however, the newly annexed settlements merely made up the losses occasioned by the decline in revenues from the original villages. For even though it can be assumed that population and agri-

Table 6 *Expenditure on Behalf of the Holy Cities According to Early Seventeenth-century Egyptian Budgets (in parā)*[1]

Type of expenditure	*1600–1*	*1601–2*	*1612–13*
Payments to the inhabitants of the Holy Cities	194,525	unknown	less than 100,000
Transportation and administrative expenses	387,409	121,263	332,856
Other	1,312,355	unknown	ca. 4,000,000[2]
Total	1,894,289	1,393,423	4,392,331
Total (in gold coins)	47,107	34,835	109,808

1 MM 5672. See Shaw (1968), pp. 268–82 on the general background. It is not clear whether the totals include the prestations of the public foundations.
2 Largely construction expenditures in Mecca; in addition, this total probably includes the expenses of two subsequent pilgrimages.

culture in sixteenth-century Egypt expanded, individual villages were often ruined by natural or man-made calamities.[20] The Meccan chronicler Ḳuṭb al-Dīn, who wrote in the second half of the sixteenth century, believed that the new additions were insufficient to make up for a marked decline in the yield of old foundation holdings.[21]

That such losses did in fact occur is apparent from an account of the Greater De<u>sh</u>ī<u>sh</u>e foundation, which encompasses the period from July 1591 until November 1592.[22] Total income for that period amounted to 10,678,643 *pāra*, a substantial sum when compared to any one of the major expenditures in the Egyptian budget of 1596–7. But more than seven million were merely arrears from previous years, and even in 1591–2, the foundation still had 6.8 million *pāra* owed to it, presumably for the most part outstanding peasant dues. For its official purposes, the Greater De<u>sh</u>ī<u>sh</u>e had only been able to spend about two and a half million *para*. Nor had the foundation fulfilled its obligations in terms of grain deliveries; the Greater De<u>sh</u>ī<u>sh</u>e foundation owed the inhabitants of Mecca and Medina back deliveries for several years. A new administrator had just been appointed, who with some success tried to get the apparatus of the foundation moving again. But in the meantime the population of the Holy Cities must have suffered severe scarcities.

Contemporary documents mention some of the manipulations which resulted in the decline of foundation-sponsored grain deliveries. The tax collectors in charge of adjacent villages often usurped the revenues from villages held by the foundations.[23] Official corruption, frequently denounced in contemporary texts, also had a role to play – but the Ottoman policy of fighting corruption by a frequent change of foundation administrators was also quite often counterproductive. The confusion attendant upon frequent changes in personnel might result in a further decrease of grain and money deliveries.

ANATOLIAN FOUNDATIONS FOR THE BENEFIT OF MECCA AND MEDINA

A carefully executed register from the late sixteenth century informs us about the geographical distribution and financial resources of these foundations.[24] It was put together because of a dispute among high-level Ottoman functionaries, and to fully understand the nature of the data it contains, the background must be explained in some detail. Most Anatolian and Rumelian foundations had been established by private persons, but their annual proceeds were collected by the central administration and sent to the Hejaz en bloc. This was certainly the most economical solution in terms of transportation costs, but the danger that foundation-owned money was used for the daily needs of the Ottoman administration was not to be gainsaid. Now Ottoman officials disagreed over the question whether the administration should pay a standard sum to the population of the Holy Cities in place of the actual revenues of the many small private foundations which constituted their due, and which varied greatly in accordance with harvests and internal security conditions prevailing in their respective localities. The very diplomatic and polite formulations used in this text do not spell out the objection, which however must have been foremost in the minds of those officials opposed to the new dispensation, namely that the Ottoman government was likely to withhold some of the donations destined for the poor of the Holy Cities, and thereby violate the dispositions of the founders, sacrosanct in Islamic foundation law. Instead, those officials who preferred to continue with the old method pointed out that there was no precedent for the new arrangement, for an occurrence which previously had been proposed as a precedent after further investigation could no longer be regarded as such. Finally the case was submitted to Sultan Murād III (reigned 1574–95), who decided that the revenues of all foundations benefiting the Holy Cities should be handed over to their legitimate recipients and all violations of the donors' intentions scrupulously avoided.

Our text was probably written with much care, as it was meant to serve Murād III as a basis for his decision. In order to facilitate judgment of the case and later checking up on the activities of finance officials, the foundations were listed one by one. The inventory covers Istanbul, Edirne and Bursa, most of Rumelia and the Anatolian provinces of Anaḍolu, Ḳarāmān, Rūm, Mar'ash and Diyārbakır. Foundations in Syria, on the island of Cyprus and in Baghdad are also recorded, so that the inventory supplies a reasonably complete record of all Mecca and Medina foundations with the exception of those located in Egypt.

In 1588–9 the Anatolian and Rumelian foundations recorded 3,375,610 *aḳče* as their regular income. If we add once-and-for-all contributions and outstanding dues from previous years, the total is 4,206,142 *aḳče* or 35,051 Ottoman gold coins. This was a modest contribution compared to the prestations of the Egyptian foundations; for, in spite of all its problems, the Greater Deshīshe alone delivered about 64,600 gold pieces. Yet given the fact that so many of the founders were private individuals, the total was quite impressive nonetheless. After all, in provincial Anatolian towns during those years, a few thousand *aḳče* would buy a house, and in Istanbul during the last weeks and months of the sixteenth century, 355 grams of bread cost an *aḳče* and a chicken 14–16 *aḳče*.[25]

In the Ottoman capital, foundations benefiting the Holy Cities, and more particularly Medina, were very popular, though this does not mean that inhabitants of Istanbul necessarily chose the poor of the Hejaz as the prime recipients of their charities. But very often foundations were established to benefit specific people, such as the family or former slaves of the donor. When these beneficiaries had died, the foundation revenue was then transferred to the poor of Mecca or Medina. Members of the Sultan's family establishing pious foundations quite often reserved a sum of money for the inhabitants of the Hejaz from the very beginning. Thus the mother of Sultan Selīm I (reigned 1512–20) ordered the annual distribution of 1000 golden *eshrefiye* coins to the poor of Medina.[26] This money was to be taken from the fees paid by the users of the public bath of Sultan Bāyezīd II (reigned 1481–1512), which was (and still is) located in downtown Istanbul.

Many Mecca- and Medina-related foundations were strongly affected by the inflation of the later sixteenth century. For in the Holy Cities the *aḳče*, the principal Ottoman silver coin of this period, was not in use, so that gold coins were generally employed for the transfer of subsidies. But as the *aḳče* was devalued *vis à vis* the Ottoman gold coin, the value of Anatolian and Rumelian prestations sank accordingly. Some founders attempted to prevent this by fixing the height of their prestation in gold currency. We possess a record of the foundation of a certain Istanbullu named Meḥmed b. Aḥmed which contained a clause of this type.[27] But this did not solve the problem: when the *akče* was devalued by 100 per cent, the foundation was obliged to increase its revenue by the same amount, if it wished to abide by the donor's stipulation. In most cases, this would have been all but impossible.

On the Balkan peninsula outside of Istanbul, foundations benefiting the Holy Cities were concentrated in and around the former capital of Edirne. In the region of Salonica and Yenidje Vardar, the descendants of Ghāzī Evrenos, who had played an important role in the Ottoman conquest of the Balkans during the fourteenth century, established a foundation for the poor of Medina.[28] But foundations of this type were much more widespread in western and central Anatolia. Bursa, another former capital of the Ottoman Sultans, possessed a large number of such foundations, even though their value was much lower than that of their Istanbul counterparts. In the region of Amasya, Tokat, Sivas and Kayseri, but also in northern and central Anatolia, a number of wealthy foundations also served the poor of Mecca and Medina. This is all the more remarkable as these cities were of some commercial importance, but, except for Amasya, had not served as residences for princes and Sultans over any length of time. The foundations of Konya Ereğlisi in southern central Anatolia, on the other hand, owed their existence to the pre-Ottoman dynasty of the Karamanids, who had developed this stopping point of caravans into a small but active town. In the sparsely settled border regions of eastern Anatolia, however, foundations benefiting the Holy Cities were scarce, apart from the commercial centre of Diyarbakır. On the island of Cyprus, recently conquered from the Venetians, Ottoman governors had established some foundations of this kind.[29] The register also contains references to foundations in favour of Mecca and Medina located in Mosul and Baghdad. But no detailed information is available on these remote provinces, where Ottoman domination was as yet insecurely established.

We can thus group the foundations benefiting Mecca and Medina in two different categories. In Istanbul, and to a lesser extent in Edirne and the larger Anatolian cities, we find numerous small foundations, many of which had probably been instituted by local merchants and, occasionally, wealthy artisans. Outside of these larger urban centres, foundations in favour of the Hejazi poor were usually instituted by Ottoman officials, and sometimes by members of the Sultans' families. In newly conquered provinces, such as Cyprus with its recent Venetian past, these foundations probably symbolized the intention to establish a firm and durable bond with the religious centres of the Islamic world.[30]

THE INHABITANTS OF MECCA AND MEDINA: A POPULATION ESTIMATE

Concerning the distribution of the pious gifts which Sultan Selīm I had assigned to the inhabitants of Mecca, we possess the account of the Meccan chronicler Ḳuṭb al-Dīn.[31] He describes how amir Muṣliḥ al-Dīn, Selīm I's envoy to the Hejaz, made a list of all the poor households in the city; his list included the names of their members, who were each assigned three gold pieces a year. By the later sixteenth century, payments were still being made according to amir Muṣliḥ al-Dīn's records. In addition (unfortunately we cannot tell whether before or after amir Muṣliḥ al-Dīn's count), the city's notables made a list of their own. This encompassed all occupied houses and all inhabitants of the city apart from merchants and soldiers – that is, women, children and servants in addition to the adult male population, a total of 12,000 persons. After registration, each of them received a share of the donations, which Ḳuṭb al-Dīn understood to be on the basis of a legal claim, and in addition a gold piece per person as a free gift. From Ḳuṭb al-Dīn's account, one may conclude that the city had 15,000 regular inhabitants at the very least, for the merchants, who had no claim to pious gifts, were usually numerous in Mecca, and many must have been heads of resident households. Unfortunately, Ḳuṭb al-Dīn tells us nothing either about them or about the soldiers.

We have no further data about the Meccan population in later years, but for Medina a few figures are available. In 1579–80 the Ottoman authorities assumed that 8000 people lived in the city in pious retreat (*müdjāvir*).[32] If each one of these people was in charge of a household of five persons, Medina should have had a population of at least 40,000 people, not counting merchants and soldiers with no claim to pious subsidies. On the other hand, many of the *müdjāvir*s of Medina must have been elderly people, who had smaller than average households. In 1594–5, 7000 inhabitants of Medina received subsidies from the Ottoman state.[33] If the criteria by which eligibility was determined had not changed in the meantime, the city's population should have contracted. A text from the mid-seventeenth century claims that during the reign of Murād III (reigned 1574–95) Medina's inhabitants totalled 6666 persons, which seems dubious in the light of previous and later figures. In 1641–2 23,200 inhabitants of the city received official support, though the authorities in Istanbul did suspect that this figure had been inflated by fraudulent manipulation.[34] A new count was therefore ordered, but no record of the results has been found. Medina probably contained more recipients of outside aid than Mecca, but this assumption is based on the fact that so much more is said in official documents about Medina, and of course there may have been other reasons, hitherto unknown, for this disproportion.[35]

THE DISTRIBUTION OF SUBSIDIES AND PENSIONS

When pensions and subsidies were distributed without incident, we know almost nothing about the process, for most of the documents relating to this issue are sultanic commands, designed to abolish this or that abuse. Usually complaints from pension recipients and local administrators preceded rescripts of this kind, but they have not survived; all that remains of the letters of complaint are the summaries at the beginning of the responses issued in the name of the Sultan. A frequent cause for complaint was the late arrival of grain deliveries, 1569–70 and 1578–81 being particularly bad years in that respect.[36] Outside of the pilgrimage season it was very difficult to earn money in Mecca, so that the late arrival of official subsidies caused distress so acute that pious inhabitants of Mecca could not afford to participate in the pilgrimage ceremony on 'Arafat, even though most of the Meccan population took part in this ritual every year.[37]

Even when subsidies finally arrived in Mecca or Medina a disappointment might be in store for the recipients, as the grain was often spoilt due to poor storage while in transit. A rescript from the year 1583 describes the *khān* located in Yanbu', the port of Medina, which was in such poor condition that, in the previous year, 3000 *irdeb* of wheat sent on behalf of the Deshīshe foundation had suffered water damage.[38] A thorough repair of the *khān* would have cost 3000 gold pieces, and the administrator of Jeddah, who had been ordered to take care of the matter had done nothing at all, protesting that everything in the Hejaz was very expensive. Moreover, the Beduins in charge of transporting the grain often stole some of it, mixing earth in the sacks so as to prevent detection of their pilfering; of course, knowledge of such tricks was not limited to Beduins.[39]

Other complaints concerned money remittances. Sometimes the Ottoman administration remitted not the coins most employed in the Hejaz, namely *pāra* and gold pieces, but a silver coin known as *shāhī* which, as its name indicates, originally was intended for the Iranian market. *Shāhī*s were minted by the Ottoman administration to make a profit from the outflow of silver to Iran, which in spite of all prohibitions could not be stopped. When coins were sent instead of bars or jewellery, at least minting dues could be charged. Somehow the *shāhī*s also became current in Syria, where peasants used them for the payment of taxes.[40] But this coin never gained acceptance in the Hejaz, and recipients of subsidies paid out in *s͟hāhī*s had a lot of trouble in consequence. Money changers, however, certainly profited from this situation.

The conflict of interest occasioned by the employment of the *s͟hāhī* for subsidies to the Hejaz was discussed by the *ḳāḍī* of Damascus.[41] This official explained that at the time of writing (1583) gold and gold coins were extremely scarce in Syria. Therefore it was unreasonable to demand that local peasants pay their taxes in money, although the *ḳāḍī* realized that the remittance of large quantities of silver coins was bound to create hardships for the poor of the Hejaz.[42] The administration tried to solve the problem by legislating the rate of exchange for the *s͟hāhī*, with what consequences remains unknown.[43] At other times the Ottoman government attempted to keep the *s͟hāhī* out of Mecca and Medina altogether, by demanding that these coins be exchanged for gold or *pāra* before remittance. If gold was scarce and expensive, however, the poor of the Hejaz were bound to lose, one way or the other.

Other conflicts arose because people who did not possess any rights to official aid managed to secure it nonetheless, or because people with political power assigned themselves much higher subsidies than those to which they would have normally been entitled.[44] Quite often, officials in charge of distribution kept a share of the subsidies for themselves. Sometimes *ḳāḍī*s and finance administrators made sure that people who did not even live in the Hejaz received grants from the foundations intended to benefit the poor of Mecca and Medina.[45] Thus a *medrese* teacher living in Damascus was being paid for teaching at the establishment founded by Sultan Süleymān in Mecca. As a result a colleague of his, who did in fact teach at the school, was unable to draw his pay.

In Medina there occurred a long drawn-out dispute involving the rights of a group of descendants of the Prophet Muḥammad known as the Banū Ḥusayn.[46] These influential families claimed one third of all subsidies sent to Mecca; they possessed a rescript from Sultan Murād III which assigned them grants-in-aid from the Des͟hīs͟he foundation. This was in itself remarkable. In the sixteenth century, when Ottomans and Safawids were frequently at war, the recipients of official subsidies normally had to be Sunnis, while the Banū Ḥusayn were Shi'is. The governor of Egypt opposed the Banū Ḥusayn's demands, pointing out that other legitimate claimants would then have to be denied their rights. For a while the opponents of the Banū Ḥusayn had the upper hand in Istanbul, and the Sultan's Council denied them official support of any kind. But the Banū Ḥusayn insisted and, in the long run, they seem to have been successful, for in the early seventeenth century we find them receiving subsidies out of the Egyptian provincial budget.[47]

AN ATTEMPT AT REFORMING THE DISTRIBUTION OF SUBSIDIES

Since complaints concerning the distribution of subsidies concentrated on Medina, an attempt at reform from the year 1594–5 also refers principally to this city. Various pious people with claims on the ruler's bounty had reported that, of 6000 *irdeb* of wheat delivered, one third was subtracted straight away (presumably this was the share of the Banū Ḥusayn); 1000 *irdeb* were reserved for the kitchen (probably the soup kitchen founded by Sultan Süleymān); and several hundred *irdeb* for administrative personnel and other expenses. This did not leave very much for the poor.[48] In the answer to this complaint, the Ottoman government laid down the principle that employees performing a service should receive a salary (*'ulūfe*), leaving all grants defined as alms for the genuine poor. When people in receipt of charities died, their rights to subsidies should not pass on to their heirs; rather, these vacant positions were to be entered into a special register for reassignment to other poor already residing in Medina. Candidates for official support could be native to the city or have moved there; what mattered was not their origin, but their piety and religious learning. Inhabitants of Medina who did not need the subsidies and invested them in trade were to be removed from the list of subsidy recipients. The same thing applied to people who were negligent in the performance of their daily prayers or whose lives were not above reproach. Slaves were to be excluded from all subsidies, presumably because their owners were responsible for their upkeep. Nothing is said about the claims of the Banū Ḥusayn, who had caused so much trouble in the recent past. Possibly the Ottoman administration hoped that the matter had resolved itself when Murād III increased the Medina subsidies by the amount of 5000 *irdeb*. Possibly the decrease of claimants discussed above should be connected with the edict of 1594–5 and the more stringent criteria ordered therein. But it is impossible to tell whether the stipulations of 1594–5 were effective for any length of time.

TOTAL EXPENDITURES IN FAVOUR OF THE PILGRIMAGE AND THE HOLY CITIES

Items of information about the different types of Ottoman expenditures in the Hejaz do not all date from the same year, and cannot therefore be used to put together a hajj-related budget for any given year. But to gain a rough overall impression nonetheless, we will add up a few figures referring to the major items of expenditure, both documented and estimated. We can assume that the Greater De<u>sh</u>ī<u>sh</u>e produced about 65,000 *akče* a year, and the Lesser De<u>sh</u>ī<u>sh</u>e about 10,000. From the foundations of Anatolia and Rumelia, about 28,000 gold pieces were obtained annually. Subsidies from the Egyptian provincial budget amounted to about 23,000 gold pieces, but often the sum really expended must have been a great deal higher, with an upper limit of about 109,000 gold pieces.[49] From the customs revenues of Jeddah, which the Ottoman administration had abandoned to the Sherif of Mecca, the latter in the 1580s could expect to collect about 90,000 gold pieces (see Chapter 7). We thus arrive at a total of between 216,000 and 302,000 gold pieces. In addition, there was the value of the grain sent to the Hejaz by the Egyptian foundations to be taken into account, while expenditures on behalf of the Syrian caravan amounted to about 80,000 gold pieces. Outside of grain deliveries, the pilgrimage thus cost the late sixteenth- and early seventeenth-century Ottoman administration anything between 300,000 and 385,000 gold pieces.

These figures become more meaningful when we compare them to other major expenditures of the Ottoman imperial budget. Between February 1606 and May 1607, 618,416 gold pieces were spent on the Ottoman war effort against the Habsburgs, excluding war matériel and a few other expenditures.[50] This is remarkable if we consider that, for the Ottoman Empire as for early modern European states, war was by far the most important item of expenditure. Of course these figures can do no more than indicate an order of magnitude, but it is still important that a sum of money roughly equivalent to one half or two thirds of annual campaign expenses was set aside for maintaining a measure of control over the Hejaz.

In return, the Holy Cities and the surrounding region produced no revenues for the Ottoman treasury, apart from the share of the Jeddah customs revenues not assigned to the Sherifs. Yet although at the end of the sixteenth and the beginning of the seventeenth century the position of the Ottoman treasury was quite precarious, as becomes obvious from the devaluations of this period, neither the Sultans nor members of their Council ever suggested that expenditures for the pilgrimage or the Holy Cities be cut down. Only in the late seventeenth century, when other wars against the Habsburgs put a severe strain on Ottoman resources (1660–4, 1683–99), do we observe attempts to cut down drastically on hajj-related expenditures.[51] By contrast, most sixteenth-century Sultans readily increased expenditures on the pilgrimage and the Holy Cities, which indicates their political importance.

The accounts also indicate that Egypt remained the source of most subsidies remitted to the Holy Cities; grain and other foodstuffs came almost exclusively from this source. Of the 300,000–385,000 gold pieces sent to the Hejaz every year, at least 120,000 or about one third were derived directly from Egyptian sources. In reality the percentage was no doubt higher: a significant share of the Jeddah customs revenues, for example, was paid by Egyptian merchants and shipowners in the first instance.

After about 1660, or 1670 at the very latest, this set of arrangements, which for one and a half centuries had enabled the Ottomans to maintain themselves in the Hejaz, was in deep trouble. The Mamluk tax collectors were less and less inclined to pass on Egyptian tax revenues to Istanbul, and after 1683 regular financing of the pilgrimage caravans became all but impossible. When, in the early eighteenth century after the war was over, Ottoman administrators attempted to reestablish control over the pilgrimage routes, it was necessary to rebuild not only *khān*s and fortifications, but, at least in Syria, the administrative structure as well.

The Istanbul authorities of the sixteenth and seventeenth centuries apparently reasoned that they needed to secure foodstuffs and a safe passage to the pilgrims, as well as subsidies to the inhabitants of Mecca and Medina, because any obvious failure delegitimized the Sultan himself. A flood of rescripts was therefore sent out to prevent corrupt practices and ensure that subsidies actually reached the intended beneficiaries:

> In the time of my late father, the ruler – may his grave be fragrant – [deliveries of money and grains on the part of different foundations as well as other payments] were not handed over on time, due to the negligence of the provincial governors and the avarice and lack of piety among supervisors and Beduin shaykhs. Arrears reached scandalous levels, so that the poor of the Holy Cities, the servitors [of the different foundations] and the pious inhabitants [of the Holy Cities] suffered great want. The Sultan has learned of their sorry plight . . . .[52]

Administrative reorganization and the appointment of a new Chief Supervisor were meant to secure that

> the Beduin shaykhs take note of the financial probity of the Supervisor and thereupon desist from their treason, and instead follow the path of justice. Then we will ensure that the wheat

> deliveries of the Deshīshe, alms and salaries reach their destinations in full and on time. In this sense, my auspicious sultanly writ has been issued and my most noble order sent forth.

Quite obviously, the legitimacy of the Ottoman Sultan was at stake here.

5

In Praise of Ruler and Religion: Public Buildings in Mecca and Medina

When the Ottomans took over Mecca in 1517, they found the Great Mosque in the shape which it had received under the early Abbasids (750–86), apart from the Ka'aba which last had been rebuilt in early Ummayad times.[1] After the Ummayad governor al-Ḥadjdjādj had overthrown the Meccan caliph al-Zubayr in 693, he restructured the Ka'aba in such a fashion as to get rid of the changes which the defeated ruler had imposed. Thereafter, the Ka'aba was a rectangular building with a flat wooden roof, the ceiling of teakwood being supported by three wooden columns. The only door was located high above the courtyard and could be reached by way of a ladder.

The Great Mosque as a whole consisted of a courtyard bordered by galleries on all four sides, with the Ka'aba approximately in the centre. Within the courtyard proper, the area in which pilgrims performed their circumambulations was clearly marked off. This part of the mosque also contained a small monument commemorating the Prophet Ibrāhīm, the well of Zamzam, from whose water the pilgrims usually drink, in addition to a number of minor buildings. Some of the latter served the prayer leaders of the four schools of Sunni religious law, which in spite of differences in matters of detail are all considered equally orthodox. In the early days of Islam, the courtyard had been quite small, but since the time of the caliph 'Umar (634–44) it had slowly been extended by the purchase of adjacent houses. The gallery, which still retains the shape given to it by the Ottoman Sultans, was begun in the days of the Abbasid caliph al-Manṣūr (reigned 754–5). Al-Manṣūr's successors al-Mahdī (reigned 775–85) and al-Hādī (reigned 785–6) completed the structure, and also built the oldest of the seven minarets which were to grace the building in later times. The remnants of the palace which Ummayads and Abbasids had inhabited while visiting Mecca were also included in the gallery. At this time the latter possessed a flat roof, and the teakwood ceiling was partly gilt. Some of the columns were of marble, while the remainder had been put together out of different varieties of stone and covered with a coating of plaster. At the end of the twelfth century the Andalusian pilgrim Ibn Djubayr recorded 471 columns and piers.[2] About the middle of the nineteenth century, the English traveller Richard Burton counted 555 supports, the increase being probably due to Ottoman additions.[3] Until about 1950, when a new building campaign entirely changed the look of the Great Mosque, these Ottoman changes and additions determined its overall appearance.

In the Islamic world the Ka'aba is regarded as a sanctuary built by God and the angels and restored several times by different prophets. This explains why, throughout the centuries, changes to the building were kept to a minimum, though rulers of the first Islamic century had fewer qualms about making such changes than their descendants. But the veneration accorded the Ka'aba did not mean that the remainder of the Great Mosque was also considered sacrosanct; on the contrary, galleries and minarets have undergone major changes in the course of time.

A significant reason for public construction in Mecca has already been discussed: the prestige of a Muslim ruler to a not inconsiderable degree was due to the buildings which he put up to the glory of God and the welfare of the pilgrims. Aging and damage, too, have often occasioned both restoration and total rebuilding. The attempt to create a dignified and even magnificent environment for the pilgrimage ceremonies did not limit itself to the Great Mosque, but encompassed the entire city of Mecca. Making necessary allowances for the different requirements of pious visitors to Medina, the same thing applies to that city as well. The two cities also had a number of problems in common: water supplies and public hygiene, traffic and transportation had to be organized in such a way as to cope with major seasonal influxes of people and animals. As building in the remote and desert regions of the Hejaz was not only difficult but expensive as well, a ruler's decision to immortalize himself in this fashion amounted to a major political statement.

PIOUS FOUNDATIONS AND CONSTRUCTION ACTIVITY IN THE OTTOMAN EMPIRE

During the fifteenth and sixteenth centuries, and to a certain extent in the seventeenth as well, Ottoman Sultans, mothers of Sultans and high officials were very active as builders. Mosques were favoured by most donors, but the larger sanctuaries were associated with soup kitchens, schools for the elementary training of children but also for advanced theological study, libraries and many other institutions.[4] The funds needed to operate such a foundation were set aside by the donor, who either constructed shops, *khān*s, mills or public baths at the same time as the mosque or *medrese* which formed the core of the foundation. Or else the donor assigned previously existing enterprises to the upkeep of favoured charities. Highly placed personages, and particularly members of the Sultan's family, often could induce the ruler to grant their foundations taxes collected from villages. Thus a not inconsiderable transfer of purchasing power from the countryside to the city was effected. The size of the foundation indicated the rank of the donor; only the Sultan, thus, could build a mosque with two or more minarets.

Public construction was centred upon Istanbul and its immediate vicinity.[5] Muṣṭafā 'Ālī, sharp-eyed and sharp-tongued as ever, has concluded that the need for services in a given place was not considered when selecting the site of a new foundation.[6] In his view, high visibility and the donor's prestige were all that counted. But the larger and more important provincial cities such as Edirne, Damascus, Cairo, Mecca and Medina also received a large number of pious foundations. Relative to their rather modest permanent populations, the two Holy Cities were even particularly privileged in this respect.

CONSTRUCTION MATERIALS

Due to the lack of many materials needed in construction, building activities in the Hejaz demanded much more organization and preparation than construction in almost any other part of the empire. Building stone was available locally, but timber, iron, bricks and marble had to be imported from distant provinces. Timber at times was secured from the northern shores of the Black Sea; in 1609–10, a Christian sea captain asked for and received permission to buy timber in the province of Kefe (Feodosiya) and more particularly Balıklagu (Balaklava) for the needs of Medina.[7] Sometimes timber could be secured from the Ottoman arsenal, which possessed monopoly rights to large wooded areas of northwestern Anatolia, still heavily forested at that time. But wars in the Mediterranean were liable to cut off timber supplies, as happened in 1570–3 during the war with Venice over the possession of Cyprus. In the building of the Great Mosque of Mecca, large quantities of Indian teak were used – a wood so hard, according to some experts, that it could be used as a substitute for iron.[8] Only some of this teak consisted of recent imports. When older parts of the Great Mosque, presumably going back to the Mamluk period, were torn down in order to make room for Ottoman projects, quite a lot of the salvaged teak was still in good condition and was therefore reused in the Ottoman rebuilding of the gallery.

Iron was used for a variety of purposes: in many monumental buildings iron hooks held together large blocks of hewn stone, while doors had metal fastenings and windows iron grates.[9] Vaults were often strengthened by iron supports which, though they protruded in an obvious and inelegant fashion, secured the structure whenever there were doubts concerning the strength of the foundations. When vaults were added to the gallery of the Great Mosque of Mecca in the second half of the sixteenth century, iron (in addition to the teak already stored in Mecca) was employed for just this purpose.[10] Moreover, iron was needed for nails, and last but not least for the shovels and other implements indispensable for the functioning of any construction site.

Iron used in Mecca usually came from the smelting furnaces in the area of Samokov, in what is today southern Bulgaria. From there it was carried by caravan to Istanbul or to a port on the western shores of the Black Sea, and from there to Egypt. The use of iron in the Hejaz was made more difficult because the lack of fuel made it all but impossible to work iron at the construction site. Thus the Ottoman central administration sent ready-made nails to the Hejaz, even though the official in charge of this project warned that serious losses would be unavoidable.[11] After all, quite a few people could use nails. . . .

Many items needed for construction or repair of the Great Mosque were manufactured in Istanbul, so that upon arrival they only needed to be put in place. Manufactured items had to fit fairly stringent specifications, and coordination was made difficult by the length of time needed to get a response to a query or request. In 1611, when the walls of the Ka'aba needed strengthening, a regular public test of the items to be employed was held in the capital. Meḥmed Agha, Chief Architect and responsible for the construction of the Blue Mosque, had designed lavishly decorated iron props to support the Ka'aba from the outside. As Aḥmed I wished to see how the supports would work, they were set up outside the Edirne gate, at the site known as the estate of Davud Pasha. Other gifts to be sent to Mecca were also exhibited, and the Sultan attended the ceremony with the Grand Vizier, the Shaykh al-Islām and many other dignitaries.[12] To make sure that the supports would accurately fit the Ka'aba, drawings had been made previously, but, for good measure, a team of artisans was also sent to Mecca.[13]

Materials to be used in decoration were also brought in from afar.

Sultan Murād III sent a quantity of gold to gild the silver doors of the Ka'aba, but we do not know whether he used gold from the treasury in the Topkapı Palace or tax revenues from less distant provinces such as Syria, which could have been reassigned to Mecca.[14] Thus a multitude of deliveries from southern Rumelia, northwestern Anatolia and Istanbul had to arrive more or less punctually in the Hejaz for construction to proceed at a smooth pace. On the whole these arrangements seem to have worked reasonably well. This was a major organizational achievement, particularly since not only construction materials, but also workmen were in short supply and had to be brought in from outside.

CONSTRUCTION WORKERS

When Ewliyā was in Mecca in 1672, he noted that the city's inhabitants did not show any interest in the practice of crafts.[15] A similar observation can be found in the travel account of the Dutch scholar Snouck Hurgronje, who was in Mecca toward the end of the nineteenth century; at that time many services needed in the city were performed by immigrant Africans.[16] Similar evidence exists for sixteenth-century Medina; a report concerning the books in the library attached to the Prophet's mosque in Medina, dated 1578, states that these books were in urgent need of rebinding. But in the whole city there was no suitable bookbinder, 'and if we do find one he will charge a lot of money'.[17] The Sultan's Council therefore decided that it was better to bring in a bookbinder from Egypt. Apparently this was considered a cheaper solution even though the bookbinder's travel money would add to the cost of his work.

Qualified workers on Ottoman construction sites in the Hejaz often came from Syria or Egypt. An account concerning repair work undertaken in 1601–2 indicates that wages paid to such workers were at a medium level.[18] Compared to their colleagues working on an official construction site in the Aegean region they were not doing too badly, but they made considerably less than could be earned on a construction site in Saydā (Sidon) in the year 1616.[19] Given the instability of prices and exchange rates during this period, however, data from different times (even fifteen years apart) and places are risky to compare.

In all likelihood many Syrian and Egyptian construction workers did not leave their native provinces voluntarily, but were drafted by the Ottoman state. In some instances the opportunity to perform the pilgrimage must have been a motivating force. To date the best documented of all building projects of the Ottoman 'classical' period is the Süleymāniye construction site. If the Süleymāniye constitutes a typical case, few slaves were employed on Ottoman official building sites, and none are recorded for the construction of the Great Mosque of Mecca. Frequently, however, artisans were called up by local *ḳāḍī*s and assigned to work on public construction.[20] Sometimes the *ḳāḍī* was told to furnish a given number of stonecutters or masons, and sometimes artisans deemed especially skilful were even requested by name.[21] It was not easy to escape such a draft, though some craftsmen tried as best they could, and the cases in which they succeeded are also those about which we know least.

Wages in public construction were determined by the Ottoman government, and were probably lower than craftsmen could get from private employers. Some artisans, however, did attempt to better their situation. Concerning sixteenth-century Istanbul, we possess a document which shows that dissatisfied artisans demanded and obtained a raise; for this purpose, strikes and refusals to work were not unknown.[22] Some craftsmen employed on public building projects in the capital simply managed to 'disappear', taking up work for private persons or else leaving the area.[23] Similar tactics were employed in the Hejaz. Certain stonecutters and blacksmiths managed to enter the suites of influential pilgrims and thus return home, much to the dissatisfaction of the authorities.

BUILDINGS AND BUILDING EXPENDITURES

High food prices, lack of materials and labourers, losses in transportation, certainly also the difficulty of supervising officials in a remote locality – all contributed to the expense of construction in Mecca and Medina. We do not have any comprehensive accounts concerning the renovation of the Great Mosque of Mecca under Selīm II (reigned 1566–74) and Murād III (reigned 1574–95). Such isolated items of expenditure as are known show that the Ottoman government was able and willing to expend large sums. In 1571, when plans were being made for the renovation of the gallery, 40,000–50,000 gold pieces were set aside for the delivery of timber alone. Masonry domes were even more expensive.[24] The same text reports that to cover the gallery by rows of domes would increase the price to about 100,000 gold pieces. From a sultanic rescript dated 1568 we learn that 50,000 gold pieces had been spent on the four *medrese*s of Süleymān the Magnificent (reigned 1520–66), recently completed at that time.[25] Additional expenses may have arisen, moreover, for at the time the rescript was drafted, the previous owners of the land on which the *medreses* had been built had not yet been compensated.

Smaller repairs in Medina were also quite costly. In 1585 the Sultan's Council planned to spend 10,000 gold pieces on repairs to the outer wall of the courtyard of the Prophet's mosque in Medina.[26] The restoration of the minor fortress of Yanbu', where the grain stores for Medina were kept prior to transportation to the city proper, was to cost 50,000 gold pieces. Repairs to 63 hospices for the reception of poor pilgrims in Medina were estimated at 32,000 gold pieces all told, which means that repairs in Medina at the end of the sixteenth century ran to a total of 92,000 gold pieces. In 1564 renewal and extension of a single hospice was estimated at a thousand gold pieces.[27]

Large sums were also expended on the pipes which carried water from the 'Arafat plateau to Mecca. Since this water carried a large amount of sand and pebbles, the pipes were often clogged, and cleaning them caused considerable expense. New pipes were also added to improve the Meccan water supply. In 1571, 60,000 gold pieces were spent on this project alone.[28] Transmitting these large sums of money to Mecca on time caused the Ottoman fisc considerable difficulty. Some of the money was sent from Istanbul, while the Egyptian contribution was also substantial. Grain left over from last year's pilgrimage caravan equally was sold to defray expenses. A sizable amount of correspondence went back and forth between different Ottoman officials, and this doubtlessly increased the expense of the project yet further.

The costliness of building in Mecca and Medina as opposed to less out-of-the-way regions becomes apparent when we compare these figures to the building expenses of two major Istanbul mosques. The Süleymāniye complex – six colleges of law, religion and medicine, a hospice, a hospital and a public kitchen, as well as the magnificently decorated mausolea of Süleymān the Lawgiver and his consort Khurrem Sultan – cost 53,782,980 *aḳče* in the course of an eight-year construction period. This is equivalent to 896,383 Ottoman gold pieces. The Sultan Aḥmed mosque (built 1609–17) cost 180,341,803 *aḳče*, but as the *aḳče* had dramatically been devalued in the meantime, this corresponded to no more than 1,381,245 Ottoman gold coins. In size and elaboration, the two complexes were comparable: around the Sultan Aḥmed mosque clustered a major complex of buildings, including a reception pavilion (*ḳaṣır*) for the Sultan, a school, a place where drinking water was dispensed and numerous shops.[29] Apparently a vizier intent on building up his image in the manner criticized by Muṣṭafā 'Ālī, indeed would have been well advised to build in

Istanbul and not in the Holy Cities; he certainly got more value for his money.[30] But of course the very expense of prestigious construction in the Hejaz contributed to the prestige of the rulers who could afford to finance it.

The high cost of a building project could be used to legitimize the ruler initiating it, as becomes apparent from a description of the repairs which Aḥmed I, also responsible for the Sultan Aḥmed mosque, undertook in Mecca. The account of Aḥmed I's repairs to the Great Mosque is found in Dja'fer Efendi's biography of the architect Meḥmed Agha, who was in charge of both projects. The author recounts that Sultan Aḥmed had a spout for rain water, made of pure gold, affixed to the roof of the Ka'aba.[31] As background information, he adds that the Abbasid caliphs, who originally had furnished the Ka'aba with a spout of silver gilt, did not possess the resources for a more valuable gift. Now this spout was in bad condition and needed to be replaced. According to Dja'fer Efendi, by contrast the Ottoman Sultan was so rich that he could easily afford not only a golden water spout but, if necessary, a golden wall all around the Ka'aba.

This willingness to employ costly materials is all the more remarkable in view of the sparing use of gold, silver and other valuables in the decoration of the great Sultans' mosques in Istanbul. In the foundation document of the Süleymāniye it is expressly stated that the ruler had decided against expensive decorations and in favour of a spacious and well-built structure.[32] In many other respects, however, the Ottoman Sultans when building in Mecca had introduced features characteristic of public construction in the capital. Therefore it is not a matter of chance if, in this particular instance, they disregarded Istanbul precedent in favour of a lavish use of precious materials. Meḥmed Agha's biographer has attempted an explanation: for the Ka'aba he uses the image of the beloved, whose beauty is enhanced by her precious jewellery.[33] This simile and his description of the Ka'aba as a whole contain allusions to mystical poetry. Thus two sets of motivations apparently played a role when the decision was made to use a profusion of gold and silver in the decoration of the Ka'aba. On the one hand, the Sultan was to be legitimized by the display of his extraordinary wealth. On the other hand two holy sites, namely the Ka'aba as the centre of the world and the grave of the Prophet Muḥammad in Medina, were to be confirmed as different in kind from any other place on earth, even the major Sultans' mosques in Istanbul. And yet at least one of the latter, namely the Süleymāniye, had been designed as a monument to the triumph of Sunni Islam.[34]

THE RENOVATION OF THE GREAT MOSQUE OF MECCA

During the first fifty years of Ottoman control, major changes were made in the Great Mosque of Mecca. The place from which the Ḥanefī prayer leader directed the members of his law school at prayer was at first marked by a small two-storey structure. But soon this building, which had been erected by a governor of Jeddah, was torn down and replaced by a building domed in the manner characteristic of Ottoman monumental construction.[35] Sultan Süleymān also had four theological schools built in the immediate vicinity of the Great Mosque; to have *medrese*s form part of major mosque complexes was another element of Ottoman building tradition.[36] The number four was chosen because of the four schools of law recognized as orthodox by Sunni Muslims. But it was quite difficult to find suitable teachers for the Ḥanbalī and Shāfi'ī schools. Possibly this lack of personnel was the reason why the Ottoman administration later transformed the *medrese* of the Ḥanbalīs into a *dār al-ḥadīth*, that is a specialized school for the study of reports concerning the sayings and doings of the Prophet Muḥammad.[37] While the Ḥanbalīs were little represented in the Ottoman Empire, a *dār al-ḥadīth* was also the crowning feature of the educational system in Süleymān the Magnificent's Istanbul foundation (built 1550–7).[38]

Thus, even though the special traditions of the Holy City were initially upheld, specifically Ottoman institutions and building types soon appeared in Mecca. But to make the new *medrese*s operate was a difficult matter. Ewliyā Čelebi had noted that Meccans were not very enthusiastic about careers of study and teaching in religious law or theological studies, and for scholars from the Ottoman core lands Mecca proved too remote for comfort and career building.[39] Under these circumstances, it was difficult to prevent the buildings from being misused as residences for influential pilgrims, some of whom even stabled their mounts there. The central administration time and again was obliged to concern itself with complaints concerning the functioning of these *medrese*s.[40]

Süleymān the Lawgiver also renovated several of the Great Mosque's minarets. When he ascended the throne, the mosque was adorned by six minarets, one of which had been built by the Abbasid caliph al-Manṣūr (reigned 754–5).[41] In spite of its venerable age, Süleymān the Lawgiver had it torn down in 1524–5 and replaced by a new one. The same fate befell a minaret from the time of the Abbasid caliph al-Mahdī (reigned 775–85). Instead of the single gallery for the muezzin which had characterized the older building, the new minaret was furnished with two galleries; again, multiple galleries were typical of the Sultans' mosques in Istanbul. Toward the end of his reign Sultan Süleymān added a further minaret which struck the eye by its great height, thereby bringing up the total to seven. But around 1597–8, according to a note in the Arabic-language chronicle of Ḳuṭb al-Dīn which was translated into Ottoman at this time, possibly by the poet Bāḳī, the minarets of the Great Mosque suffered severe damage.[42] Unfortunately Bāḳī, or whoever else penned the note, does not specify what kind of damage this may have been. A fire seems the most likely possibility. Nor is there any information about subsequent repair work.

The most important undertaking of this period was the total renovation of the galleries surrounding the courtyard of the Great Mosque. As the Ka'aba had retained its shape since Ummayad times, the galleries and the minarets were the obvious focus for rebuilding. Moreover they determined the appearance of the mosque as a whole. A building with a large central dome, the most striking feature of Ottoman Sultans' mosques, could not be accommodated in the Great Mosque of Mecca. But it was possible to use a series of small-scale domes to cover the galleries.[43] This feature is also typical of the fully developed mosques of the Ottoman classical period, where the visitor walks from an exterior open courtyard into a second interior space lined by porticoes, where the ablution fountain is normally located.[44] Yet the strict symmetry of Ottoman interior courtyards could not be reproduced in Mecca, where a large number of ancient and highly decorative gates existed which could not be moved at will. Moreover, in consequence of the Meccan courtyard's great size, its character as an open space was a permanent feature, while in many Ottoman Sultans' mosques, and particularly in the Süleymāniye, a broad gallery combined with a small amount of unroofed space almost created the illusion of a closed room.

Due to the importance of this building project, which was executed in the reigns of Selīm II (reigned 1566–74) and Murād III (reigned 1574–95), there was a considerable amount of official correspondence, part of which has survived. The decision to build a domed gallery was probably taken during the Cyprus war (1570–3), when timber could not be imported and the Sultan still wanted to go through with the project as quickly as possible.[45] Therefore, locally available materials had to be used, particularly stone and mortar. Despite their haste, the Sultan and his advisers seem to have hesitated some time over the final shape of the gallery. In a rescript which postdated the first discussion of the domes by a few months, there were renewed references to a gallery in the 'old style', that is, with a flat roof.[46] In March 1573, however, the decision to build a domed gallery had finally been taken.[47] In the following year, the architect in charge of the project left Istanbul for Mecca.[48]

Unfortunately all we know about this personage is his name, Meḥmed, and the fact that at the time in question he was a palace official (*čavush*). This is a different person from the Meḥmed Agha who built the Sultan Aḥmed Mosque in Istanbul at the beginning of the seventeenth century – and, as we have seen, was also later active in Mecca. If he had been involved in the building of the domed gallery in his youth, his admiring biographer Dja'fer Efendi would not have failed to mention the fact. Meḥmed Čavush was not the first architect to work on the gallery project, however, as 34 domes had been built before he even left Istanbul.[49] At this time the Sultan's Council was still deliberating the number of domes to be erected. In a rescript dated 1573 the idea of a structure of 400–500 domes was ventilated; but in the end only 152 were actually built.[50]

The final shape of the gallery floor also was the subject of much deliberation. In Mamluk times the ground was covered with pebbles. The Ottoman structure at first followed the Mamluk example but, by about the year 1577, the authorities in Istanbul were debating a more magnificent solution.[51] As a reason for changing the traditional arrangement, it was claimed that most of the worshippers in the Great Mosque were poor people, who did not bring their own prayer rugs. For these people prostration in ritual prayer was most uncomfortable, as the sharp pebbles lacerated their legs. Certain descendants of the Prophet and other notables therefore applied to the *ḳāḍī* of Mecca, who passed on their wish for a more comfortable arrangement to the Ottoman central administration. Thereupon the Sultan ordered a floor covering consisting of marble slabs. But when the slabs had already been cut, certain inhabitants of Mecca strenuously objected to the new solution. Possibly the real reason was that the luxurious appearance of the gallery in its new form had aroused objections among the more piety-minded inhabitants of Mecca.

The authorities in Istanbul did not insist on putting in the marble slabs. According to the new order, the *ḳāḍī* of Mecca was to invite the inhabitants of the city (obviously the more prominent among them) and certain building specialists to a conference. After the participants had come to an agreement, the *ḳāḍī* was to notify the Istanbul authorities of the result. Thus the central administration attempted to secure the consent of the more prominent inhabitants of the city before new building projects were undertaken. This show of consideration must have been due to the religious prestige of Mecca on the one hand, and to the enormous distance from the centres of Ottoman power on the other. For no evidence of similar consultations has come to light where the cities of Anatolia or Rumelia were involved; at least in written texts, everybody pretended to believe that the Sultan only had to command for his order to be instantly obeyed.

In the following years, the reconstruction of the gallery proceeded apace.[52] Already in August–September 1576 the completion of the work was celebrated by a commemorative inscription. The text was written in Istanbul, but to have it inscribed on a slab of marble the authorities looked to a craftsman already present in Mecca or at least someone who could be brought in from Egypt. The whole affair was not without its political implications, for the *ḳāḍī* of Mecca was enjoined to find a master who could write a script that was not only elegant, but legible as well. 'But you [the *ḳāḍī* of Mecca and the administrator of Jeddah] must pay attention to the calligrapher and have [the text] written in such a fashion that nobody reading it has any doubts. The whole affair should be taken care of in this fashion. You should also write to us in which place the inscription has been put up.'[53] This may serve as some consolation to modern historians and epigraphers, who know the problems involved in deciphering a perfect-looking inscription; apparently contemporaries were in no better position. In the end the inscription was put up close to the gate of 'Abbās, a frequently used entrance into the Great Mosque.

LIGHTING, PERFUMING AND DECORATING THE GREAT MOSQUE

Chance has preserved a rescript from the last years of Süleymān the Lawgiver (1564–5), which gives us some idea of the manner in which the Great Mosque must have appeared to worshippers. Unfortunately, however, this text antedates the rebuilding of the gallery by a few years.[54] An official in charge of the Meccan water supply, by the name of Ibrāhīm, had complained to the central government that the six *ḳanṭar*s of wax assigned to the illumination of the mosque during night prayers were insufficient for the purpose. Therefore the mosque was only lit on dark nights, while at other times pilgrims were forced to rely on whatever light was available. This was not a desirable situation, as many pilgrims were elderly and handicapped, often even unable to see the *imām* in the dark. It therefore was suggested that the yearly allotment of wax be doubled. Some of this wax came in the shape of ten large candles, each weighing 10 *vuḳiye* according to the standard of Rūm, probably about 12.8 kg. Eight of these candles illuminated the Ka'aba, while the courtyard was lighted by small hanging lamps. These were probably similar to the ones seen on a European etching of 1719, where a ring of such lights is shown as surrounding the Ka'aba.[55] Throughout the mosque courtyard, 387 such lamps (*ḳandīl*) had been distributed; however, as olive oil recently had been in short supply, 285 lamps remained unlighted. There were also complaints about the fact that most of the mosque illumination was extinguished after night prayers, since visitors to the mosque kept coming at any time. The administrator therefore asked for a 150 *ḳanṭar* increase in the amount of olive oil allotted to the mosque.

In his response, the old Sultan emphasized his benevolent interest in all pilgrims, and promised to send ten large candelabras, as well as the wax and olive oil required for keeping the mosque lighted throughout the night. In addition, the text is interesting because it mentions the measures intended to prevent misuse of the Sultan's gifts: the *ḳāḍī* was to enter the donation into his register and future judges were enjoined to abide by the stipulations of the rescript. However, in the absence of the Meccan *ḳāḍī* registers, we have no way of knowing how long these instructions really were carried out. There seems to be some room for doubt, as a rescript dated March 1568 refers to golden candelabras sent to the Holy City as a gift. They had not been properly recorded and were now regarded as lost, while wax and olive oil also had not been used for their appointed purposes.[56]

In 1564–5 Ibrāhīm, the administrator of water resources already referred to, requested a donation of 250 gold pieces to pay for the perfumes which were twice a year sprinkled over the Ka'aba. Up to Süleymān the Lawgiver's last years, this ceremony had not in any way been supported out of official funds, and Ibrāhīm now suggested that sandalwood, rose water, amber and musk be supplied.[57] When committing himself to make this donation every year, Sultan Süleymān expressed the hope that this act of his be recorded among his meritorious deeds; presumably he had both this world and the next in mind. Yet his death apparently prevented these gifts from arriving with any regularity. In 1569–70 the new Sultan's Council had to concern itself with a petition by Mecca's influential Ḳāḍī Ḥüseyin, to the effect that for two years no money for perfumes had arrived from Jeddah, so that it had become necessary to borrow 500 gold pieces.[58]

The two texts establishing Sultan Süleymān's donations are remarkable for their discussion of motivation, which otherwise so often is absent from Ottoman official records. They show that religious motives and considerations of political legitimation were inextricably intertwined in the minds of the Sultans and their officials.

Discussions concerning religious and political aspects of the pilgrimage also occurred in connection with the various coverings used in the Great Mosque, the largest of which was the Ka'aba covering. Down to the reign of Aḥmed I (reigned 1603–17), this piece of fabric was sent from Egypt, as had already been the practice in Mamluk times. From the time of Aḥmed I, the lavishly decorated coverings sent whenever a new ruler ascended the Ottoman throne were made in Istanbul, leaving only the 'ordinary' coverings, which were prepared every year, to be manufactured in Cairo.[59] Generally the coverings were black, as had been the custom instituted in Abbasid times; for black was the colour of this dynasty. But in the late sixteenth century, the Ottomans for a while experimented with a white covering, for in the Meccan sun, black dye rapidly faded, giving the covering an unsightly appearance. Samples accordingly were sent to Istanbul, where it was decided to henceforth use black lettering on a white ground. No document so far has been located which explains why this eminently practical reason did not in the long run prevent a return to a black covering.[60]

Sixteenth- to eighteenth-century illustrations of the Ka'aba generally show a covering that is only slightly decorated, mainly by a band of cloth with an inscription mentioning the name of the reigning Sultan, although in the later sixteenth century Ottoman artists seem to have experimented for a while with a different design. From a rescript dated December 1577/January 1578, we learn that at this time it was customary to add a band decorated with versets from the Koran to the bottom of the covering. The Sultan's Council now ordered a change of design, however, which involved leaving out the Koranic inscription. The reasoning behind this prohibition was that when a large number of worshippers pressed around the Ka'aba, the inscription was bound to be trampled underfoot. Unfortunately we do not know whether at this time the covering was still white or had reverted to its original black colour.[61]

Other coverings used in the Great Mosque were those veiling the three columns bearing the Ka'aba ceiling. In 1566–7, the columns themselves had been in bad condition and the Sultan's Council had ordered their repair. Evidence from 1592–3 refers to the custom of renewing the column hangings at the accession of a new ruler. During the reign of Murād III, which by that time was already drawing to a close, this custom had been neglected. Now the ruler consented to pay for new hangings and for some other urgent repairs as well, but there obviously was some concern at the prospect of yet further expense.[62]

MECCAN FOUNDATIONS OUTSIDE THE GREAT MOSQUE

In the second half of the sixteenth century, the Mamluk foundations of Sultans Ḳā'it Bāy, Ḳānṣūh al-Ghūrī and Čaḳmaḳ were still in existence, even though certain administrators supposedly had stolen most of the revenues. In the case of Ḳā'it Bāy's foundation, the deficit thus incurred amounted to 2000 gold pieces, while the *ḳāḍī* Ḥüseyin Mālikī, at that time also in charge of the Mālikī *medrese*, stood accused of having misappropriated 600 gold pieces. As a result, the foundations were operating at less than optimum efficiency, and certain services essential to the cleanliness of the area surrounding the Great Mosque were not being performed.[63] By the end of Murād III's reign, both the upper and the lower level of the *medrese* founded by Ḳā'it Bāy were in ruins, and the same applied to the rooms and chambers situated along the pilgrims' way between Ṣafā and Marwa, which belonged to the same foundation. But these buildings, along with other foundations dating back to the Mamluk period, were considered to be capable of repair, at least in part.[64] Nor was the foundation of the Mamluk amir Djānībeg in much better case. Three chambers belonging to this foundation were so ruinous that they were in immediate danger of collapse, and the reporting official felt that the structure endangered passers-by and might even place the Great Mosque in jeopardy.[65] In almost all these cases, the administration in Istanbul blamed the embezzling of foundation administrators, presumably Mamluks for the most part. With hindsight, their depredations may be viewed as part of an appropriation process, as a result of which Egyptian revenues increasingly were retained by the Mamluks, and which was to gather yet further momentum in the seventeenth century.

Rather more active was the soup kitchen which Süleymān the Lawgiver had established in the name of his deceased consort the Khāṣekī Khurrem. No information is available on its architectural form, but there were frequent discussions on the grain it was to receive from Egypt. In early 1589 there seems to have been a gigantic corruption scandal. Almost 700,000 *pāra* of Egyptian revenues pertaining to the foundation had not been collected; unjustified claims of shipwreck had been made to cover up irregularities by the administrators, who had been aided in their trickery by an organizational confusion which may well have been deliberate.[66]

We possess some evidence on the operation of the foundations established by the Grand Vizier Soḳollu Meḥmed Pasha (died 1579); a hospital he founded will occupy us in another context. But he was also the founder of a lunatic asylum, which he financed in an unusual manner: he had one of his ships sold, and obtained a promise from the Sultan that the provincial treasury of Egypt would lend him enough money to make up the total of available funds to 10,000 gold pieces. Meḥmed Pasha's foundation also contained a public bath, still functioning in the 1670s, although there had been complaints in connection with some 'funny business' concerning the replacement of the larger of the two boilers. The Grand Vizier had determined that any surpluses from the revenue-producing parts of his foundation should be spent toward the repair of the buildings. This rule and the overall wealth of the foundation may explain why, in spite of complaints concerning incompetent or corrupt administrators, the institution was able to function for a hundred years and more.[67]

Murād IV had been only moderately active in furthering public construction. But among his buildings in Mecca there was a lodge (*tekke*) held by members of the Naḳshbendī order of derwishes, who received stipends for praying for the Sultan's soul. In 1643–4, only a few years after the founder's death, there already were complaints that these stipends were not being distributed according to the register of official subsidies (*ṣürre*), and that people of political influence were using the foundation to reward their own adherents. By the middle of the seventeenth century, a Mewlewī derwish lodge was also in operation, founded by the Ḳapudān Pasha Mūsā. This lodge apparently received some of its support from faraway Bosnia, and the complaint was heard that local holders of military tax assignments retained the Mewlewīkhāne's revenues for their own benefit. According to the custom of Ottoman Anatolia and Rumelia, the foundation also received the interest from a sum of money that a benefactor had assigned to it; but in this case as well, the Mewlewī derwishes had difficulty obtaining what was due to them.[68]

ATTEMPTS AT URBAN PLANNING

With the completion of the gallery, which is in use to the present day, albeit dwarfed by the enormous additions of the 1950s and 1960s, financial means became available for another ambitious project. In the reign of Murād III (1574–95) it was decided to remove the town quarters immediately adjacent to the mosque; apparently an open square was meant to take their place. Here again, so it seems, the model of the great Sultans' mosques of Istanbul, Bursa and Edirne was at the back of Ottoman planners' minds.[69] For a 'classical' Ottoman mosque not only was flanked by *medrese*s, libraries, soup kitchens and similar institutions, but also possessed an outer courtyard where no houses could be built, although these areas sometimes were used as cemeteries. These outer courtyards isolated the mosque from the mass of urban houses and ensured its heightened visibility. The Great Mosque of Mecca, by contrast, had no remarkable façade apart from a number of monumental gateways, and often houses crowded in the immediate vicinity of the sanctuary. Thus Murād III's project aimed at creating a completely new urban form. It is not surprising that well-to-do Meccans who owned these houses, and during the pilgrimage season rented them to pilgrims at a good price, were less than enthusiastic about this project.[70] These people were able to mount a degree of opposition, the outlines of which can be dimly perceived through the surviving documentation. At the other end of the social scale, poorer pilgrims were also affected. Quite a few hostels serving the needs of this group had been located near the Great Mosque, and now they were demolished one by one.

House owners and administrators of pious foundations received compensations from the Treasury, as the Sultan would not have gained religious merit if the land and buildings in question had been acquired in a way regarded as unjust by Islamic law.[71] An estimate was made of the buildings' value, and the sum of 27,000 Ottoman gold pieces set aside for compensation purposes. Unfortunately nothing is known about the fairness or otherwise of the assessment process, nor can we tell whether the former owners could acquire new houses in other parts of the city. At first a mode of payment was adopted that placed poorer owners at a grave disadvantage, for the Egyptian finance administration was put in charge of compensation and effected payments in Cairo. People without contacts in Egypt were bound to suffer grave losses if they tried to convert documents issued by Cairene finance officials into ready cash locally. At the last moment, however, the central administration decided to effect payment in Mecca after all.[72]

WATER SUPPLIES

This wholesale restructuring aimed to provide the Great Mosque with an environment that was not only imposing but also clean and free from unwelcome smells. These were difficult problems in a hot, periodically overcrowded city where water was at a premium. The first precondition was an improved water supply, which involved both an increased volume of water to be brought into the city and a better distribution of the available water over the different parts of Mecca. The main water pipes, which led from the plateau of 'Arafat to the Great Mosque, were being repaired in 1564–5.[73] By April 1571, work was still continuing, as 3000 gold pieces had been earmarked for wages; at that time the Egyptian stonecutters and blacksmiths had not been paid for a full five years. Yet, during this period, the stonecutters had prepared enough stones to secure the completion of the project.[74]

Some of the delays were due to technical difficulties. A rescript from the year 1580 discusses the fact that the water channel had not been made as smooth as would have been necessary.[75] As a result, the water did not flow regularly but was collected in pools, and very little of it arrived in the Holy City. To rectify this mistake an important sum of money was set aside. But even if there were no technical defects, the pipes were liable to get clogged with the sand and gravel carried along by the water. In 1573, Ḳāḍī Ḥüseyin of Mecca pleaded in favour of the cleaning personnel employed by the water administration, whose modest pay was insufficient in a time of scarcity.[76] In addition, the foundation used slaves as cleaners. In 1573 there were 42 ''Arab' (that is, presumably, black) slave women employed at this task, the remnant of a contingent of a hundred donated some time previously by an Ottoman princess; the remainder either had died or else run away. In addition, Süleymān Pasha on his voyage to India had acquired 40 ''Arab' (in this case, probably, southern) Indians. Of these 40, 22 people survived at the time of the rescript; but since the text mentions their salaries (*'ulūfe*) they may have come to the Hejaz as free labourers, or else they were manumitted in the course of time. In 1573 the remaining slaves were also freed.[77]

Water was distributed to individual quarters with the help of special devices; in 1568 these were in the course of construction. We possess a sultanic rescript in which an Egyptian specialist in this art was ordered to travel to Mecca and participate in the task.[78] Certain quarters had been given pious foundations which allowed the inhabitants to make better use of the available water. In 1567–77 we find the Grand Vizier Soḳollu Meḥmed Pasha building a public bath, and the *ḳāḍī* of Mecca was instructed to aid him in this undertaking.[79] Previously Sultan Süleymān had established a foundation intended to supply the inhabitants of Mecca with drinking water. But by 1585 the Sultan's Council had to deal with a complaint that for 20 years this foundation had not been providing any water, which means it stopped working at about the time of the founder's death.[80] The foundation's employees, meanwhile, had not failed to draw their pay. In 1581 the Sultan and his Council expressed their dissatisfaction at the Meccan water supply: after so much treasure had been expended, a *kurna* full of water still cost four or five *pāra*.[81]

In addition to the establishment of Ottoman pious foundations serving the Meccans' need for water, those remaining from Mamluk times were restored. However, the amount of 15,000 gold pieces which was demanded for this purpose seemed excessive to the central administration; we do not know how much money was ultimately assigned.[82] In addition, there was the perennial problem of preventing well-to-do residents of the city from diverting the water to their own gardens and houses, an issue all to familiar from the Ottoman core provinces as well.[83]

Water supplies in Jeddah were even more precarious than in Mecca, and the inhabitants largely depended on cisterns. In 1573, there were plans to instal water pipes, as Sultan Süleymān had stipulated as much in his will, and his son Selīm II made an effort to honour his father's wishes. But the experts asked for their professional opinion were not sanguine. The pipe would have to be 79,910 *arshın* (63,768.18 metres) long, and some of it would have to be cut into solid rock. In addition, the land around Jeddah was saline and salt was liable to get into the water, making it bitter. As a result, the project was given up, and additional water reservoirs were commissioned as a palliative.[84]

OTHER URBAN SERVICES

A further precondition for keeping the streets of Mecca and particularly the mosque courtyard clean and orderly was to lodge even the poorest pilgrims in hostels of one sort or another.

> The poor people who come to pay a visit to the noble Ka'aba do not have a determined spot [in which to spend the night]. Therefore they settle in a corner of the noble sanctuary and this is dirtied, so that lice are propagated. . . . Therefore Her Highness the late princess had purchased a piece of land close to the soup kitchen she had established, and suitable for the construction of a hostel for the afore-mentioned people.[85]

This rescript from the year 1556 refers to a topic which was to gain importance in subsequent years, namely the construction of simple housing for pilgrims who otherwise would have spent the night outdoors or on the mosque premises themselves. When a poor pilgrim fell sick, the situation became particularly difficult.

> We hear that certain sick and helpless persons spend both day and night in the noble sanctuary because they do not have the force to leave [the premises]. Now my . . . Grand Vizier . . . has found a suitable house in the vicinity of the Great Mosque. It consists of a rectangular courtyard whose sides have been roofed

> over. This he has purchased from the [previous] proprietor for a [suitable] price. Also, he has had a public bath built in the vicinity of the Great Mosque, and the income it produces should be spent on the things needed by these sick people. It should also be used to purchase shrouds for the dead.

However, the problem of finding appropriate lodgings for all pilgrims was made more difficult by the Sultan's ambitious project of restructuring, to which quite a few of the existing hostels had been sacrificed.[86]

Another difficult problem was the cleaning of the Meccan streets. This was important since the dirt, if not removed, in time found its way into the Great Mosque, located as it is in the lowest part of the city.[87] In 1577 the mosque courtyard had just undergone a thorough cleaning. 'But if people throw their garbage into the street, in the event of a flood the places just cleaned will fill up again, so that the cleaning has to be repeated.' Therefore the Sultan's Council ordered *ḳāḍī* and Sherif to make sure the inhabitants of Mecca deposited their garbage in a place outside the city limits designated expressly for the purpose. Unfortunately, we have no way of knowing how this worked out in practice.

Thus the Ottoman administration was concerned with both aesthetic and hygienic problems. However, these two categories are characteristic of twentieth- and not of sixteenth-century thinking. Ottoman administrators were simply trying to ensure that the pilgrimage took place in a dignified atmosphere consonant with the importance of the event. Apart from dirt and evil smells, quite a few other phenomena were regarded as inimical to the solemnity of the pilgrimage, such as high houses which afforded a view into the sanctuary, and particularly the use of the courtyard of the Great Mosque for purposes not immediately related to worship.[88] It seems that Ottoman administrators regarded casual and quasi-domestic use of the mosque courtyard as a sign of disrespect toward the sanctuary. That Iranian inhabitants of Mecca had a different view of proper use of the mosque courtyard only made the problem more intractable: 'Some Iranians known for their heretical views . . . disturb the pious who have assembled for worship in the courtyard of the mosque. In the evening they come with their womenfolk and families, with their cushions and cradles to sit down in the mosque court, and there is no end to their inappropriate behaviour.'[89] In this respect at least we observe certain parallels to Christian Europe in the early modern period. Both churchmen of the post-Tridentine Church and Ottoman administrators were concerned about establishing a sharper division between the sacred and the profane areas of life, and ensuring that behaviour at holy places was marked by restraint and a show of respect and decorum.[90]

To permit pilgrims to concentrate on their religious experience, the Ottoman administration also needed to solve problems which today would fall within the province of the police. Traffic posed its own special difficulties. Thus the way between the hills of Ṣafā and Marwa, on which the pilgrims hurry to and fro in memory of Ibrāhīm's repudiated wife Hādjar/Hagar, had long since become an urban business street. Traders displayed their goods, and their stalls constituted a great obstacle to the movement of the pilgrims. To limit the damage, the Ottoman authorities prohibited the establishment of new shops.[91] But the previously existing shops continued to operate, and only in the twentieth century was the street between Ṣafā and Marwa incorporated into the sanctuary and reserved for the exclusive use of pilgrims.

Other problems were connected with the markets where 'cooks, sellers of cooked sheeps' heads, butchers and other people of dubious respectability assemble and try to attract the custom of the pilgrims. Sneak thieves also make use of the opportunity to steal the purses of the Muslims and rob them of their money.'[92] Yet the market was necessary, for the pilgrims could not have fed themselves without its existence. Therefore the Council of the Sultan merely decided to banish it to a locality remote from the Great Mosque. But in other parts of Mecca, too, makeshift huts and tents where food and coffee were offered for sale cluttered up the public thoroughfare and hindered the pilgrims at their devotions.[93] While the Ottoman central administration made every effort to keep the public thoroughfares open, the success of its efforts depended upon the cooperation of the Sherif and, last but not least, on that of the merchants themselves.

The available rescripts convey the impression that the Ottoman central government had a notion of what constituted a well-organized pilgrimage city, and was trying to realize this conception as a whole. Appreciable sums of money were invested in the city's infrastructure so as to create conditions allowing pilgrims to fulfil their religious duties in a dignified setting. By the creation of a city specifically geared to the needs of pilgrims and closely supervised by *ḳāḍī* and Sherif, the Ottoman political class attempted to legitimize the Sultan's rule. Unfortunately, and for reasons which at present remain unknown, almost all the evidence concerning Ottoman urban planning is confined to the second half of the sixteenth century. As to the seventeenth, the only project on which we possess evidence concerns the Great Mosque. However, here at least the available sources allow us to figure out the political considerations behind a major rebuilding project.

THE REBUILDING OF THE KA'ABA

The reconstruction campaigns of the sixteenth century had left the Ka'aba untouched. Apart from a few medieval repairs, this was still the building erected by al-Ḥadjdjādj after the defeat of al-Zubayr in 693. However, by the late sixteenth century the first warnings were heard that the Ka'aba was structurally in poor condition.[94] But some theological and legal experts were opposed to the idea of tampering with the building in any way, and the Ottoman administration accepted these views without demur. Only the young Sultan Aḥmed (reigned 1603–17), who was responsible for one of the last major mosques in the 'classical' style, decided to do something to support the greatly weakened structure of the Ka'aba. Even then the walls were left untouched. Instead, as we have seen, the building was supported from the outside by a set of braces, an iron belt on supports intended to contain the outward pressure of the walls.[95] Moreover, the rainpipe of the Ka'aba was replaced; this was not a merely utilitarian measure, as the spout is located at a place where the faithful prefer to pray and hope for the fulfilment of their prayers. In addition, most of the roof of the Ka'aba was replaced and damage to the walls repaired. Precious materials were used in abundance. Apart from the installation of a rain spout made of pure gold, already mentioned in another context, the three columns in the interior of the Ka'aba received a decoration made of gold and silver. Moreover a silver tablet over the entrance to the building was replaced by a tablet made of gold.

Even so the restoration of Sultan Aḥmed's time did not really strengthen the Ka'aba's structure. This became apparent in 1630, when Mecca suffered a serious flood.[96] While occurrences of this kind were quite frequent, this particular flood was so destructive that contemporary observers thought it without precedent. Due to its geographical location the Great Mosque of Mecca has suffered from flash floods down to very recent times. In many desert areas, rainwater does not enter the earth's crust but will flow down the surface in *wadı*s. The Great Mosque is situated in the middle of such a *wadı*, which is normally dry but fills up rapidly in case of precipitation. In 1630 not only the mosque courtyard but the entire lower city were under water, and many people were drowned. The chronicler Süheylī reports that the water came up to the key in the lock of the Ka'aba door, which is situated high above the ground.[97] For three entire days the water remained in the mosque courtyard and, when it finally withdrew, a mud layer as deep as the height of a man had been deposited. This mud soon dried and turned hard as stone, so that it had to be specially moistened before finally it could be shovelled away.

The walls of the 'Ancient House' were too weak for this additional stress and a subsequent investigation showed that it was about to collapse. Thereupon the Sherif called a meeting of the prominent inhabitants of the city.[98] While such assemblies of notables did not possess a corporate existence and at first glance seem quite informal gatherings, at least in Mecca they were frequently convoked and played an active role in the 1630s rebuilding of the Ka'aba. So we may assume that similar meetings had accompanied previous construction projects too. But, apart from the chronicle of Ḳuṭb al-Dīn, sixteenth-century sources are oriented toward the central administration and not toward local personalities, which explains why we only hear about assemblies of notables in connection with a later event, namely the restoration of the Ka'aba. Moreover, as changes of any kind to the building fabric of the Ka'aba were being challenged from a religious point of view, the Ottoman administration may have felt more need for consultation than in the case of earlier projects.

It was probably this assembly which decided to give the surveyor and construction expert 'Alī b. Shams al-Dīn the responsibility of saving the Ka'aba from collapse.[99] The administrator of Jeddah was requested to furnish some timber which happened to be in the port, and this soon arrived. According to a declaration by the supreme *müftī*s of the four schools of law, the restoration of the Ka'aba was a religious responsibility which the Sherif had to undertake in the Sultan's place. But representatives of the Ottoman central administration were approached directly as well:

> Sherif Mas'ūd hurried to send one or two messengers to the province of Egypt, in order to truthfully and in all the necessary detail notify Meḥmed Pasha, the governor of Egypt who knows no equals, as a representative of the Sultan. The messengers began their journey on Monday and reached Cairo at the end of the noble month of Ramaḍān. They were granted an audience with the governor, and submitted a statement by the inhabitants of Mecca and a petition by the Sherifs. After having informed himself about the situation, the aforementioned vizier forwarded the statement and the petition to the Sultan's palace and thus informed His Majesty, the ruler.[100]

But the governor of Egypt, due to his special responsibility for the affairs of the Hejaz, also took action independently. He ordered the remittance of further construction materials from Egypt and sent over Riḍwān Agha, the commander of his Circassian Mamluks.[101] To emphasize the importance of his mission, the latter was promoted to the rank of *beg*. At first Riḍwān Beg was meant to represent the governor merely until further orders were received from Istanbul. But later he was confirmed in office[102] and if Süheylī's account of the situation is more or less realistic, Riḍwān Beg should be considered the person actually in charge of the Ka'aba restoration.[103] This would mean that the decision not to attempt any further half-measures, but to take down the walls of the Ka'aba stone by stone, and then to rebuild the structure according to the old plan, was taken by Riḍwān Beg himself. Or, if the plan originally had been devised by someone else, he at least was responsible for its execution.

Riḍwān Beg was not an architect but an administrator and a political coordinator: he had to make sure that everything needed for the construction project was brought in from Egypt on time, and for that purpose needed to maintain good relations with the governor and the Mamluks of Egypt. But the consent of the Meccan notables was also indispensable and could never be taken for granted. Just when the mosque courtyard had been cleaned up to some extent, and the work of taking down the walls of the Ka'aba stone by stone was about to begin, the Shāfi'ī chief *müftī* voiced his objections.[104] In the latter's opinion, a step of this importance could only be undertaken after the Sultan had given his formal consent. Riḍwān Beg then proceeded to furnish himself with a legal opinion to the contrary, which certain Meccan scholars supplied in short order – there was even another Shāfi'ī *müftī* in this group. From the moment in which it was possible to fully assess the damage to the Ka'aba, many scholars had encouraged the authorities to proceed as rapidly as possible.

The technical aspects of the job concerned building experts and surveyors. We hear nothing of architects sent from Istanbul, who so often had been active in Mecca during the sixteenth century. Probably the experts consulted were Syrians or Egyptians who happened to be in Mecca at the time. Their main concern was to protect themselves from future recriminations by informing the notables as quickly as possible of every step taken. Thus a meeting was called before the walls of the Ka'aba had been taken down completely, in which Riḍwān Beg participated along with the Sherif of Mecca and other prominent personalities. Here the experts formally declared that even the remaining sections of the Ka'aba walls lacked solidity: 'Do not blame us in this matter and do not say: Why did you not tell us that before!'[105] However, certain scholars were still opposed to the dismantling of what remained of the Ka'aba. Riḍwān Beg responded by soliciting another legal opinion, which explicitly incorporated the opinion of the experts. Only when this latter opinion also favoured the project, did he allow the workmen to proceed. In the course of all this, building experts and surveyors appear to have played only a subordinate role. As a perusal of their biographies shows, people like

Sinān the Architect (about 1498–1588) or Meḥmed Agha, the builder of the Sultan Aḥmed Mosque, seem to have been assertive personalities with considerable self-confidence.[106] But nothing of the kind is apparent from the behaviour of the Meccan craftsmen.

Süheylī's chronicle reflects the administrative mechanisms which made possible the taking down and later rebuilding of the Ka'aba. He has also recorded the actual progress of the work in amazing detail.[107] As a first step, the Ka'aba was surrounded by a kind of fence. While pilgrims could continue to circumambulate it, the building remained invisible and was only unveiled when reconstruction had been almost completed. After demolition all elements of the building were preserved with great care. The more valuable pieces were guarded in a treasury, which had been installed in one half of the building known as the 'Drinking water room of 'Abbās'. At this time, the golden and silver decorations were taken off the iron braces which had supported the Ka'aba walls from the early seventeenth century until the flood of 1630. More than a hundred *baṭmān*s of gold and 120 *baṭmān*s of silver were recuperated in this fashion. Unfortunately, the *baṭmān* varies from one place to the next. But if we interpret these figures as meaning Egyptian *baṭmān*s, which is a distinct possibility given the Meccan dependence on Egypt, the decorations of Aḥmed I's supports should have contained 81 kilogrammes of gold and 98 kilogrammes of silver.[108] The iron was refashioned into supports built into the structure proper so as to give it greater solidity.

When the Ka'aba completely had been taken down, only the Black Stone remained in its original position. But as even the piece of wall supporting the Black Stone was not considered very durable, molten lead was poured into the cracks of the stones which had burst.[109] Then the rebuilding phase could begin; Süheylī claims that twenty rows of stone were needed before the level of the Ka'aba's interior ceiling had been reached, and four more courses were necessary to arrive at roof level. A twenty-fifth course served to complete the building. In every case Süheylī has recorded the time at which a new row was begun, and the section of the building at which the masons began their work. A few stones were replaced by newly cut ones, so that in the end, the builders were left with fifty stones from the old building.[110] Our chronicler has also recorded when the teakwood which served for the roofing of the Ka'aba was carried into the mosque courtyard, and the time at which the carpenters cut it into the size required for the building. He also recounts how the three columns supporting the ceiling were placed in the building along with their bases. Even the fastening of the iron holders for the lamps illuminating the interior was recorded, along with the reinstallation of the door and the two flanking colonettes.[111]

CHANGES TO THE BUILDING FABRIC OF THE GREAT MOSQUE

For no other building project of the Ottoman and indeed of the Islamic world do we possess quite such a detailed account. This is due to the fact that the Ka'aba in its original shape was regarded as a creation of God Himself, which later had been renovated by several prophets.[112] This view also explains why several religious and juridical scholars objected to the Ottoman restoration projects. As the ideal solution, most scholars and administrators alike regarded a restoration which stabilized the Ka'aba for future generations but kept interference with the venerable building to an absolute minimum. But a minority apparently considered that natural decay of the building should be allowed to run its course.

In all the discussions, the opinion of the building experts was important, since only they could decide whether a given piece of wall still was solid or not. But their opinion only became practically relevant when it had been accepted by a majority of juridico-religious scholars. Apparently Riḍwān Beg, who represented the Ottoman authorities at the building site, from the very beginning had decided in favour of complete reconstruction. He then made sure to get the appropriate legal opinions whenever he needed them. This proceeding, though comprehensible from a twentieth-century point of view, was not the only option available at the time. When at the end of the sixteenth century the Ka'aba's poor structural condition had first been discussed in Ottoman administrative circles, the people in charge made no prior commitment to reconstruction, and ultimately allowed themselves to be swayed by the opponents of restoration. And even though Riḍwān Beg favoured a radical solution, he apparently made no attempt to change anything in the arrangement of the Ka'aba itself, or, if he did change some minor detail or other, the chronicler was careful to pass it over in silence. In this part of the mosque, the standards applied were quite different from those encountered in the case of the gallery, where, as we have seen, Abbasid, Mamluk and Ottoman building styles could be applied in juxtaposition.

CEREMONIES ACCOMPANYING THE RESTORATION

Agreement between Sherifs, the *müftī*s of the four recognized schools of law, the generality of juridical and religious scholars, the other prominent inhabitants of the city and Riḍwān Beg, as a representative of the Ottoman administration, thus never could be taken for granted, but constantly had to be reestablished. This situation was reflected in a sequence of ceremonies which indicated the more important phases of the restoration process. Robes of honour were distributed at fairly frequent intervals.[113] The latter ultimately came from Sultan Murād IV, but were forwarded to Mecca by the governor of Egypt. Such robes were also distributed by the Sherif of Mecca, the most prominent recipient being Riḍwān Beg himself. The latter also distributed such robes in his own right, namely when the restoration of the Ka'aba had been completed and his own official duties terminated. Riḍwān Beg gave a robe to the Sherif and to a market overseer who presumably had directed Meccan administrative personnel.[114] In addition, the 'Opener of the Noble House' received a robe of honour; to the latter's family, the Banū Shayba, the keys of the Ka'aba had been entrusted from time immemorial. All these personages belonged to the inner circle of Meccan notables. More remarkable is the fact that the Sherif also honoured the surveyors and building specialists, who were of much more modest stature, while Riḍwān Beg distributed robes to both the chief mason and the chief carpenter.[115] This gesture is consonant with a declaration of Riḍwān Beg's at the beginning of the construction period, in which he promised satisfactory wages to all the people employed on the building project. However we have no way of knowing to what extent his promises were acted upon in practice.

The distribution of robes of honour was accompanied by public prayers for the Sultan.[116] But such prayers were a frequent occurrence and often took place without any distribution before or afterwards. Prayers for the Sultan marked off almost all the phases of the Ka'aba restoration, and were said for the continuation of the Sultan's rule and thereby for the continued existence of the Ottoman state. To refuse participation in such prayers was considered an act of rebellion. In his biography of the architect of the Sultan Aḥmed Mosque, Dja'fer Efendi tells us that rebels would be consigned to hell as they refused to pray for the ruler; while he was referring to the Ottoman–Iranian conflict and not to the Hejaz, the assertion tentatively can be regarded as valid in the Meccan context as well.[117] By participating in these prayers the Meccan notables recognized the rule of the Ottoman Sultan, and because the reconstruction of the Ka'aba politically was a disputed act, allegiance to a remote suzerain had to be reasserted over and over again.

In the scenario of the ceremonies legitimizing the rule of the Ottoman Sultan and the reconstruction of the Ka'aba, Riḍwān Beg had assigned himself a prominent place. Thus he personally concerned himself with the metal casing designed to protect the Black Stone from further damage. Later he examined whether the door of the Ka'aba had been inserted properly, and in person climbed on to the roof of the mosque (here the gallery probably is intended) to establish which parts of it needed to be repainted. When work on the Ka'aba had been completed, he in person ascended the roof in order to let down the covering which protects and veils the sanctuary. These gestures make visible the support of the Ottoman administration, whom Riḍwān Beg represented in Mecca, for the whole restoration project.[118] On a more personal level, this also was an opportunity for Riḍwān Beg to demonstrate his personal humility and piety. This latter element is stressed by the chronicler Süheylī, who states that after his term of office in Mecca had ended, Riḍwān Beg voluntarily renounced the title of *beg*, because whoever held it could not avoid shedding blood.[119] This highly placed Mamluk thus behaved in a way appropriate for a religious scholar, and it is interesting to see that the mixture of roles was viewed by Süheylī as a positive and not as a negative character trait.

Riḍwān Beg's key role in the restoration project is reflected in the fact that, at the end of his tenure of office, he received as a gift an entire covering of the Ka'aba, which had been used for a year but now had been replaced by a new one.[120] The Sherifs, the Banū Shayba as gatekeepers of the Ka'aba and other Meccan notables normally possessed the right to shares of this valuable silk brocade, which they had cut up and sold to well-to-do pilgrims. Thus in a sense they could be considered as the donors. Riḍwān Beg reciprocated by gifts of money to the Meccan notables. He did not retain the covering, however, but passed it on to the Sultan's treasury. This gesture presumably was meant to once again document the concord prevailing between the ruler, his representative Riḍwān Beg, and the more influential inhabitants of the Holy City. By donating their shares in the Ka'aba covering, the Sherif and the other Meccan notables also may have wished to acknowledge Riḍwān Beg's zeal and commitment, while at the same time recognizing him as a *primus inter pares*.

Sultan Murād IV (reigned 1623–40), who was not known as a great builder, only participated in this venture in an indirect fashion. When officials on the spot in Mecca needed help, not the Sultan but the governor of Egypt was their main recourse. Only a few documents from the Registers of Important Affairs refer to the project. As was customary in such cases, the commemorative inscription in gold and lapis lazuli put up in Mecca at the end of the building campaign, and mentioned by Süheylī, also records the name of the ruler.[121] More remarkable was the fact that the new inscriptions referred to the Sultan's predecessors who had taken an active share in the reconstruction of the Great Mosque, namely Murād III (reigned

1574–95) and Aḥmed I (reigned 1603–17). Two separate inscriptions were set up in their honour. In addition, there was a further inscription which mentioned all the rulers who had acquired religious merit in contributing to the building of the Great Mosque throughout its history. Thus Murād IV was placed at the end of a long and distinguished series of pious rulers and could not fail to derive additional legitimation from this fact.

Süheylī describes yet another ceremony which symbolically concluded the building campaign; the implements which had been used in the course of the work, and at a later date the scaffolding timber as well, were buried outside the city. It is a pity that the chronicler has not interpreted this ceremony for us; the only hint he gives comes from his use of the term 'pertaining to Süleymān, solomonic', which would seem to indicate that he was thinking of an analogy to the temple of Salomon.[122] The term 'salomonic' also reminds us of Süleymān the Lawgiver (reigned 1520–65), in whose symbolism Salomon played a major role. Probably the timber and implements were buried to preclude their use in any profane undertaking.

THE CASE OF MEDINA

Information on construction in Medina is a great deal more sketchy and, above all, limited to the last quarter of the sixteenth century. It is therefore probable that the specifically Ottoman character of Medina, which is apparent from nineteenth- and twentieth-century photographs, only came into being in later centuries. Repairs to the Great Mosque are first documented for 1575–6, when Ḳāḍī Ḥüseyin, at that time officiating in Medina, received a sultanic rescript complimenting him on the successful completion of a building project in the Prophet's mosque (*Ḥarem-i muḥterem*).[123] Unfortunately, our text does not indicate the type of work done. In 1580, urgent repairs had to be effected to the dome of the small building in the mosque courtyard, which for centuries had been used as a treasury, for the building fabric showed dangerous fissures.[124] This was one of the more ancient sections of the mosque, as due to its location in the courtyard it had been spared by the fires of 1256 and 1481. Another text from 1585 speaks about repairs to the mosque wall reaching as far as the Bāb al-Nisā, which had been put up in the time of the Ummayad caliph 'Umar b. 'Abd al-'Azīz. These repairs were to cost 10,000 gold pieces and therefore should have been substantial.[125] However, our text was written at the time when the financing was still being debated and actual work probably had not yet begun. Preparations in 1585 were well enough advanced for the *naḳḳāshbashı*

Luṭfullāh, described as having previous experience with official buildings in Medina, to be appointed as the person responsible for the project (*mu'temed*).[126] In the following year, discussion was still continuing. Now it was estimated that only 3000 gold pieces would be needed, which indicates that either the first estimate was unrealistically high, or that the project had been scaled down drastically.[127] By 1588, something concrete definitely had been undertaken, for we learn about timber brought in from (or rather by way of) Egypt, which had been used for repairs to the mosque wall.[128] Roofs also were leaking and urgently needed repairs at this time, and, even worse, the books in the library were being eaten by bugs so that a library room with wooden bookcases was deemed indispensable to limit further damage.[129] By 1588–9, construction was in progress, for the central administration had sent another *naḳḳāshbashı*, a certain 'Aṭā'ullāh, to supervise the undertaking as *emīn*.[130] His work was to be checked by a *nāẓır*, a man of the Palace probably without specific skills related to construction. As this *nāẓır* had been a finance director in his earlier career, in Medina he also must have been responsible for securing the necessary cash. Workmen apparently were secured by drawing them off from projects in Mecca; the *ḳāḍī* of this city was enjoined to send unskilled labourers, masons, stonecutters, blacksmiths and even an architect or skilled builder. Architects employed on the site were accorded 30 *pāra*s a day 'to pay for their meat', in addition to 10 *irdeb* of wheat every month. Masters and unskilled labourers were assigned a money wage (*üdjret*) of 12 *pāra* and a monthly food allotment of 5 *irdeb* (1588–9).[131] Further changes to the mosque compound are recorded for 1594–5. The area reserved for the reciters of prayer in the Rawḍa was broadened to accommodate two additional rows of people, and a school for the study of the Prophet's sayings and doings (*dār al-ḥadīth*) was built adjacent to the *ḳıbla* wall of the mosque, not far from the gate of Bāb al-Salām.[132]

Not only the building fabric, but also the interior decorations were refurbished at this time. In 1577–8, the *shaykh al-ḥaram* pointed out to the central administration that the door curtains and the coverings over the Prophet's tomb and the graves of his associates all were in urgent need of renewal.[133] A list of all the textiles currently in the mosque was forwarded to Istanbul, where it possibly may still be found in one of the less accessible corners of the archives. In 1594–5 the covering for the Prophet's grave was manufactured in Istanbul, while the curtains and other items were ordered from Egypt.[134] Unfortunately it is impossible to determine whether in the intervening years the old decorations had continued in use or whether this was already the next renewal of the set.

Discussions about the financing of these different projects reveal some of the treasures possessed by the mosque, and which must have been donated over the course of several generations.[135] We learn that golden lamps weighing 697 *mithkāl* and silver lamps weighing 51,120 *dirhem* were no longer in a usable condition, and therefore should be sent to Egypt to be melted down. Once converted into money, these treasures could be used to finance further construction. Moreover there were donations from various Sultans, in the shape of both money and jewellery. In the last months of Murād III's reign (1594–5) the Sultan complained that his father had donated 40,000 gold pieces for the institution of various pious foundations, but that, after construction was completed, the remainder of the money found its way into the Egyptian provincial treasury.[136] It is most unfortunate that no archival evidence has been found to date on the gifts of treasure which Sultan Aḥmed I lavished upon the Prophet's grave, and which apparently remained there until the Ottoman–Wahabi war of the early nineteenth century.

On the extensive foundations of the Mamluk era there is little evidence. In 1588–9 a local administrator claimed to have spent a large sum on repairs to the foundation of Sultan Ḳā'it Bāy, but we do not know on what type of work.[137] A lunatic asylum bearing the name of Nūr al-Dīn Shahīd, presumably the ruler of Aleppo and opponent of the Crusaders (died 1174), was still operating in 1576. But there were complaints that for the last seven or eight years, the institution had been unable to obtain the medicines it needed; and the Sultan's Council believed that this might be due to the depletion of the foundation's Syrian revenues.[138]

We possess somewhat more documentation on a number of smaller sanctuaries, *medrese*s and other pious foundations which the Ottoman Sultans sponsored in Medina. Thus, in the first years of Selīm II's reign (1567–8), there was a plan to construct a residential courtyard surrounded by cells on the famous cemetery of Bāḳī, near the grave of the third caliph 'Uthmān.[139] The people residing there were to spend their time reading the Koran; possibly the site, which up to this point had been deserted and rather neglected, was chosen because the founder of the Ottoman dynasty bore the same name as the third caliph. Other negotiations concerned the wish of Meḥmed Agha, the head of the Black Eunuchs, to establish a pious foundation in Medina. The latter had selected a ruined school from Mamluk times, which he was planning to restore and complete. In the rescript which at present seems to be the only record of this foundation, the Sultan's Council stressed that, above all, the descendants of the founder or the administrators of the foundation would have to be consulted.[140] If the previous foundation was ruined beyond hope of repair, and the property in question could be acquired by way of exchange, well and good. If not, some other way should be found to enable the Chief Eunuch to set up his foundation.

More important from a practical point of view was the provision of places to sleep for the poorer visitors who crowded into the city on their way to and from Mecca, and who quite often elected to stay in Medina for the remainder of their lives. A rescript from the year 1579 describes their plight: as they were unable to find lodgings, they lived on the street, and in winter many of them perished.[141] It was now suggested that the courtyard of the storehouse where the city's grain was being kept was both vacant and suitable for the purpose, and that a room with a stove or fireplace could easily be added. Moreover, the land already belonged to the Ottoman state, and so the governor of Egypt was ordered to begin construction immediately. In 1585 there was talk of yet another project, namely to repair the 63 hostels (*rıbāṭ*) currently existing in Medina.[142] Unfortunately, no rescripts that have been located to date permit us to establish how much of this ambitious project actually was carried out.

Sultan Murād III, whose activity as a sponsor of public construction in Mecca has been discussed, was also active in Medina. His foundation consisted of a *medrese*, accompanied by other establishments. Ewliyā Čelebi mentions a public bath, while a rescript of 1586 records that the Sultan also had planned to build a drinking water fountain with its own special conduit.[143] But the depredations of a local shaykh, who claimed to have served on the project and lavishly remunerated himself for his services, rather held up the progress of the building. Certainly Murād III's *medrese* was functioning in 1607–8, when the foundation had been attached to the office of the *ḳāḍī* of Medina.[144] In return for teaching in the school, the *ḳāḍī*s received a supplement to their salaries from the Egyptian revenues of the foundation. In the reign of Aḥmed I (1603–17) the accounts were still conscientiously audited. At one time the Chief Black Eunuch, *ex officio* the supervisor of all foundations established by the Ottoman family, caught out a *ḳāḍī* who had collected his pay for days on which he had not actually taught, and reported him to the Sultan's Council. Disputes concerning the appointment of senior students as teaching assistants (*dāniṣhmend*) and the assignment of living space to students prove that the *medrese* was still active in 1678.[145]

In addition, Murād III's foundation also boasted a public kitchen, and this too was operating in 1678, for at that time the foundation administration was deeply involved in a dispute with some of its neighbours concerning the disposal of waste water.[146] Complaining of the bad smell, the neighbours finally obliged the foundation administrators to construct a closed conduit for this water. By the time the rescript was issued, the latter were busily engaged in sabotaging this solution, claiming that it was too expensive and troublesome. The bread produced by the foundation originally had been intended for its servitors, but by the late seventeenth century, the right to procure it had become quasi-private property, an abuse the central administration had great trouble repressing. Partly this may have been due to the fact that the community of pious people Murād III had established in the village of Ḳubā', outside of Medina, was no longer very active. Although derwish lodges and similar communities normally were among his favourite haunts, Ewliyā Čelebi, who produced a vivid account of this village and its gardens as they appeared in the early 1670s, fails to mention Murād III's lodge.[147] At the end of the sixteenth century however, this particular foundation had been in much better condition; with a revenue of 15 gold pieces and a grain assignment, the foundation had managed to attract a scholarly shaykh who taught theological subjects, and was rewarded for his work by a very substantial supplementary income.[148] Probably the decay of Murād III's Ḳubā' foundation was due to the fact that Egyptian revenues were being withheld by the Mamluks, a problem which we have encountered in other contexts.

The mosque of Ḳubā' itself, which was visited by pilgrims because it had been founded by the Prophet Muḥammad when he first established himself in Medina, was also the object of the Ottoman Sultans' solicitude. In 1576 the mosque was in ruinous condition, and the order to estimate the cost of restoration indicates that ordinary repairs were not deemed enough, and that rebuilding of certain parts might well be necessary. Ewliyā Čelebi mentions the existence of domes and vaults, which may well date from this late sixteenth-century rebuilding.[149]

RELIGION, ART AND POLITICS

We have very little idea what impression pilgrims of the late sixteenth and early seventeenth centuries received when confronted with all this new construction. It is not easy to determine even how many people outside the Hejaz knew about the buildings. They were described in official documents, town chronicles and the biography of the architect Meḥmed Agha.[150] But the pilgrimage guide of Meḥmed Yemīnī from the seventeenth century has nothing to say about new construction in Mecca and Medina.[151] Except for the traveller Ewliyā Čelebi, few Ottoman authors of the time have produced extensive descriptions of the Meccan Great Mosque in its new shape.[152] We know very little about the reading habits of seventeenth-century Ottomans, but it is probable that short tracts of the kind written by Yemīnī were more widespread than the voluminous travel account of Ewliyā Čelebi, for instance, which only became famous in the nineteenth century. The Ottoman official documentation was totally inaccessible to contemporaries, of course. Thus most educated Ottomans must have found out about the buildings undertaken by Ottoman Sultans in Mecca only when they personally came to the city as pilgrims, or heard about them from friends and neighbours. This explains why the building inscriptions constituted a major source of information, and were regarded by the Ottoman central administration in this light.

The Ottoman government viewed its building projects as an opportunity to marshall the support of the influential families of the Hejaz, from the Sherif downwards. Much time and energy was spent on this matter, and the dissent of a single scholar was taken so seriously that major negotiations were undertaken for this reason alone. This applied particularly to the reconstruction of the Ka'aba, but the reorganization of the city's physical structure and its urban services likewise could only work if the notables of the Holy Cities could be persuaded to cooperate.

This situation differs in important ways from the practices we know from Anatolia and Rumelia, to say nothing of the Ottoman capital itself. For in the Ottoman core areas, where centralized political control was more intense, etiquette required the authors of official documents to pretend that the Sultan only needed to issue an order and it would be unquestioningly obeyed. Real-life situations were much more complicated, and political negotiations, between factions within the Ottoman administration but also between tax-paying subjects and officials, were by no means unknown. When an entire town quarter was moved to make room for the Yeñi Dj̲āmi' in Istanbul, there must have been negotiations about relocations and compensations.[153] Complaints by inhabitants forced to move indirectly are reflected in the praise of Sultan Aḥmed I by the biographer of Meḥmed Ag̲ha, who lauds the Sultan for having selected a building site where he could establish his foundation without evicting too many people. But it is in itself remarkable that, in the extant documentation, these negotiations are only alluded to, and there is no explicit discussion of the subject as a whole.

If the Holy Cities thus received special treatment, this was due first and foremost to the great distance which separated them from Istanbul, and the expense of crossing great stretches of desert. As a result, Ottoman forces in the Hejaz remained modest, and control by the centre depended on factors which we today would call 'ideological' more than on the existence of a conventional military–administrative framework. Here the religious significance of the two cities came into play; because of their role in providing an infrastructure to the pilgrimage, inhabitants of the Holy Cities did not pay any taxes, and were subsidized by the public treasury and pious foundations. This arrangement made it possible for Ottoman power to maintain itself and, in this context, visibility was an important factor. Public building constituted a means of making the presence of the Sultan immediately apparent to visitors and residents of Mecca and Medina, and this must have been the political rationale for lavish spending in the Hejaz.

To create an environment in which the pilgrims might fulfil their religious obligations in a dignified manner and without encountering too many distractions, the Ottoman Sultans attempted to enforce a whole set of urban measures. Similar efforts otherwise were only undertaken in the Ottoman capital cities, that is successively in Bursa, Edirne and particularly Istanbul. Certain ideas about the city, such as the attempt to isolate a mosque from its environment by means of an open space, seem to have been transferred wholesale from Istanbul to Mecca. The same can be said of the dome, that characteristic element of Ottoman architecture. Attempts at applying Ottoman conceptions of design did not, however, extend to the Ka'aba, except for minor decorative features, such as the ornamentation of lintels or inscriptions.

On the other hand, the lavish use of precious materials, so characteristic of Ottoman projects in the Hejaz, was not a feature of the Sultans' mosques of Istanbul. Apparently, in the Holy Cities, where a visible sultanic presence was of paramount importance, it was considered necessary to emphasize the ruler's wealth and his willingness to spend it on lavish gifts to the sanctuaries. By thus inviting comparison with the rich buildings put up by the Mamluk Sultans, the Ottoman rulers attempted to legitimize their domination.

6

The Pilgrimage as a Matter of Foreign Policy

The pilgrims visiting Mecca every year came not merely from within the borders of the Ottoman Empire, but from all parts of the Islamic world, which reached from Tangier and the Niger all the way to China. In the sixteenth and seventeenth centuries, however, certain countries which today furnish large contingents of pilgrims were islamized only to a limited degree. Thus pilgrims from western Africa, Malaya or the Indonesian islands were not as visible in Mecca as they were to become in the nineteenth century. But subjects of the Shah of Iran and the Mughal Emperor of India were present in appreciable numbers, and this posed a special challenge to the Ottoman Sultan. On the one hand the pilgrimage was obligatory for every Muslim possessing the necessary means. Thus the Ottoman Sultan, whose claim to legitimacy to some extent depended upon the fact that he protected the pilgrims, was obliged to make and keep Mecca accessible to all Muslims.[1] This was also the image the Sultans presented to the outside world: 'No Muslim and believer in the unity of God', says one sultanic rescript, 'should be hindered in any way if he wishes to visit the Holy Cities and circumambulate the luminous Ka'aba.'[2]

At the same time, political considerations also had a role to play, as certain Muslim rulers might try to influence events in Mecca openly or in an underhand fashion, to say nothing of possible spies. In the period which interests us, this particularly concerns subjects of the Shah of Iran, a religious and political rival of the Ottomans with whom the Sultans of the time were frequently at war. Sheykh al-Islām Ebūssu'ūd Efendi, the foremost *müftī* of the Ottoman Empire and trusted adviser to Süleymān the Magnificent (reigned 1520–66) even went so far as to deny that the Shi'is of Iran were Muslims.[3] When the Ottoman Empire and Iran were at war, Iranian pilgrims were not permitted to enter Ottoman territory and therefore unable to perform the pilgrimage. Even in peacetime the entries and exits of Iranian pilgrims were carefully checked by the authorities. A rescript from the time of Süleymān the Magnificent, dated 1564–5, expresses these intentions most graphically: 'It is not permissible to enter my well-guarded territories at any time outside of the [pilgrimage] season.' The same text also explains how the entering and exiting pilgrims were to be controlled in practical terms: 'May they all appear at the previously determined time. Their arrival should be reported to [the Ottoman authorities] so that [the pilgrims] can be met at the border.' The Iranian pilgrims then were to be taken to Mecca through sparsely inhabited territories. Whenever it was inevitable that they pass through inhabited regions, contact with the population was to be kept to a strict minimum.[4]

SAFE CONDUCTS FOR HIGH-RANKING PILGRIMS

Non-Ottoman pilgrims of some social status often made things easier for themselves by procuring an official *laissez-passer*. These documents in Ottoman parlance were called *yol emri* and, in many cases, copies were entered into the Registers of Important Affairs.[5] They constitute an important source for Ottoman policies toward distinguished visitors. As most of these texts conformed to a more or less standard format, divergences from the norm, which also occur occasionally, are of some interest. Normally the text explains that such-and-such a pilgrim, coming from Samarkand, Tashkent or some other remote place, was on his way to Mecca or else returning home. All *ḳāḍī*s, provincial governors and other administrators were requested to not cause the pilgrims any difficulty. In practice this meant that couriers on official business did not have the right to demand the mounts of the pilgrims and their servitors for their own use. Sometimes local authorities also were requested to furnish an escort along particularly dangerous stretches of road, as well as guides to show the way. Many travel permits also state that the pilgrims possessed the right to purchase foodstuffs in the localities along their route, and forbade local administrators to curtail this right under any pretext. This clause was probably aimed at *ḳāḍī*s and other officials in provinces where there was a scarcity for either natural or man-made reasons.[6] Especially prominent visitors sometimes were to be given an official reception. There were also *laissez-passer* which benefited not a group of individual pilgrims, but the inhabitants of an entire town.[7]

HIGHLY PLACED LADIES ON DIPLOMATIC MISSIONS

The foreign pilgrims whose *laissez-passer* we encounter in the Ottoman registers were all people of some standing, and often their position in spiritual or worldly hierarchies was recognized by the Ottoman authorities. Probably the special treatment often granted to them presupposed some research and verification of credentials on the part of the Ottoman government. But matters became even more delicate when members of ruling dynasties visited the Holy City as pilgrims, particularly if these visitors happened to be female. Thus Shah Ṭahmāsp of Iran sent his consort, the mother of Prince Ismā'īl, to the Hejaz.[8] Akbar, the Mughal emperor of India, was represented by one of his wives, Salīma, and by his aunt, the court historian and memorialist Gul-badan Bēgam.[9] Of course, the two ladies were accompanied by a numerous suite. Female members of the Ottoman dynasty also visited Mecca with some frequency, while no Sultan ever performed the pilgrimage. The only prince ever to do so was Prince Djem (1459–95), unsuccessful competitor of Bāyezīd II, who visited Mecca when he was already in exile, and the Hejaz still a Mamluk dependency.[10] Presumably the rationale was that the Sultan never should be too far away from the political centre of the empire and the Habsburg and Iranian frontiers. Princes, on the other hand, might have used the pilgrimage as an opportunity for political activity not readily controlled by their royal relative. Thus Ottoman princesses could be regarded as the politically least troublesome representatives of the dynasty.

In 1572–3 the Ottoman dynasty appeared in the Hejaz in the person of Princess Shāh Sulṭān, whose safe conduct specified that she wished to visit Jerusalem before proceeding to Mecca and Medina.[11] The governor of Damascus was enjoined to treat her as an honoured visitor and aid her in procuring the supplies needed for the journey. For the trip to Jerusalem, he was to furnish a special escort, and make sure that the princess was assigned a place in the first section of the pilgrimage caravan, the place normally favoured by distinguished travellers (see Chapter 2). While the governor, as the immediate superior of the pilgrimage commander, was requested to pass on this order through the regular channels, the commander also received a rescript of his own, in which his responsibilities were detailed once again. A notable difference between the two rescripts concerns the way in which supplies were to be procured. In the text addressed to the governor, much stress was placed on the honour and deference due to the princess and no mention was made of the manner of payment for her supplies. On the other hand, the order to the caravan commander was more matter-of-fact in tone, and explicitly stated that the princess would pay for her necessities. Quite possibly, the central authorities expected her to receive all supplies in Damascus, and here she probably paid very little, as even much less exalted personages received grants-in-aid toward their pilgrimages (see Chapter 2). On the other hand, last-minute purchases en route may well have been regarded as the princess's own responsibility.

Where foreign rulers were concerned, motives for sending a high-born lady as a pilgrim must have differed from case to case. Such visits already had a long history. The twelfth-century pilgrim Ibn Djubayr noted the presence of the 25-year-old wife of Nūr al-Dīn, ruler of Aleppo, who apparently attracted a good deal of attention by her magnificent suite and the number of her clothes, but also by the abundance of her charities.[12] Ibn Djubayr had many positive things to say about the Malika Khātūn, who in this context was very much a public personality. Seen from the political point of view, her visit was probably successful, as she had managed to bring her husband and father to the attention of the pilgrims, and made sure that the caliph al-Nāṣir did not monopolize the Meccan political stage.

Visits of high-born ladies from outside the Ottoman Empire presumably involved a gesture of trust toward the Sultan and also the Sherif of Mecca, as the honour of a foreign dynasty was entrusted to the Ottoman authorities for a few weeks or months. At the same time the household of a princess aroused less suspicion than that of a visiting prince, and such suspicion, even if once aroused, was more difficult to act upon; politeness demanded that no one pry too closely into the movements of a royal woman. This situation at times must have facilitated diplomatic contacts. A good example concerns an Iranian princess, who fell ill in the course of her pilgrimage and had to extend her stay. The Sultan's Council was unable to make out whether this was a real or a 'diplomatic' illness. While the authorities attempted to send the greater part of her suite home, basically there was little they could do, except await their visitor's recovery.[13]

The members of 'ordinary', non-royal embassies also sometimes combined the pilgrimage with their official duties. Thus the ambassador of the Khān of Tashkent in 1571–2 was given permission to travel to Mecca. His *laissez-passer* also specified that he should be assigned a safe place in the caravan, in this case in the very centre.[14] But otherwise we hear of no special privileges to be accorded to the ambassador.[15] Quite possibly the authorities in Istanbul regarded his ruler as a remote prince of minor importance, whose only merit was his proven Sunni orthodoxy. Ambassadors of more powerful rulers presumably were escorted to Mecca with somewhat more pomp and circumstance.

INDIAN PRINCES AND PRINCESSES IN MECCA

Ever since the Timurid prince Bābur (lived 1483–1530, ruler of India 1526–30) had brought all of northern India under his control, the Mughal court showed a close interest in the affairs of the Hejaz. The Indian court chronicler Badāōnī, a contemporary of Bābur's grandson Akbar, who lived in the second half of the sixteenth century, mentioned Bābur Khān's rich gifts to Mecca.[16] We possess a letter from Bābur's son Humāyūn (reigned 1530–56) to the Ottoman Sultan Süleymān the Magnificent; but this letter contains so many unrealistic assumptions that it is difficult to believe that it was ever sent.[17] Humāyūn, or whoever drafted the letter in his name, wrote about the Mughal prince's wish to meet Sultan Süleymān in Mecca, and embark upon a campaign with him against the Safawids. None of this ever materialized; neither Humāyūn nor Sultan Süleymān ever set foot in the Hejaz. Humāyūn, throughout his rule in India, was fully occupied in stabilizing his throne; and Süleymān campaigned against the Safawids without Mughal aid.

Humāyūn's son Akbar at first continued to show interest in pilgrimage affairs. In the 1570s he even announced that poor people wishing to perform the pilgrimage would receive a subsidy out of the ruler's funds.[18] He also founded a hospice for pilgrims in Mecca; certainly, a foundation bearing his name was seen by Ewliyā Čelebi in 1672.[19] In later years, however, the ruler moved away from Islam and invented a Hindu–Islamic syncretistic religion which became known as Dīn-i Ilāhī (Divine Religion). He also changed his mind with respect to the Mecca pilgrimage: the court chronicler Badāōnī reports that at this time highly placed personalities who demanded permission to undertake the pilgrimage had to brave the ruler's disfavour.[20] Only people whose attachment to Islam made them unwilling to adapt to court life under the new dispensation were sometimes told to travel to the Hejaz and stay there until further notice.[21] This was in accordance with what was by then an established Mughal custom; even in the reign of Humāyūn, political exiles had settled in the Holy Cities. They included the ruler's brother Kāmrān, blinded after an unsuccessful rebellion, and the latter's wife Māh Čiček Bēgam.[22]

While Akbar was still at least outwardly a Muslim, he also established a presence in the Hejaz by sending two prestigious female members of his family to Mecca as pilgrims. They stayed for several years, performing the rites of pilgrimage a total of four times, and only returned to India in 1582. This prolonged visit caused considerable apprehension in the Sultan's Council, and in 1580–1 a rescript referred somewhat obliquely to ostentatiously distributed alms and religiously dubious practices.[23] It appears that Mughal diplomacy regarded the Sherif of Mecca as a sovereign ruler with a multitude of political contacts, who controlled a territory which in a sense was common to all Muslims. Quite apart from accusations of heresy against many highly placed Indians, this situation explains the mistrust with which the visit of the two Indian princesses was regarded in Istanbul.

THE POOR INDIANS' TOWN QUARTER

Not only very highly placed, but also extremely poor people came to Mecca from India.[24] In all likelihood, not all the people who performed the pilgrimage due to Akbar's munificence ultimately returned home. We can draw this conclusion from a rescript dated 1578–9, which mentions that a large number of Indian pilgrims had arrived in Mecca in 1577 and 1578. The poorest of these pilgrims, for whom the authors of the rescript devised a number of vituperative epithets, had to spend the nights in the Great Mosque itself. Others settled in a quarter close by. That they were unwelcome to the Ottoman authorities is obvious; at least in part this must have been due to the resulting difficulties of provisioning. Moreover, the presence of a large number of destitute folk disturbed the plans which Sultan Murād III had made for the restructuring of the Meccan city centre (see Chapter 5). The plan was to pull down all private houses located within a certain distance of the mosque, and the poor and often smelly town quarter of the Indian pilgrims was a prime target. To the regret of the authors of the rescript, it was not considered possible to expel the Indians en masse; but at least they were to be transferred to a less centrally located part of the city, where the smells they generated would not waft into the Great Mosque. Unfortunately we possess no further evidence about the poor Indians and their town quarter, and thus cannot determine how many people were transferred, how they reacted to this traumatic event and where they finally reestablished themselves. It is even possible that they found local protectors, and the town quarter was left in place after all.

THE DANGEROUS JOURNEYS OF INDIAN PILGRIMS

Salīma and Gul-badan, in spite of their high status at the Mughal court, had to wait for quite some time before Akbar could secure the necessary Portuguese safe conduct; their return, too, was delayed by untoward circumstances, including a severe storm.[25] Many ordinary pilgrims, whose troubles no historian has recorded, must have lived through similar trials and tribulations. Ever since the Portuguese had established themselves in certain ports on the western coast of India (1498–1510), Indian and Arab shipowners, if they wished to avoid molestation, had to procure the same kind of safe conduct that Akbar tried to secure for the royal women – at one point through the (ultimately unsuccessful) mediation of certain Jesuit priests. Safe conducts were expensive, but shipowners found without one by a Portuguese man-of-war risked the loss of their ships. Muslim shippers in the Indian Ocean were more affected than Hindus or members of other religious groups, as Portuguese officials were accustomed to regarding Muslims of whatever background as their principal enemies. Economic motives also were of some importance, as in southern Asia traders on the high seas were mainly Muslims; thus measures taken against a Muslim merchant hit not only the Muslim but also the competitor.

To protect Indian pilgrims efficiently, a navy would have been necessary, but neither the rulers of south Indian port towns nor the Mughals were willing to spend money on such a venture. They therefore welcomed outside help; even Hindu princes were ready to cooperate with the Ottoman warships sent in 1538 by Süleymān the Lawgiver (reigned 1520–66) to drive the Portuguese out of the Indian Ocean. But this campaign ended in failure. In the first years of the reign of Süleymān's successor Selīm II (reigned 1566–74), before the decision to conquer Cyprus had been taken, projects for an active intervention in the Indian Ocean briefly revived. Plans were even made for a Suez Canal to link the Mediterranean and the Red Sea, and the justification for the whole undertaking was the protection of pilgrims. In the end, however, the war against Venice was given priority, and Ottoman presence in the Indian Ocean remained minimal. Indian pilgrims continued to suffer reprisals until the decline of Portuguese power in the seventeenth century forced the viceroys of Goa to seek good relations with the Mughal rulers: a prerequisite for such an improvement was the cessation of attacks on pilgrim ships on the part of Portuguese naval commanders.

As pirate attacks became more frequent in the seventeenth century, it is debatable whether Indian pilgrims gained very much from this new state of affairs. These pirates were English, Dutch or even Portuguese, and particularly attacked ships on the return voyage. For they were mainly attracted not by trade goods or potential slaves, but by the gold and silver which, due to the balance of trade constantly favourable to the Indian subcontinent, ships returning from Arabian or Persian Gulf ports were likely to carry (see Chapter 7). Even so, the overland route was not practicable for Sunni pilgrims, as the risks incurred in traversing Shi'i Iran were also quite high. In official correspondence between the Mughal emperors and the Shahs of Iran this matter was sometimes discussed, but the problem never received a workable solution.

If Mughal rulers abstained from any military intervention in order to increase the safety of Indian pilgrims, this abstinence also reflected the international situation. Throughout the sixteenth century, relations between Safawid Iran and the Uzbek khanates of Central Asia were quite tense, while, on the other hand, the Mughal rulers were concerned about possible attacks on the part of Uzbek princes against their vulnerable northwestern frontier. In order to maintain a political balance, the Shah of Iran therefore seemed a potential ally, and the closure of the land route to Indian pilgrims apparently formed part of the price paid for this alliance by the Mughal rulers.

IRANIAN PILGRIMS: A CASE OF POLITICAL MURDER

Even though the Ottoman administration regarded certain Indian pilgrims as a source of political instability, Iranian visitors to the empire were viewed with even graver suspicion. This is demonstrated by the tragic end which befell the pilgrimage of the Safawid vizier Ma'ṣūm Beg, who ventured onto Ottoman territory in 1568–9.[26] At that time the two rival empires were still at peace, and Ma'ṣūm Beg therefore had been accorded permission to visit Mecca. But Ottoman officials in eastern Anatolia soon informed the central power that the vizier had appointed functionaries of the Safawi order of derwishes, which at this time still played a role in the politics of the Shahs. From the Ottoman point of view, this activity was perceived as a major threat: before Shah Ismā'īl I made himself ruler of Iran in 1501, the Safawids had been a family of derwish shaykhs influential in eastern Anatolia as well as western Iran, both in the military and the political sense. Before losing eastern Anatolia to the Ottoman Sultan Selīm I (reigned 1512–20) after the battle of Çaldıran (1514), Shah Ismā'īl had controlled this area, and retained quite a few partisans particularly among the nomadic and semi-nomadic sector of the population. Ma'ṣūm Beg's attempt to integrate these partisans of the Shah into a formal organization therefore should be regarded as part of a deliberate and far-reaching policy.

The Ottoman central government countered this threat by having Ma'ṣūm Beg murdered. However, the peace with Iran was not to be endangered by this act of violence, and the governor of Damascus therefore staged an attack by Beduins, who could then be blamed for the fatal result. During the uncertain peace of those years, when a new war was soon to begin, other emissaries of the Shah to Anatolia suffered the same fate, but Ma'ṣūm Beg's high position ensured that his tragedy is better documented than most.

THE CLOSED ROAD FROM BASRA TO MECCA

As the story of Ma'ṣūm Beg's mission demonstrates, high-level Ottoman administrators were much worried about the possibility that Shi'i pilgrims to Mecca might make contact with the adherents of the Shah on Ottoman territory. This concern also is expressed in the very impractical route that many Iranian pilgrims were required to follow. For most Iranians it would have been easiest to travel to Baghdad and from there to the Iraqi port of Basra, which was in Ottoman hands. After crossing the Persian Gulf, the pilgrims would already have been on the Arabian peninsula, even though the latter needed to be crossed from east to west before reaching the Hejaz. But the alternative which the Ottoman authorities imposed upon the pilgrims was far longer and more dangerous. According to an exchange of letters between the Sultan's Council and certain notables of Basra, which is documented in a rescript dated 1564–5, all Iranian pilgrims were required to take the 'official' caravan routes by way of Damascus, Cairo and Yemen.[27] The notables of Basra lobbied for a caravan of their own, but their request was rather sharply turned down.

Apart from possible infiltration on the part of the Shah's emissaries, the Ottoman authorities presumably were concerned also about Portuguese expansion plans on the eastern coast of the Arabian peninsula. In Basra, al-Ḥasā and Bahrain, certain amirs supported the Portuguese as a counterweight to the Ottomans, and in this fashion hoped to preserve their independence. But while this was a probable concern of the central administration, it was never expressed in the rescripts which have been examined to date. It is nonetheless quite possible that the Ottoman authorities feared, rather than the Iranians, the expansion of the Bahraini Shi'is into the Hejaz, and that this constituted the major reason for the closure of the Basra route.[28]

On the other hand, the cessation of legal connections between Basra and Mecca generated political problems of its own. The notables of the province of al-Ḥasā, a fairly recent acquisition, no doubt suffered economic disadvantages due to this regulation. They therefore exerted pressure upon the Ottoman governor to have the route reopened. No doubt it was to the advantage of the Ottoman authorities to gain the loyalty of the influential families of this outlying border province. Moreover, the governor of the province also needed to establish his office as a recognized institution, for Laḥsā, as the Ottomans called al-Ḥasā, had been elevated to the status of a fully fledged province (*beglerbeglik*) only in 1554. The districts which made up the new province were controlled by local shaykhs, who had ruled the area before the coming of the Ottomans. If not won over to the Ottoman side, it was not unlikely that, at the next opportunity, they would go over to the Shah of Iran or even to the Portuguese. Given the need to find a compromise between these conflicting interests, the Sultan's Council experienced some difficulty in drafting a coherent policy. A rescript dated 1570–1 expresses the administration's hesitations with a frankness quite unusual in this type of document: after mentioning earlier pilgrim travel along the Basra–Mecca route, the text explains that it was later closed to shut out *Ḳızılbash*, that is, heretics from Iran or the Arabian Gulf coast, who were liable to cause disturbances among the pilgrims.[29] But whether a reopening really increased the danger of infiltration admittedly was open to some doubt. Sensibly enough, the authors of the rescript pointed out that it was mainly *bona fide* pilgrims who were kept away by the closing of the route. Real spies probably would find ways and means of insinuating themselves, no matter what precautions were taken. Financial considerations also were of some importance, as the pilgrims paid various taxes en route. Even though the rescript does not contain a clear decision, it seems that the Sultan's Council at this time was willing to risk the reopening of the Basra route.

In 1573–4 pilgrims from Basra finally could reach Mecca by direct travel.[30] This meant that certain groups of Beduins must have been willing to guarantee the safety of the pilgrims, and we do in fact learn that Beduins from Nedjd had protected pilgrims during previous years and were now offering their services for the coming year as well. But already by 1575–6, the pilgrims of Basra could no longer travel by way of Laḥsā. This measure was probably taken as a precaution. Shah Ṭahmāsp was known to be ill, and the continuance of the peace would be in doubt after the death of the ruler who had concluded it. Shah Ṭahmāsp did in fact die the following year and, by 1577–8, the two empires were again at war.[31] These events formed the backdrop to the closure of the Laḥsā route to all pilgrims, not only to Iranians. In one rescript, the Ottoman authorities even admitted that, under the present circumstances, it was all but impossible for pilgrims from the Gulf area to get to Mecca.[32] But it is unlikely that, before the end of the war in 1590, anything was done to solve the problem.

At the same time, the closure of the Basra–Mecca route quite obviously did not prevent Iranian spies from entering the Ottoman Empire. In 1580–1 a rescript refers to supposed Safawid agents, who were accused of having suborned military commanders at the frontier and sown trouble among the pilgrims assembled in Mecca.[33] The governors of Laḥsā and Basra were requested to employ their most capable counter-espionage agents in this affair, but also to make sure that ordinary traders were not molested. Unfortunately, the text does not tell us who these favoured merchants were. Since the war was still continuing, they must have been neutrals, probably Indians who brought spices and cottons into the country and purchased the famous pearls of Bahrain. After all, the customs duties paid by these merchants constituted an appreciable source of revenue.

The interests of merchants trading in Laḥsā were also defended by the local Ottoman governors, who had these customs revenues in mind. Before the Ottoman–Iranian war, the taxes of the province's principal port had been farmed out for three quarters of a million *akče*, but the interruption of pilgrimage travel also dried up this source of revenue. At least for a short time the provincial administrators were successful, for in 1580–1 the route was reopened to Sunni pilgrims.[34] But it is difficult to envisage how Shi'is could have been excluded in practice, particularly since many Iraqi Ottoman subjects as well as Bahrainis were Shi'i Muslims.

In later times the route from Basra by way of Laḥsā presumably was opened or closed according to political exigencies. Ewliyā Čelebi, in his pilgrimage account of 1672, explicitly mentions pilgrims from Basra. They had probably arrived by the direct route, because if they had made the enormous detour by way of Damascus, Ewliyā, who himself had travelled with the Damascus caravan, would not have failed to mention the fact.[35]

COMBINING TWO PILGRIMAGES

Shi'i pilgrims from Iran often combined their journey to Mecca with a visit to the Iraqi pilgrimage centres of al-Nadjaf and Karbalā'. In al-Nadjaf they visited the tomb of the caliph 'Alī (reigned 656–80), the Prophet's son-in-law and his fourth successor after the Caliphs Abū Bakr, 'Umar and 'Uthmān. Karbalā' is the site of the tomb of Imām Ḥusayn, son of the Caliph 'Alī and the grandson of the Prophet by his daughter Fāṭima. Without ever ascending the throne, Imām Ḥusayn was killed in an uprising in the reign of the Ummayad caliph Yazīd (reigned 680–3). In the Shi'i world view, these personages were the rightful heirs of the Prophet Muḥammad and leaders of the Muslim community. Given geographical proximity, there were probably more Iranian pilgrims to al-Nadjaf and Karbalā' than to Mecca. This can be concluded from the fact that, in the rescripts of the sixteenth century, the former are mentioned much more frequently than the latter.

In order to obtain an overall view of Ottoman official attitudes toward Muslim pilgrims, the two pilgrimages should be studied together.

A rescript from the end of 1568 or the beginning of 1569 makes it abundantly clear that the Ottoman authorities, even if they had wished to do so, often would have been unable to prevent Iranian pilgrims from visiting the graves of the Caliph 'Alī or Imām Ḥusayn.[36] In the case under discussion, a group of Iranian hajjis had returned from Mecca by way of Medina. After visiting the Prophet's tomb, they hired a guide and travelled to Baghdad. When the Sultan's Council was informed of this move, its members professed to be shocked. The Ottoman governor was reminded by special rescript that Iranians were forbidden to visit Baghdad. We have no other record of such a prohibition, and possibly it had been issued in a purely *ad hoc* fashion. But all of this cannot have had much of a practical effect; for, by the time the rescript reached its destination, the Iranians may well have completed their business and returned home.

The mother of Shah Ismā'īl II (reigned 1576–7), whose pilgrimage has already occupied us in a different context, also visited al-Nadjaf and Karbalā', probably in 1563–4.[37] Her visit, like that of other Iranians, was governed by a set of regulations probably taking shape at the time and officially issued in 1565, at the very end of Süleymān the Lawgiver's reign. The original version apparently has not survived, but we possess a confirmation from 1573–4, which probably reiterates the principal stipulations of the original.[38] Semi-official representatives of the Shah seem to have resided both in al-Nadjaf and Karbalā', whose principal function it was to distribute alms – a manner of establishing a presence on the territory of a foreign ruler not unknown in Mecca. It was, however, not permitted to the two representatives to establish soup kitchens for the poor, even if only Iranians were to benefit from the Shah's largesse. In Istanbul it was argued that any pilgrim could take care of himself or herself for the span of five to ten days, and a longer stay was regarded as undesirable anyway. These regulations obviously were intended to keep down the Shi'i presence to an absolute minimum. Baghdad probably was regarded as an especially sensitive area; the city had only been conquered by the Ottomans in 1534, and presumably many Baghdadi Shi'is continued to sympathize with the Safawids.[39]

Certain Iranians, however, did settle in the Iraqi pilgrimage cities and even acquired houses and land. In 1578, when the Ottoman and Safawid rulers once again went to war after the death of Shah Ṭahmāsp, several of the Shah's subjects fled Karbalā', and their houses were confiscated by the Ottomans.[40] In Mecca there also existed a community of Iranian residents, who aroused the ire of the Ottoman authorities by their casual behaviour in the courtyard of the

Great Mosque (see Chapter 5).[41] But whether this community survived the Ottoman–Iranian wars of the late sixteenth and early seventeenth centuries remains unknown.

PIOUS GIFTS AS A SOURCE OF DIPLOMATIC RIVALRY

In times of peace Safawid rulers occasionally sent pious gifts to the major sanctuaries located in Ottoman territory. Such donations were made mainly to the mausolea of the Caliph ʿAlī and his son Imām Ḥusayn, but gifts to the sanctuaries of the Hejaz, too, are documented. As the Ottoman rulers also sent gifts, rivalry between the two rulers occasionally ensued concerning the manner in which these gifts were to be exhibited. Thus a rescript dated 1573–4 informs us that the Shah, or else his active and influential sister the princess Perīkhān, had asked for permission to have the two Iraqi sanctuaries covered with carpets from Iran.[42] This demand was politely rejected; but when gifts from Iran did in fact arrive at a sanctuary, the Sultan's Council usually felt that it was not appropriate to reject them.[43] Thus a silver censer and a candelabra donated by Princess Perīkhān were consigned to the storehouse of the Iraqi sanctuaries.[44] Unfortunately, our sources do not permit us to determine whether they were ever exhibited in public.

PILGRIMS FROM CENTRAL ASIA

The Timurid principalities of Central Asia in the sixteenth century were governed by Sunni rulers, many of them in constant conflict with the Safawid Shahs of Iran. Due to the frequent wars between the Iranian ruler and the Khān of the Uzbeks, Sunni pilgrims could not travel to Mecca by the direct route, and all politically feasible detours were enormously long and difficult. Certain pilgrims reached Mecca by way of Istanbul, and returned to their Central Asian homelands by way of Delhi. Apparently one of these pilgrims was asked by the Ottoman authorities to deliver an official missive from Sultan Aḥmed I (reigned 1603–17) at the court of the Mughal ruler Djihāngīr (reigned 1605–27). However, Akbar's son refused to recognize the credentials of this improvised ambassador.[45]

Central Asian pilgrims generally travelled from Bukhara and Samarkand through the steppe to the Caspian Sea. After a stopover in Astrakhan, they continued their journey through present-day southern Russia, until they arrived at one of the Ottoman ports of the northern Black Sea coast, such as Kefe (present-day Feodosiya) or

Özü (Ochakow).[46] If everything went well, the pilgrims then crossed the sea and ultimately arrived in Istanbul, where they could join the hajj caravan to Damascus. Some pilgrims might avoid the Istanbul detour and disembark in one of the ports of northern Anatolia, such as Sinop or Samsun.[47] But in that case they needed to traverse Anatolia from north to south, often on less frequented routes, to meet the Damascus pilgrimage caravan somewhere near Eskişehir or Konya. Given the bad state of the routes linking the Black Sea coast with central Anatolia down into the third quarter of the twentieth century, it is unlikely that the pilgrims who chose this route saved much time, quite apart from the much greater risk of being robbed on the way.

Before the Central Asians entered Ottoman territory in the narrow sense of the word, they needed to pass the steppes controlled, at least to some extent, by the Tatar Khān of the Crimea. This latter khanate was one of the successor states of the Golden Horde, which originally had been founded by Chingiz Khan and his sons during the thirteenth century. By the sixteenth century, the Crimean Tatars frequently were at war with the rulers of Moscow, and recognized the Ottoman Sultan as their suzerain, who appointed and occasionally dismissed their khāns. But the latter retained a good deal of political initiative, and among other things claimed to be the patrons and protectors of all Tatar pilgrims to Mecca. When one of the latter died en route, the Tatar Khān's representative, who accompanied every caravan setting out from Damascus, took charge of his effects, and the Ottoman official in charge of heirless property had no right to intervene (see Chapter 2).[48] At first this ruling probably applied only to the subjects of the Tatar Khān, but later it was extended to all Transoxanians.

As a protector of the pilgrims, the Tatar Khān at times intervened to protect them from excessive taxation. We possess a document dealing with a complaint from pilgrims to Mecca, of whom a prince of the Nogay Tatars had demanded high customs duties in the Black Sea port of Azak (Azov).[49] In response, the Ottoman provincial governor of Azak was ordered to bring the matter to the attention of the Tatar Khān. The authorities in Istanbul apparently assumed that the Khān would exert pressure on the Nogay princes and remind them of the Sultan's commands concerning the treatment of pilgrims. But it is difficult to determine to what extent this expectation was realistic, as the Nogay princes often regarded themselves as the opponents of the current Tatar Khān.

On the long route of the Central Asian pilgrims, Astrakhan was a much frequented stopover. In 1554–6 this city had been conquered by Czar Ivan IV and since then formed part of Russia.[50] When the

Czar attempted to stop the passage of pilgrims, the Ottoman Sultan intervened, partly because his title of caliph obliged him to concern himself with the problems encountered by all pilgrims, even if they were not subjects of the Ottoman state. Moreover, the ruler of the Central Asian khanate of Khiva had urged the Sultan to interfere in the region's political conflicts. A letter from the Khān of Khiva complained about the oppression that merchants and pilgrims suffered from both the Safawids and the Russian Czars; only if the Ottoman Sultan were to take Astrakhan, would these problems find a solution. This demand was taken seriously in Istanbul, since it immediately concerned the Sultan's prestige in the entire Islamic world. The problem of pilgrim transit through Astrakhan apparently contributed to the decision of Sultan Selīm II (reigned 1566–74) to lay siege to the city; but the Ottoman army failed to take it.[51]

Other factors doubtlessly contributed to the decision to go to war over Astrakhan. By the second half of the sixteenth century, Ottoman policy on the northern frontier involved maintaining a balance of power between the Nogay princes, the Tatar Khān and the Czars. Ottoman Sultans and viziers, even at this early period, may well have been worried about the possibility that the Czars would establish themselves on the Black Sea coast, and interpreted the conquest of Astrakhan in this sense. But even so it would be an error to underestimate the importance of pilgrim transit. The Ottoman Sultans could not legitimize themselves by their role in early Islamic history, nor could they put forth a claim, still of some importance in Turco-Tatar circles, of being descended from Chingiz Khan or Tamerlane. Thus their legitimacy depended on practical services to the Islamic community at large, and, among the latter, service to the pilgrims was of special importance.

Among the Central Asian pilgrims who got themselves a *laissez-passer* from the Ottoman administration, we find a good many derwishes. Some of the latter claimed descent from famous personages of Islamic history. Thus a shaykh from Bukhara supposedly was descended from the mystical poet Aḥmad-ı Yasawī, who lived in the twelfth century.[52] Another shaykh from Transoxania declared himself the descendant of 'Umar, the second caliph and successor to the Prophet Muḥammad.[53] This was a rich man, who travelled in the company of his family and sixty derwishes, who in turn had brought their own families along. This style of travel strongly differed from that of Ottoman pilgrims, who normally did not even take their wives. But the Transoxanian shaykh may have been special in other respects as well. His *laissez-passer* contains the clause that the provincial administrators of the regions he traversed should supply him with foodstuffs and camels, while no mention is made of any payment on his part. As most *laissez-passer* specify payment, it is quite possible that the shaykh made his pilgrimage as a guest of the Ottoman Sultan. Another guest of honour was the shaykh 'Abd al-Ḳahhār 'Ulvī; the rescript referring to his case specified that he was to receive high honours from both the Ottoman governor of Kefe (Feodosiya) and from the Tatar K͟hān as well.[54]

PILGRIMS FROM THE FAR WEST

In Ottoman documents from the sixteenth century, references to pilgrims from the North African provinces of the Ottoman Empire are rare, and the same applies to Morocco. This may be explained by the route followed by these travellers, who passed through Cairo and not through Istanbul, so that their problems were less likely to come to the attention of the Sultan's Council than those of the Tatar pilgrims. Seventeenth-century travellers often reached Egypt after a voyage on a French or English ship, for these offered better protection against attacks on the part of Maltese corsairs. There was also a caravan which traversed North Africa from west to east, and, after taking a rest in Cairo, pilgrims could join the annual pilgrimage caravan.[55] Among religious scholars of North Africa it was common practice to combine the pilgrimage with a visit to the major centres of the Islamic world, and even to produce a written account of their travels. Therefore we should not conclude merely from the scanty evidence in the Istanbul archives that few North Africans took the trouble to visit Mecca.

Some official information concerning pilgrims from Morocco can be gathered from two rescripts mentioning the name of Sultan 'Abd al-Malik (reigned 1576–8), who was a protégé of the Ottoman Sultan.[56] Like other Muslim rulers, he maintained an envoy in Mecca, whose job it was to distribute alms in the name of the Sultan. The Ottoman authorities accorded him the privilege of selecting the recipients without any outside interference. But the text also makes it clear that the Sultan's Council did not regard the envoy as a fully fledged ambassador, but as a simple servitor of the Moroccan Sultan.[57]

Within a short time after his arrival, the Moroccan envoy ran into trouble, probably due to the none too elevated standing of the ruler who had sent him. The Moroccan had acquired a house in Mecca, but Ḳāḍī Ḥusayn, former *ḳāḍī* of Medina and acting *s͟hayk͟h al-ḥaram*, one of the most powerful men in the city, took it away from him under one pretext or another.[58] Thereupon the envoy complained to Istanbul, and the Sultan's Council apparently sympathized with his plight. But it is not clear whether Ḳāḍī Ḥusayn was in fact obliged to return the house.

A rescript protecting the heirs of deceased Moroccan pilgrims was probably due to the activities of the unfortunate envoy. This privilege resembles that issued to the Tatar Khān, assuring the Moroccan ruler that the estates of his deceased subjects would be turned over to the heirs and not confiscated. Given the atrocious reputation of the officials who farmed the collection of heirless estates (see Chapter 2) this exemption from their attentions constituted a significant advantage.[59]

POLITICS AND THE PILGRIMAGE

If politics consists of the skill of conciliating contradictory interests, Ottoman hajj policy did not deviate from the standard definition. An Ottoman Sultan who wished to fulfil the expectations of the political class, that is *'ulemā* and other public officials, needed to protect both domestic and foreign pilgrims from hunger, lack of water, Beduin attacks, hindrances imposed by foreign rulers and excessive taxation. In this context, the Ottoman rulers also acted as suzerains of the Sherifs. The Sultans were not the only Muslim rulers to maintain a presence in the Hejaz, however, as the Mughals and Moroccan Sultans sent envoys to oversee official almsgiving, to say nothing of the pilgrimages of members of different royal families. The Ottoman ruler's claim to preeminence might result in his controlling and limiting the charity of certain foreign rulers, especially if the latter's donations were so lavish as to imply a bid for support from Hejazi notables, particularly the Sherifal dynasty. But on the other hand, to limit the gifts of foreign rulers might lead to the disaffection of potential beneficiaries. This had to be prevented, often by the accordance of Ottoman largesse. For many Meccan families appreciably benefited from the donations of foreign rulers; in addition, the Sherifs passed on a sizable amount of the donations they received to the Beduins of the Hejaz. Under these circumstances, the hostility of politically active personages in Mecca or Medina might result in Beduin attacks on the pilgrimage caravans, and thus the attempt to secure Ottoman control indirectly might lead to a loss of legitimacy. The Sultan's Council and the relevant provincial governors therefore needed to proceed with circumspection.

Somewhat different political problems arose in connection with votive gifts. When the Ottoman Sultan or a foreign Muslim ruler donated carpets, candelabras, books or other items of value, these gestures must be understood as not merely religious but political as well. Between the Ottoman rulers and the Safawid Shahs these donations occasionally aroused a good deal of rivalry. Competition would have been even more intense if the Safawids had not preferred to concentrate their attention on the Iraqi mausolea of the Caliph 'Alī and his son the Imām Ḥusayn. To the Ottomans as Sunni rulers these personages certainly were venerable because of their relationship to the Prophet Muḥammad and their role in early Islamic history. But their graves were regarded as less important than the Prophet's mosque in Medina and the Great Mosque of Mecca. The Ottoman Sultans certainly attempted to establish a Sunni presence in Iraq by adorning Sunni sanctuaries, such as the grave of the derwish saint 'Abd al-Ḳādir al-Djīlānī; conversely the latter sanctuary was destroyed whenever the Safawids managed to conquer Baghdad and hold it for a more or less extended period.[60] But on the other hand, no Ottoman Sunni would have objected to the decoration of the mausolea which commemorated the graves of the Prophet's descendants in Iraq.[61] Thus the different but not necessarily contradictory priorities of Ottomans and Safawids with respect to Islamic sanctuaries certainly kept diplomatic rivalry between the two ruling houses within manageable limits.

In the second half of the sixteenth century, Ottoman Sultans and their advisers showed a particular interest in the pilgrimages of derwishes and religious scholars from Central Asia. This again needs to be viewed against the backdrop of the Ottoman–Safawid conflict. Pilgrims from Central Asia could not take the closest route to Mecca, because the Safawids, locked in long-term conflict with the Uzbeks, prevented their passage. Detours through India or Istanbul were so difficult, however, that only people for whom religion was the dominant commitment, even in their everyday lives, were willing to take this burden upon themselves. Thus most Central Asian pilgrims who visited the Ottoman Empire were either religious scholars or derwishes. Such people in the eyes of their Ottoman opposite numbers must have appeared as heroic representatives of Sunni Islam *vis à vis* the heretic Iranians. Views of this kind probably explain why some of these Central Asian pilgrims were received with so much pomp and circumstance.

Pilgrims from Safawid Iran were affected by the conflict between the two great Muslim empires in yet a different fashion. Although no Ottoman rescript ever claimed that the pilgrimage route from Basra was closed in retaliation for the difficulties laid in the way of Central Asian pilgrims, it is not inconceivable that this motive had a role to play. On this issue, however, the Ottoman government again attempted to conciliate mutually incompatible interests. On the one hand the amirs of the Arabian peninsula in their desert fastnesses were to be prevented from establishing contacts with the Safawids, and possibly even with the Portuguese, in order to escape Ottoman control. At the same time, the wishes of the notables of Basra had to be taken into consideration, whose economic interests were at stake and who controlled a strategic port city of great importance to the Ottoman Empire. What at first glance appears as Ottoman indecisiveness, on further consideration turns out to be an attempt to find a viable compromise between these diverging political aims.

7

The Pilgrimage in Economic and Political Contexts

At all times, the pilgrimage was located at the intersection of several far-flung networks, primarily social and religious, but political and economic as well. Yet neither the Ottoman state, nor its predecessors dominating the Hejaz in the Middle Ages, fully controlled all these networks. Therefore the political elites, both Ottoman and Mamluk, were faced with a number of difficult tasks. As we have seen in the previous chapters, the safety of the pilgrims could only be assured if Ottoman administrators succeeded in satisfying, and where necessary intimidating, armed Beduins on the verge of famine, unruly janissaries and a local population accustomed to imperial largesse. As force could be used only in emergencies, the scope for various kinds of political action was considerable.

For this purpose a regional administrative apparatus was created, which, from the central government's point of view, was more difficult to control than its counterparts in the Ottoman core regions of Anatolia and Rumelia. The Sherifs functioned as the most important element. Accordingly, they demanded to be recognized as independent rulers, even if these claims were not accepted in Istanbul. To counter their ambitions, the Ottoman administration appointed the *ḳāḍī*s of Mecca and Medina, the administrator of Jeddah, the *agha*s of Medina, and lesser officials as well. Last but not least, the notable families of the Holy Cities, if handled with circumspection, might serve as a support for Ottoman power.

To maintain equilibrium, the Ottoman central administration had to take into account not only political relations, but also foreign trade. Here the possibilities for official intervention were severely limited. Yemeni traders in the Middle Ages, and southern Indians from the seventeenth century onward, delivered foodstuffs and other necessities to the Hejaz. But the arrival or failure to arrive of these merchants could be controlled only in a very limited sense by Sultans and viziers, whether they resided in Baghdad, Cairo or later Istanbul. Portuguese attacks, the activities of European pirates or bad rice harvests in southern India could all endanger the supply of food in the Hejaz, and the Ottoman administration possessed but limited means to counter these threats.

In the present chapter, we will investigate the manner in which politics and foreign trade affected different aspects of the pilgrimage. We will be dealing with the attempt of a highly organized and bureaucratized state of the early modern era to influence interregional and international trade in the interests of pilgrims and permanent inhabitants of the Hejaz, and thereby to legitimize its own existence in the eyes of both domestic and foreign pilgrims. We will also discuss both the cooperation and occasional resistance this official Ottoman policy encountered from traders, local notables and the Sherifs themselves.

THE SUBJECTION OF THE HEJAZ

In 1517 Ṭumān Bāy, the last Mamluk Sultan of Egypt, was hanged at the gates of Cairo upon the orders of the Ottoman Sultan Selīm I (reigned 1512–20).[1] Ṭumān Bāy's predecessor Ḳānṣūh al-Gh̲ūrī (reigned 1501–16) had been killed in battle; after 1516, Syria was in Ottoman hands. These facts severely limited the options of the Sherifs of Mecca who, as princes of local importance only, had governed the Hejaz ever since the tenth century. A text from the year 1517 clearly demonstrates that, at the beginning of the sixteenth century, the Meccan food supply closely depended on the arrival of grains from Egypt. A short time previously the Portuguese had staged an incursion into the Red Sea, with dire consequences for life in the Hejaz. 'The situation in this place really is worthy of commiseration. Before these accursed unbelievers arrived, a *ṭuman* of grain sold for 20 *as̲h̲rafī* coins. When the news arrived, the price increased to 30 on the very same day, and to 40 a day later. It still continues to rise, and people say that it will reach 100.'[2] This was the report of the Ottoman naval commander Selmān Re'īs from Jeddah, and it explains why the Hejaz submitted to Ottoman domination without a shot being fired.

The presence of the Ottoman fleet in the Red Sea equally contributed to the rapid submission of the Sherifs.[3] In order to stop the advance of the Portuguese into the Red Sea region, Sultan Ḳānṣūh al-Gh̲ūrī had asked the Ottoman ruler Bāyezīd II (reigned

1481–1512) for military and naval support. The Ottoman fleet, commanded by amir Ḥüseyin al-Kürdī, lost a battle against the Portuguese before Diu in 1509 and failed to drive them away from the western coast of southern India. But the amir rapidly fortified Jeddah, and this certainly influenced the last-minute decision of the Portuguese commander to leave the city in peace. Meanwhile relations between Ḥüseyin al-Kürdī and the reigning Sherif Barakāt seriously deteriorated, and, after a series of clashes, the Sherif had the Amir drowned near Jeddah. According to Meccan chronicles, Sultan Selīm himself had ordered the killing. But the Ottoman naval commander Selmān Re'īs, who was in Jeddah in 1517, felt that this act ran completely counter to Ottoman political traditions and was the sole responsibility of the Sherif.

MECCAN SHERIFS AND OTTOMAN GOVERNORS

Possibly Sherif Barakāt did not wish to discuss the killing of amir Ḥüseyin al-Kürdī with Sultan Selīm I, when the latter conquered Cairo in the same year.[4] In any case he did not in person travel to Cairo, but sent his very young son Abū Numayy to offer his submission to the Ottoman Sultan. Selīm I accepted this solution without ever travelling to the Hejaz himself, and the Sherifs were recognized as dependent princes. No Ottoman governors resided in Mecca or Medina, although small detachments of soldiers from Egypt were garrisoned there. In the second half of the sixteenth century, after Ottoman control had stabilized in the Hejaz and Egypt, a low-level provincial governor (*beg, sandjakbegi*) resided in Jeddah on the Red Sea coast and represented the Ottoman government *vis à vis* the Sherif of Mecca.[5] The hierarchical superior of the governor of Jeddah was the *beglerbegi* of Egypt, and later the equally remote governor of Ḥabeshistān (Ethiopia).

Given the great distances involved, the governor of Jeddah often possessed more room for manoeuvre than other Ottoman provincial governors. But many *'ulemā* and other well-connected personages, whose salaries were paid out of the revenues of the port, sometimes found this situation highly undesirable, and were able to limit the port administrator's freedom of action by calling on the central administration to intervene. In 1594, the Chief Black Eunuch was appointed *nāẓır* (supervisor) of the port of Jeddah, whose main job it was to make sure that the beneficiaries of official largesse did in fact receive their money. Since the Chief Eunuch continued to reside in Istanbul, a substitute was appointed who presumably came to reside in Jeddah itself. We do not know whether this arrangement was meant to be permanent, or limited to the frequent periods in which the governorship was vacant, as it had been when *'ulemā* and other beneficiaries allegedly were unable to collect their money. But whenever a new governor and port administrator arrived, coping with the Chief Eunuch's representative must have posed some delicate problems.[6]

The most distinguished holder of this position was probably the historian Muṣṭafā 'Ālī (1541–1600), who, even though he did not make the kind of career he considered appropriate to his merits, was appointed to governorships several times, and ended his career in 1600 as an administrator of Jeddah. 'Ālī had established amicable relations with the reigning Sherif, to whom he showed the literary work he was then in the course of completing, certain sections of which the Sherif was alleged to have endorsed with enthusiasm. These good relations also may have been due to the fact that 'Ālī was willing to regard the Sherifs as a sovereign dynasty.[7]

The Sherifs' attempts to be recognized as more or less independent princes have occupied us in another context (see Chapter 6); we now need to consider how the authorities in Istanbul reacted to such claims. Even though territorial limits in the desert were bound to be somewhat vague, the Ottoman administration had a working notion of the area the Sherifs were supposed to control, and distinguished this territory from provinces under direct administration. This is apparent from two rescripts dated 1573–4, which relayed instructions concerning the peasants of the oasis of Khaybar.[8] The latter had complained about mistreatment on the part of some 'rebellious Beduins', who came to the oasis at harvest time, allegedly robbed grain and dates, raped women and wounded or even killed some of the inhabitants. Now the peasants had offered to accept a garrison and in addition pay 2000 gold pieces to the provincial treasury of Damascus in exchange for protection. In the rescript addressed to the governor of Damascus, it is expressly stated that the responsibility for protecting the inhabitants of the oasis lay with the Sherif; only if the latter declared himself unable to do anything about the matter, would the central administration consider direct intervention. At the same time the Sherif received an official letter which reminded him that the local fortress commander was his own man, and that he would have to shoulder the responsibility of punishing the robbers.

Khaybar was a remote outpost, which even in the second half of the nineteenth century, the Ottoman government did not really control; and presumably the Sherif was enjoined to intervene because the administration did not wish to commit troops to this venture. Quite apart from practical considerations, it is noteworthy that the Ottoman government, even at the height of its power, did not claim that the Sherif's lands simply constituted Ottoman territory, where the nearest provincial governor could do whatever he considered necessary. At least in this limited respect, the Ottoman Sultan thus accepted the claims of the Sherifs to control a certain stretch of territory with minimum interference from the outside.

At the same time, the Sherifs of Mecca were appointed, usually for life, by the Ottoman Sultan.[9] In case of conflict, Sherifs could be deposed, but the successor had to be taken from the same family. Most Sherifs possessed a large number of brothers and nephews, and therefore had to be prepared for the eventuality of being ousted. It was not unheard of that a deposed Sherif might succeed in regaining office at a later period.

Among the Beduins the Sherif family had allies and thus could put together an armed force of its own. In 1585 the Ottoman central government did not contradict the Sherif's claim that from his revenues he must support 20,000 to 30,000 adherents and dependants.[10] Probably the Sherif paid subsidies to the Beduins, so as to have a claim on them in case of need. Given the difficulty of feeding large numbers of people in the Hejaz, a standing army would have been out of the question.

From the central administration's point of view, it was the function of this armed force to prevent attacks on the pilgrimage caravan. But a Sherif who got into trouble with an Ottoman caravan commander could make another use of his Beduin auxiliaries. Ewliyā Čelebi has given a full report of just such a case. In 1670–1, that is, a year before the traveller's visit, a newly appointed governor of Jeddah felt offended by the reigning Sherif, and serious conflict was the result.[11] Pilgrims engaged in their devotions in the courtyard of the Great Mosque felt so threatened that they closed the gates on the inside, while the Ottoman governor sent a small armed force to the mosque. The soldiers ascended the mosque roof, by which Ewliyā presumably meant the gallery surrounding the courtyard of the Great Mosque. But the Beduins in the service of the Sherif climbed the heights of Abū Ḳubays not far from the city centre, the *medrese*s immediately adjacent to the mosque itself and even the galleries of the minarets, firing into the courtyard. According to Ewliyā, two hundred dead and seven hundred wounded were the result. Even if we concede that his figures often were somewhat exaggerated, this incident shows that the Sherifs did not readily submit to Ottoman domination. As to the Sherif responsible, Ewliyā has left a somewhat comic account of his deposition; but ultimately the latter was able to reestablish himself as a ruler of Mecca.[12]

Thus the authorities in Istanbul possessed some experience of the troubles a Sherif might cause if so inclined. Accordingly they mostly used persuasion rather than force, and the rescripts addressed to the Sherifs often were replete with fulsome compliments. When certain tax collectors active in Jeddah aroused complaint, and the Ottoman administration decided to depose and banish them, the Sherif's cooperation was actively solicited (1575–6).[13] Another Sherif, who by his prudent intervention had managed to prevent a dispute between pilgrims and inhabitants of Mecca from getting out of control, received a robe of honour at the accession of the new Sultan Aḥmed I (reigned 1603–17). This was normal practice; but, amidst a formidable array of compliments, the Sherif was also informed that the current commander of the pilgrimage caravan had been stripped of his office. Although the text does not say so expressly, it does seem that the Sherif previously had intimated his dissatisfaction with this official.[14]

During the Ottoman conquest of the Yemen (1568–71), and in the following years, the Sherifs sometimes were requested to support the Ottoman war effort.[15] From the Ottoman point of view, the Sherifs benefited from the conquest of Yemen, as the latter secured their domain from a possible Portuguese attack. The lands under the control of the Sherif also increased, as some of the newly conquered areas were annexed to their domain. To the Ottomans, the Sherifs were important in this context mainly because they could furnish horses. Central Arabia at that time was already famed for these animals, which in the nineteenth century were to attract several adventurous English visitors. In 1579 the Sherif was requested to send three hundred horses against an appropriate payment; presumably he found these animals among his allies the Beduins.[16] At the same time, the Sherifs were to ensure communications between Yemen, where Ottoman rule always remained problematic, and the core areas of the Ottoman domain. On the caravan routes leading to Mecca, pilgrims and couriers travelled to the Hejaz and, along with them, news of recent political developments reached the authorities in Egypt and Istanbul.

Thus, in spite of their dependent position, the Sherifs constituted an important ally whose wishes had to be taken into account. The central authorities could never take the cooperation of these princes for granted, while tensions between the two powers could prove costly to the central government and very dangerous to the pilgrims. This explains why the Ottoman Sultans, in spite of their overwhelming military superiority, preferred to treat the Sherifs with circumspection.

OFFICIALS AND NOTABLES IN THE HOLY CITIES

Apart from the governors and port administrators of Jeddah, other centrally appointed Ottoman officials counterbalanced the activities of the Sherif. For these men, the Hejaz constituted a more or less extended stage in their careers, but not the site of their further official lives. Many indeed might hope to later achieve high office in Istanbul. The *ḳāḍī*s of Mecca and Medina had gone through the *cursus honorum* of teaching in a sequence of *medrese*s and officiating in ever more important cities as judges *cum* administrators. But, as we shall see, even these officials were sometimes absorbed into Hejazi society, and their ability to function as a counterweight to the Sherif could not be regarded as a matter of course.

In the judicial hierarchy, the rank of the *ḳāḍī*s of Mecca and Medina gradually grew more exalted. In the sixteenth century the two offices were not named among the highest-ranking *mewlewiyet* (provincial *ḳāḍī*ships), which allowed the incumbents nominal salaries of five hundred *akče* a day. Therefore, the judges of the Holy Cities seem to have ranked well below their colleagues of Damascus, Cairo and even Jerusalem. But by the middle of the seventeenth century, the *ḳāḍī*ships of the Holy Cities had been included among a small group of select and high-ranking offices, while most of the other sixteenth-century *mewlewiyet*s had fallen far behind. In the second half of the eighteenth century the rank of the *ḳāḍī*s of Mecca and Medina had become even more exalted; now the *ḳāḍī* of Istanbul was the only judge to precede them in the hierarchy.[17]

Presumably this development should be taken as one more indication of the growing official regard for religious law which we can observe in the Ottoman Empire of that time. In the sixteenth century, respect for the *sheri'at* had not precluded a wide scope for legal regulation based on the will of the Sultan (*'örf*).[18] From the seventeenth century onwards, however, the impact of religious law on crucial sectors of life such as the regulation of land tenure was clearly growing. Admittedly this widening application of the religious law was not a unilinear development; in other aspects of Ottoman life, the seventeenth and eighteenth centuries witnessed a measure of 'secularization' as well. Yet a growing respect paid to the *sheri'at* presumably induced Ottoman administrators to emphasize the role of the Holy Cities, and the *ḳāḍī*s benefited from this ideological trend in terms of a quite mundane increase in rank.

Even in the sixteenth century, the *ḳāḍī*ship of Mecca, at least, was occasionally granted to personages of the highest rank in the Ottoman juridico-religious hierarchy. Mīrzā Makhdūm had been a teacher of Prince Ismā'īl, the heir-apparent of Iran. He emigrated to the

Ottoman Empire in 1546 and returned home when his former charge ascended the throne. While in Iran, Mīrzā Makhdūm held high office, but, upon the death of Shah Ismā'īl, he returned to the Ottoman realm, where he was appointed *ḳāḍī* of Istanbul in early 1586. But when his mother died of the plague that same year, he decided to undertake the pilgrimage. While still on the way to the Hejaz, he was appointed *ḳāḍī* of Mecca with the honorary rank of army judge (*ḳāḍī'asker*) of Rumelia. Once in the Hejaz, he married off a daughter to a scion of the Sherif family, and when he died while in office there, he was publicly mourned with great solemnity.[19]

Mīrzā Makhdūm's political role did not even come to an end with his death. In 1588 the Sultan's Council responded to a declaration of the reigning Sherif to the effect that the *ḳāḍī* before his death had made no less than three wills, in all of which he had appointed the Sherif his executor.[20] The deceased's only heirs were his wife and his young daughter, who was still a minor and presumably identical with the bride who recently had entered the Sherifian household. This would explain the reigning Sherif's interest in the *ḳāḍī*'s inheritance, as the latter apparently had been a man of means. The story of Mīrzā Makhdūm is of interest for our purposes, as it shows that even Ottoman 'career' officials might form close social ties in the Hejaz, and thereby become less effective in their role as counterweights to the Sherif. But at the same time the personal prestige enjoyed by Mīrzā Makhdūm reflected upon his office and may well have enhanced Ottoman legitimacy. So it is quite possible that the tenure of office of this unusual scholar, whom his biographer clearly regarded as somewhat eccentric, was regarded as an asset rather than a liability by the Ottoman central government.

Apart from the *ḳāḍī*s, an important role, at least in Medina, was played by the *shaykh al-ḥaram*. This official sometimes was a member of the *'ulemā*, but at other times he was one of the eunuchs who served the Prophet's tomb. It was the *shaykh al-ḥaram*'s responsibility to appoint and dismiss the eunuchs and maintain discipline among them. A major part of this duty was to take charge of the court cases involving eunuchs (*aghāwāt*). This probably meant securing their appearance in court whenever this was demanded, for it is difficult to see what other involvement *shaykh al-ḥaram*s who were not members of the *'ulemā* could have had in judicial affairs explicitly connected with the religious law. If a member of the *'ulemā*, technically the *shaykh al-ḥaram* could have functioned as a judge. The closest analogy that comes to mind is that of a janissary commander who also had jurisdiction over his men. But it seems that the *shaykh al-ḥaram* punished recalcitrant *aghāwāt* primarily by taking away their positions.[21]

The *shaykh al-ḥaram* also had other responsibilities. Thus he oversaw a number of Medina residents who every year were paid ten gold pieces out of official funds in order to perform the pilgrimage in the name and place of the Sultan, to whom they transferred the religious merit gained by this act.[22] Certain *shaykh al-ḥaram*s also took on financial responsibilities. A text from the year 1585 concerns complaints that revenues sent to Medina had not reached their destination, and the *shaykh al-ḥaram* who authored the complaint was a provincial finance director by profession.[23] In emergencies the *shaykh al-ḥaram* also took charge of public grains arriving in the port of Yanbu', had them remitted to Medina and then distributed among the inhabitants of the city. He also sent reports to Istanbul concerning the manner in which official donations of grain had been disposed of. Thus the *shaykh al-ḥaram* had responsibilities extending not only over the Great Mosque proper, but over the city of Medina as well. Presumably he took over certain functions normally assigned to an Ottoman governor, as there was no such official in Medina, and the Sherif was represented only by a deputy of limited powers and responsibilities.

A balance of power in the cities of the Hejaz could be achieved if the Ottoman central authorities managed to forge links with high-ranking members of the local population, who might not always agree with the political tendencies of the reigning Sherifs. Certain administrative positions could be created *ad hoc*, and furnished opportunities for patronage; such advantages could be enjoyed both by people of local influence and by migrants to the Hejaz from the Ottoman core lands. Some of the latter came to the Holy Cities to retire from official life. But we do not hear of large numbers of former Ottoman courtiers fallen from favour, comparable to the Indian exiles of the sixteenth century. Presumably the Ottoman central administration regarded the establishment of malcontents in the Holy Cities as much too dangerous.

Numerous documents concerning the political and religious elites of Mecca and Medina record disputes concerning the allocation of officially granted revenues. It seems that these struggles for control over outside resources constituted the major element of political life in the Holy Cities. But this may be in part an optical illusion, as other processes, such as the formation and dissolution of family alliances, did not normally concern the Ottoman central government. We have already discussed the attempts of the Ḥusaynīs to retain a share of the *ṣürre*, and the at least temporary disadvantages they suffered on account of being Shi'is (see Chapter 4). Other distribution problems arose when deliveries were in arrears, and people close to the centres of political power made sure that they were served first whenever some grain or gold became available. When beneficiaries died, local administrators were not supposed to redistribute the all-important documents of entitlement (*berāt*) on their own initiative, and even less were these documents to be passed on to heirs. The Ottoman central administration quite obviously intended to reserve this source of patronage to itself.[24] But the frequency with which divergent practices were discussed in sultanic rescripts suggests that reality often must have been rather different from official commands. Thus several *ḳāḍī*s of Damascus were found out after they had assigned pensions ranging between ten and 50 gold pieces each to selected inhabitants of the Holy Cities, so that the pension fund no longer sufficed.[25] But even when officials duly reported candidates for the Sultan's bounty, they were not devoid of influence. Residing in faraway Istanbul, members of the Ottoman central administration had no means of knowing which candidates deserved official largesse, unless they received information from officials with local knowledge.

As a relationship to an Ottoman administrator had to be established before a person could successfully apply for imperial largesse, certain poor and pious people lacking such contacts automatically were excluded. In the rescripts emitted by the Sultan's Council, problems of this kind often were summarized in pithy phrases. We hear that 'wealthy people with power and influential backers' managed to get hold of official largesse, or that 'the vacant assignments are not given to the deserving poor but to the rich [or: to the notables]'.[26] Remarkably enough, the assignment of pensions to people already possessed of other resources was not considered an abuse unless there were poor people on record who thus were deprived of their rights.[27] Probably the alms granted to Meccans at least in part were meant to secure the loyalty of influential personages of the Holy Cities, and maybe even to cement their ties to individual Ottoman officials active in the Hejaz. Given the paucity of Ottoman military forces in the area, these links were essential if administrators were to function at all. At the same time, the unchecked use of religiously motivated alms for political purposes was bound to delegitimize the Sultans, and could not be countenanced either.

Another manner of discussing the conflicts between different candidates for sultanic largesse is connected with the statement that 'insiders' rather than 'outsiders' should receive positions and grants. In the political literature of the time variations on this theme frequently were encountered. A given author might demand the exclusion from the Sultan's service of this or that group of officials, because they had been recruited through channels of which he did not approve. In such instances, the writers of 'advice to princes' and similar texts normally championed meritorious 'insiders' over unqualified 'outsiders'. In the case of the sultanic alms remitted from Istanbul, the crucial 'in-group' consisted of 'the poor of the Holy Cities'. This term presumably denoted a residential group, although we cannot be too certain of its limits. And then there is the unsolved problem whether residence in the Holy City, the status of a freeman or freewoman, poverty and a life devoted mainly to pious purposes were sufficient to make a person a member of the in-group, or whether other conditions, less clearly spelled out but no less significant, had to be met as well. In the later sixteenth century, outsiders might pose their candidacy in a formal fashion. This was known as *mülāzemet*, due to an analogy to *'ulemā* who, temporarily out of office, applied for a vacancy in the judicial hierarchy. According to a rescript from 1576, such 'outsider' candidates had in fact been able to secure pensions in the past, but the practice was now forbidden since it hurt the interests of the established 'poor of the Holy Cities'.[28]

In addition, there were disputes over the control of *waḳıf*s, of the kind which frequently occurred in the Ottoman core lands as well. In 1567, the administrator of the Sultan's mother's Egyptian foundations in favour of the Hejazi poor had his books audited, and it turned out that he owed the foundation 10,000 gold pieces and 10,000 *irdeb* of wheat. Apparently the administrator had not used this gold and wheat for what we today would call 'private' purposes, but may have acted under duress. In Istanbul, it was assumed that some of the arrears were really the debts of certain Egyptian military men to the foundation. This probably means that the administrator had been using the foundation resources to improve his own political position.[29] A much later rescript, dating from the year 1657, relates accusations against the man in charge of the Syrian pious foundations on behalf of the poor of Medina, who supposedly had retained for himself a large share of what he should have paid to the beneficiaries.[30] In this case, we cannot even guess what happened to the money.

THE MECCAN SHERIFS AND THE CUSTOMS OF JEDDAH

The Sherifs collected one half of the Jeddah customs revenues, and this income constituted their financial base; the other half accrued to the Ottoman provincial governor.[31] How the Sherifs acquired this lucrative prerogative is open to debate. Sayyid Daḥlān Aḥmad and Ismail Hakkı Uzunçarşılı, two twentieth-century scholars, maintain that the Sherif actively supported the Ottomans when the Portuguese raided the port in 1542 and was granted one half of the Jeddah customs as a reward.[32] There exists, however, a much more colourful account of these events, which we find in the chronicle of Ibrāhīm Pečewī (1574–1649 or 1651).[33] According to the latter, the Grand Vizier Sinān Pasha, who had a major share in the Ottoman conquest of Yemen, visited Mecca in about 1570. Of the reigning Sherif Abū Numayy b. Barakāt he demanded a letter to the Ottoman administration confirming his military successes in Yemen, but the Sherif had been gravely offended by an earlier incident and was in no mood to oblige him. Before embarking on his campaign, Sinān Pasha had paid an earlier visit to the Hejaz, and had been received by the influential Ḳāḍī Ḥüseyin in the name of the reigning Sherif. As a welcoming gift he had been offered some rare cups and vessels, probably imported from Iran, where Chinese porcelain was being imitated in the shape of fayence, or even directly from China itself. But Sinān Pasha, of whose harshness and lack of finesse his old enemy Muṣṭafā 'Alī also had a great deal to say, had the costly pieces trampled underfoot by his horse, and this insult was not forgiven by the Sherif. Only after considerable hesitation did the latter allow himself to be persuaded to write the letter to the Sultan which Sinān Pasha demanded of him, and this act netted him the right to half the Jeddah customs. Ibrāhīm Pečewī concludes his story with the remark that the dues demanded from merchants doubled as a result.

No document found in the Ottoman archives allows us to determine which one of these stories is true, or from what date onwards the Sherif began to collect a share of the Jeddah customs duties. But by 1575–6 he definitely was in possession. This is apparent from a sultanic rescript responding to a complaint by the Sherif about shippers and shipping on the Red Sea. If the Sherif had not had a financial stake in this matter, he would scarcely have bothered to correspond with Istanbul about it.[34]

In those years, when Ottoman power in the Yemen was still in the process of consolidation, numerous Ottoman soldiers were stationed in the area, who had to be supplied from overseas, mainly from Egypt. As a result, there was a lot of boat traffic on the Red Sea, particularly since many ships brought back to Egypt spices from India and South Asia, which could be purchased in the ports of Yemen. In spite of all attempts to eliminate Muslim shipping, the Portuguese, who in the first half of the sixteenth century had established themselves on the western coast of India and in 1511 conquered the port of Malacca on the Malayan peninsula, had not been able to prevent the continuing arrival of South Asian spices in the Red Sea region. The centuries-old trade routes crossing the Indian Ocean continued to flourish.[35] We know of contacts not only between the Yemen and India and between Egypt and the Yemen, but also of more or less direct linkages between the Egyptian port of Suez and the western coast of India.

Direct connections, however, suffered from the actions of Ottoman provincial administrators operating in Yemen, who were anxious to have Indian goods unloaded in the ports under their jurisdiction, and thus to benefit from customs duties. Not only Suez, but even Jeddah lost traffic as a result of these policies. The Sherif countered by demanding an order from the Ottoman government forcing all shippers to put in at Jeddah. This the Sultan could not be persuaded to command, although the Sherifs were to renew their attempts in later years.[36]

TRADE AND TRAFFIC BETWEEN INDIA AND THE ARABIAN PENINSULA

If the trade of Yemen with the Red Sea ports had been insignificant, this dispute probably would not have arisen. Apart from the spice trade, the importation of Indian cotton fabrics increased the traffic of the Red Sea ports; in the course of the seventeenth century, these cottons were to become very popular not only in Europe, but in the Ottoman Empire as well.[37] We have no information on the quantities of textiles imported into Ottoman territory, but we know that in southern India whole villages specialized in production for the Arab provinces, while others worked for European, South Asian or Iranian customers. Indian terms for various textiles entered Ottoman Turkish as loan words, as happened in France and England. Jeddah was a major centre of the textile trade.

Fabrics exported from India to the Arabian peninsula were manufactured by weavers and spinners who did not themselves market their products, but depended on merchants.[38] Some scholars therefore have discussed the possibility that southern India possessed a proto-industry comparable to that which developed in certain parts of eighteenth-century Europe. Most researchers today prefer to emphasize the differences between the two cases rather than the similarities. Even so, the dominant role of merchants in the productive process is a feature which Indian textile manufacture shares with its European counterpart, while in Ottoman textile production, this type of control was much less widespread.

Certain Indian traders of the seventeenth century owned their ships, which they might send from the port of Surat on the Malabar coast to Mocha in Yemen. These shipowners did business in the grand style: the Surat merchant ʿAbd al-Ghafūr in 1701 owned 17 ships, which among other places visited Manila and China.[39] ʿAbd al-Ghafūr concentrated on the Surat–Mocha route, and it is probable that a significant share of the textiles arriving in this Yemeni port ultimately reached Mecca with the pilgrimage caravans. Armenian merchants resident in India also sent their ships to the Red Sea region; in the last quarter of the seventeenth century, the Surat trader Khodja Minas participated in this trade with ten ships of his own.[40]

After 1650, Indian merchants began to invest in shipping on a large scale. In earlier years, that kind of investment had been something of a rarity; usually, Indian traders had freighted ships belonging to the major rulers of the subcontinent, but sometimes even to minor princes. Nor did ships belonging to Indian rulers disappear, even after 1650; in 1662, a ship owned by the queen of the southern state of Bijapur appeared in the port of Aden, carrying 1500 passengers and 400 bales of goods.[41] The bales were so large that they had to be carried into the city by a detour, as they did not fit through the harbour gate. The ruler of the city of Cochin, which also served as one of the more important Indian bases for the Portuguese trade toward the end of the sixteenth century, often sent ships to Jeddah, protected by a Portuguese safe conduct. But the most important shipowners were the Mughal rulers residing in Delhi and Agra.[42] Not only did they place ships at the disposal of merchants, they also participated in the Hejaz trade in their own right. The Emperor Shāhdjahān (reigned 1627–58) several times sent valuable goods; at one time his wares were worth 240,000 rupies. In 1650 he had invested 150,000 rupies in trade goods sent to the Arabian peninsula, and the Sultan of Gujerat also sent valuable goods to the Hejaz. These ware were sold at a high profit, one hundred per cent being not at all unusual. However, this profit did not return to India, but was distributed in the Hejaz in the shape of alms.

In spite of the distance, even rulers of states on the eastern coast of India quite frequently sent their own ships to the Arabian peninsula.[43] From 1580 onward, the Sultan of Golconda dispatched one ship a year from the southern Indian port of Masulipatnam, often with a cargo of 600 tons and more. Portuguese safe conducts for these ships demanded complicated negotiations; often they were issued in exchange for deliveries of rice to the Portuguese settlements of the Estado da India. Practical difficulties were numerous. When, at the beginning of the seventeenth century, the Dutch came to be active in the Indian Ocean and soon supplanted the Portuguese, the Sultan of Golconda declared that from now on it would be the responsibility of the Vereenigde Oostindische Compagnie to protect Jeddah-bound ships from Portuguese reprisals. The reasoning behind this demand was that the Sultan, who did not possess a navy of his own, had made enemies of the Portuguese by permitting the Dutch to trade.[44]

Between 1610 and 1620 the Golconda ship regularly visited the Arabian peninsula and returned without incident. As ballast it carried a load of rice, which was distributed to the poor of Mecca in the name of the Sultan. But in 1621 and 1625 the ship from Masulipatnam to Jeddah was captured by the Portuguese. When the Sultan threatened reprisals, the Dutch hurried to provide pilots and guards. But political changes in Golconda from the 1630s onwards resulted in a change of the ships' destinations; now they were dispatched to the Persian Gulf instead. In the following decade, contact with the Arabian peninsula was occasionally resumed. But from the middle of the century onward, most Indian merchants began to freight English merchantmen, whose captains seemed more successful in coping with the numerous freebooters now scouring the Indian Ocean. After 1665 there is no further evidence for direct contact between Masulipatnam and the Arabian peninsula, although the export of cotton textiles from the area continued to flourish.

Aside from trade goods, the Indian rulers' ships transported pilgrims to Mecca. Presumably most of the 1500 passengers on the ship belonging to the queen of Bijapur had embarked with that aim in mind. The ships belonging to the Mughal ruler were explicitly defined as pilgrims' ships.[45] Even such ships, however, transported a large amount of trade goods, as most pilgrims financed their journeys by carrying wares they hoped to sell. Moreover, there was migration in both directions. Thus several *seyyid* families from Hadramaut in southern Arabia established themselves in India, and these family links must have been useful in business as well.[46] In the sixteenth century the port town of Calicut on the coast of western India boasted a large group of Arab merchants, many of whom settled permanently in the city and built themselves magnificent houses.[47] They differed from other Indian merchants of this early period by owning ships, which they used in the spice trade and the transport of pilgrims. But the Arab immigrants of the western coast never succeeded in gaining the position which Iranian migrants acquired in the seventeenth-century sultanate of Golconda.[48]

Arab scholars and merchants also migrated to southeast Asia. Portuguese writers of the sixteenth century demonstrate that even the policy of the Estado da India, profoundly hostile to Muslims, did not succeed in preventing this development. However, Muslim scholars settling in the port of Malacca while it was under Portuguese control often pretended to be merchants.[49]

TRAFFIC IN BULLION AND PRESSURE ON MERCHANTS

Trade balances in the sixteenth- and seventeenth-century Middle Eastern trade with India were consistently unfavourable to the

Ottoman realm and Iran. Even though Arabian horses and Shirāzī wine or essence of roses were sold in India, the demand for these goods could not possibly compare with the massive importation of textiles, spices, drugs and dies into both the Ottoman Empire and Iran. The resulting difference had to be paid for in bullion. Since European trade with the Ottoman Empire was equally unbalanced Ottoman merchants in their turn received considerable amounts of gold and silver. Much of the silver Ottoman merchants paid their Indian suppliers ultimately came from America by way of Europe. Or if we look at it differently, a considerable share of the silver entering the Ottoman Empire did not remain there, but was drawn off to India. This situation for Indian rulers seemed highly desirable, for there never was any lack of precious metals for minting, a serious difficulty for most other states of the early modern period.[50] After returning from Iran or from the Red Sea area, the Indian merchants could simply go to the nearest mint, and for a reasonable fee have their gold or silver transformed into coins.

Conversely the Ottoman political class regarded the loss of bullion as a great danger, even though the export of silver to Iran seemed more threatening than the loss resulting from trade with India.[51] Export of bullion, therefore, was frequently prohibited, but this was not done for the reasons which have become familiar from English or French mercantilist authors of the seventeenth century. In the Ottoman realm nobody advocated a policy of exporting as much as possible and importing nothing except raw materials. Quite to the contrary, down to the nineteenth century, most members of the Ottoman political class were in favour of encouraging imports as a source of customs revenues.[52]

Ottoman economic thinking has been characterized as 'provisionism', incidentally a term applicable to many sectors of economic policy in pre-industrial Europe as well.[53] After the state had taken its share, raw materials and foodstuffs were to benefit primarily the inhabitants of the region where they had been produced. Ottoman administrators differed from mercantilist thinking in that they viewed exports at least potentially as a danger source, while imports eased the supply situation and were desirable for that very reason.

In spite of this generally positive view of imports, however, the Ottoman administration wished to prevent the outflow of gold and silver, for the consequences of a lack of specie for trade were well-known. Yet there never were any serious attempts to stop trade with India and replace it by other, less deficit-prone trades, even though the eighteenth-century historian Na'īmā suggested just such a course. Though as an official historian he was reasonably influential as a writer, his impact on practical politics remained minimal.[54]

In this context we must understand the admonitions and recommendations which the Ottoman administration addressed to the Sherif of Mecca in 1575–6, when the latter had complained about the lack of ships putting in at the port of Jeddah. The authorities in Istanbul disapproved of the violence exercised by local commanders in Yemen, who forced merchants and shippers to visit the ports they happened to control. A rescript to the governor of Yemen supposedly had been issued with the express intention of preventing such occurrences.[55] But the Sherif equally did not have the right to force anyone to visit Jeddah, as all merchants could do business wherever they preferred.

While taxes collected in Yemen were forwarded to Istanbul, however, the temptation to use violence against shippers arriving from India was built into the system. Instead of money, the provincial governors sent spices either to Cairo or else to Istanbul, and that was only possible when, by fair means or foul, enough spices could be secured in the ports of Yemen. Considerations of this kind may have induced the Ottoman central administration in 1582 to start demanding money and not spices as taxes from Yemeni ports.[56] For at a certain point the pressure on Indian shippers in order to secure these spices came to be self-defeating: forced to sell their goods at disadvantageous prices, merchants were liable to abandon trade with the Arabian peninsula altogether.

Members of the Sultan's Council apparently assumed that the loss of shipping in Jeddah had reasons similar to those with which they were familiar in the case of Yemen. When the Sherif repeated his complaint in 1590, the response from Istanbul was even more drastic than that given in 1575–6: as the Sherif often had forced the merchants to sell him their goods at low prices, it was not surprising that there was now a loss in shipping.[57] Probably the Sultan's Council realized that revenues due to the central treasury also suffered from the Sherif's high-handed policies, as the Ottoman administration had reserved one half of the Jeddah customs revenues for its own use. However, the Sherifs often were quite successful in retaining even the share they should have forwarded to Istanbul.[58]

A PORT IN CRISIS

While Mediterranean trade of the early modern period is documented by a variety of Ottoman and European figures, we possess only very few numerical data on Red Sea trade, and most of our information is qualitative rather than quantitative.[59] The few figures extant all concern the activity of the port of Jeddah. Around 1590–1 the port administrator and governor of the province claimed that, in the past, yearly revenues had amounted to 90,000 gold pieces (*flōrī*).[60] However, it is impossible to determine whether by that figure he meant the entire revenues of Jeddah, or the 50 per cent share which theoretically should have accrued to the Ottoman central administration. To estimate the value of the goods which must have arrived in Jeddah at that time, we will base our calculation on the customs rate of 2.5 per cent demanded from Muslim merchants in many parts of the Ottoman Empire. Admittedly there is no guarantee that all traders doing business in Jeddah were Muslims, but the vast majority probably were. Under these circumstances we arrive at an estimate of goods worth 3,600,000 gold pieces. If the text refers not to the total revenue, but only to the central administration's share, it would be necessary to double this figure. But since we have no information on the customs rates actually applied, this is no more than a very rough estimate.[61]

In 1590–1 the Jeddah port administrator declared that he had been able to collect only 46,000 gold pieces during the past year; this means that, during the 1580s, the traffic must have dropped by half. Apparently the Sultan's Council assumed that this was a long-term development and not just a passing crisis, for its members tried to find alternative means of financing projects hitherto supported out of the Jeddah customs revenues.[62] Pečewı remarks that an additional load was placed on merchants doing business in Jeddah by granting the Sherif a share in the customs revenues, and thereby indicates that he was familiar with the port's difficulties.[63] In all likelihood, this chronicler also assumed that the abuses of officials had a share in the crisis.

It is doubtful that these abuses were the only reason. From a recent study of Indian trade during the early modern period, we learn that links between Masulipatnam and the Arabian peninsula were being forged in the 1580s.[64] If, in spite of this additional trade, the commerce of Jeddah was declining, we must assume that the newly developing trade with the eastern coast of southern India could not compensate for losses in trade with the western coast, particularly Surat and Calicut. European pirates certainly had a share in the decline of trade. Ottoman rescripts of the time mention the need to protect ships arriving from India from Portuguese attack.[65] It is also possible that Jeddah was losing trade to the ports of Yemen, and the Sherif may not have been altogether mistaken in accusing the Ottoman port administrators of that province.

MECCA AND CAIRO

As the Holy Cities depended on foodstuffs from Egypt, and Mamluk traditions continued to be important in many aspects of their inhabitants' lives, contacts between the Hejaz and Cairo were particularly close. The governor of Egypt, who at least for a while was the immediate superior of the administrator of Jeddah, was expected to keep himself informed of developments in the Holy Cities and pass on this information to Istanbul.[66] However, the distances involved and the relatively independent position of the Sherif made it impossible for the Pasha of Egypt to play a major role in the day-to-day events of the Hejaz.

Quite frequently the governor of Egypt was requested to make sure that the money and foodstuffs which the Ottoman Sultans sent to the Hejaz arrived on time.[67] The crucial aspect of the governor's role was to control abuses in the administration and taxation of the villages whose contributions financed life in the Hejaz (see Chapter 4). Very often, however, these attempts at control ended in failure, and peasants mistreated by tax farmers and provincial administrators fled, disorganizing the delicate supply system of the Hejaz. Once collected, foodstuffs and money were transported to Mecca and Medina under the governor's supervision. But complaints concerning failures in this area, such as delays and missing shipment, were not addressed to the governor but to the Sultan himself, in spite of the distances involved. The Sultan's Council examined the complaint and, if necessary, sent instructions and admonitions to the governor of Egypt. As a result, the central administration could easily check on the performance of one of its most important provincial officials. On the other hand, it often took a long time before the governor received orders to intervene in a particular issue.

TRADE IN FOODSTUFFS, RED SEA TRAFFIC AND THE PORT OF SUEZ

Connections between the Hejaz and Egypt were not limited to the official sector. Merchants also played a key role, as official subsidies were not sufficient to supply all the pilgrims and permanent residents of the Hejaz. Private trade is, however, very inadequately covered by the available sources; only the documents dealing with the problems of transportation on the Red Sea provide a certain amount of information.

Shipping on the Red Sea constituted one of the major bottlenecks;

for changing winds and numerous coral reefs only permitted ships leaving Suez to reach Jeddah, Yanbu' or one of the minor anchoring points at certain times of the year.[68] Shipbuilding was expensive due to the lack of timber, so that this basic raw material had to be imported from Anatolia, the territories north of the Black Sea or even India. Both owners and people leasing a ship therefore were tempted to earn back their expenses as quickly as possible by overloading. From the times of Ibn Djubayr to those of the Victorian traveller Richard Burton, we find numerous complaints about the avarice of ships' captains and their unwillingness to take responsibility for the safety of passengers and cargo.[69] To make a bad matter worse, boatbuilders had devised frames, which seem to have resembled those found on outrigger canoes, which made the ship wider and permitted the accommodation of even greater loads.[70] Under these circumstances shipwrecks were frequent, and the high rate of losses increased the price of goods marketed in Mecca and Medina.

Due to the lack of ships and boats, merchants came to compete for shipping space against the administrators of the Egyptian pious foundations, who delivered foodstuffs to the Holy Cities free of charge.[71] Theoretically this problem should not have arisen, as the larger foundations owned their ships. But often these ships were insufficient or unavailable, as they had been contracted out for jobs quite unrelated to the foundation's activities. For the foundations often ran out of cash, and then the rent for the use of ships paid by traders or even public officials was a welcome means of balancing the budget. Grain traders were not at all unhappy if the free food to be distributed by the foundations arrived late, for prices in the markets of Mecca and Medina increased in consequence.

Opportunities to create artificial scarcities in Mecca and Medina were abundant.[72] The key figure in such manipulations was the farmer of the Suez customs who, in theory, was also responsible for making the owners of Red Sea ships adopt elementary security precautions. About the farmers of the Suez customs, accusations of corruption were common enough. We thus hear of a farmer who supposedly had embezzled 7000 gold pieces.[73] Other complaints concerned Suez customs farmers who allegedly had given the order to unload grains belonging to Egyptian foundations from ships ready for the voyage to Jeddah, so that space became available for the wares of merchants.

In 1577–8 the key role of the *emīn*s of Suez in the traffic to Mecca and Medina was given as the reason for entrusting only Muslims with that office. Previous Jewish holders of the position were accused of not supplying the pilgrims with the necessary ships, so that the latter were in danger of missing, or had already missed, the time of the pilgrimage. Given the welter of accusation and counter-accusation in the hotbed of intrigue that was the port of Suez, and the absence of documents concerning later years, it is difficult to place this event in its proper context.[74]

There was a major difference between Mecca and Medina, on the one hand, and all other Ottoman cities including Istanbul on the other: only in these two cities, and nowhere else, was a large portion of the food supply secured by mechanisms other than private trade. In ordinary Ottoman cities, the inhabitants depended on the services of merchants bringing in grain for their very survival, and this situation explains why Ottoman administrators, even if they controlled the activities of traders, still regarded them as necessary and therefore worthy of protection. Due to the special situation of the Holy Cities, however, the Ottoman administrators dealing with the Hejaz tended to regard private trade mainly as a potential source of abuses, to be supervised with suspicion.

Supplying the Holy Cities became somewhat easier when, from approximately the second half of the seventeenth century onward, Indian rice became available in sizable quantities – though rice still was not the item of mass consumption that it was to become in the nineteenth century.[75] In this early period we hear of rice distributed as alms in the name of the Sultan of Golconda, rather than of private dealers in rice. Quite possibly, the inhabitants of Mecca and Medina first became accustomed to the consumption of rice because it came as a free gift. Only after they had become familiar with this grain, and the possible ways of preparing it, were people ready to spend money on the purchase of rice, and only then did opportunities open up for commerce.

MECCA AND DAMASCUS

Where food supplies were concerned, the links of the Hejaz to Syria were far less important than those to Egypt. Politically speaking, the governor of Damascus also played a less important role down to the eighteenth century, as long as this official did not regularly appear in the Hejaz in person as commander of the pilgrimage. In exceptional instances, however, governors of Damascus were active in Hejazi politics in the seventeenth century as well, even to the point of deposing an unruly Sherif. Ewliyā Čelebi, no friend of that particular dynasty, witnessed such an event in 1672 and gave a long and elaborate description of an Ottoman expedition directed against Sherif Sa'd, who was invited to present himself before the pilgrimage commander and Damascus governor Ḥüseyin Pasha.[76] The Pasha and his entourage were kept waiting for quite some time, and Sherif Sa'd did not appear; he had taken flight and was duly deposed.

Damascus merchants certainly profited from the pilgrimage. But they had dealings mainly not with the Hejazis but with the pilgrims, who bought from them their mounts, riding utensils, clothes and foodstuffs. To gauge the volume of the business thus generated, we may evoke the train following Ewliyā Čelebi to the Hejaz, which had been assigned to him by the Damascus governor: several slaves, six camels, a mare, four camel litters, a tent, as well as food and fodder for men and horses.[77] Nor was this the ultimate in luxury; for while Ewliyā came from a family with connections at court, he himself had never held high office. Admittedly the governor of Damascus had not paid the full market price for the slaves, animals and travel gear he placed at Ewliyā's disposal, but no doubt other wealthy pilgrims paid the full price for comfortable travel. Of course the artisans and merchants of Cairo benefited from the Egyptian pilgrimage in similar fashion. As other trade opportunities were much greater in Cairo, however, the caravan trade probably was less prominent in the city's economic life than its Damascus counterpart.

Many pilgrims purchased their needs at the caravan fair of Muzayrib, a few stops to the south of Damascus on the route to Mecca.[78] In the nineteenth century this was to become a major commercial centre, and one of Syria's earliest train lines linked this locality with Damascus.[79] From a rescript dated 1637–8 we learn that the fair lasted ten days and that, at least in principle, goods acquired by the pilgrims for use on the journey were supposed to be exempt from taxes and customs dues. Things often were quite different in practice; in the 1630s, the governor of Damascus usually sent a market administrator and some soldiers to Muzayrib to collect taxes. The latter demanded dues from both buyers and sellers which amounted to 25 per cent of the purchase price. In addition, the administrator made the merchants pay 40–50 *ghurush* merely for the privilege of displaying their wares in a stall. As a result the fair was not much frequented, and this constituted a grave inconvenience to the pilgrims. Indirect evidence for this state of affairs is provided by the Edirne scholar 'Abd al-Raḥmān Ḥibrī, whose pilgrimage to Mecca fell in the year 1632. 'Abd al-Raḥmān Ḥibrī certainly travelled in style, but his entire outfit had been bought in Damascus; in Muzayrib he only rented the necessary camels.[80]

In the rescript of 1637–8 the Pasha of Damascus was held responsible for the sad state of the Muzayrib fair: to reactivate business, he was ordered to stop collecting taxes from the pilgrims' necessities. All other goods were to be taxed 'at the rate which has been customary for a long time'. This last remark is important for the modern historian, as here we have the oldest reference to the fact that things not immediately needed by pilgrims could be purchased in Muzayrib. Possibly the authors of the rescript were thinking of the well-known textiles of Damascus, which may have found a market in Mecca and Medina as well.[81] However, the sultanic rescript of 1637–8 apparently had little immediate effect. Ewliyā Čelebi, who visited Muzayrib in 1672, only noted that the place was fortified and that pilgrimage stores were kept there, and said nothing about a fair.[82] Derwish Meḥmed Edīb, whose pilgrimage report dates from the year 1682, very briefly mentions the locality, and thus probably did not notice anything remarkable either.[83] Muzayrib's revival must date from a much later period.

TRADERS IN MECCA AND THE MINA FAIR

As the centre of the hajj, Mecca was more specialized in its functions than any other city of the Ottoman Empire; the city lived off the pilgrims, the Sultan's subventions and trade. While almost all cities of the early modern period possessed an agricultural hinterland, this was absent in the Meccan instance. Even the gardens in the city's immediate vicinity were not very productive. Artisans were also in short supply, and our sources do not mention the craft guilds so characteristic of Ottoman towns, Cairo included. Craftsmen to work on the numerous Ottoman building projects usually were brought in from Syria and Egypt. Ewliyā Čelebi noted that the Meccans only applied themselves to commerce.[84] But the normal base for local trade was also missing, as there were no agricultural products of the immediate vicinity that could be marketed in Mecca, nor local manufactures. Meccan trade for the most part was long-distance trade.

Trade in Mecca took place in two locations:[85] in the city itself during the days which preceded and followed the pilgrimage ceremonies, and in the settlement of Mina/Munā, where the pilgrims spent several days on their return from the plateau of 'Arafat.[86] In Mecca two covered markets were at the disposal of traders, the smaller of these being known as the Syrian or Damascene market, probably because of the goods and traders to be found there. During the pilgrimage season, these covered markets were insufficient, and then the entrances of houses or, if sun shades could be installed, even the façades were turned into temporary shops. Ewliyā Čelebi claims that in this fashion the number of shops increased to six thousand, but his figures often should be taken with a grain of salt. Even if he does exaggerate, the pilgrimage season must have been the occasion for a good deal of petty trading, as many pilgrims sold a few wares to help finance their long and expensive journeys. Others for the same reason sought to purchase goods which they hoped to sell profitably in their home towns. Unfortunately, we know nothing about the way in which these 'amateurs' went about finding a market for their goods, whether they made use of brokers or other intermediaries, or whether Meccan merchants ever sold goods on commission.

The fair of Mina was held in the context of a general celebration, for at this time most of the prohibitions pilgrims had to respect while performing the rites of pilgrimage were temporarily suspended. Ewliyā has described the experience: officers of the pilgrimage caravan and public criers announced that buyers and sellers were under the protection of the Ottoman Sultan, and called upon the sellers to lay out their wares. The Sherifs, who owned a residence in this locality, had it illuminated for the occasion, and artisans and pilgrims decorated shops, coffee houses and tents in the same fashion. Many valuable textiles could be purchased in the shops, and Ewliyā claims that there he encountered people from all four corners of the Islamic world. Precious stones and aromatics were available in profusion; some traders even went so far as to decorate their shops with them.[87] As no dues were collected at this fair, many people may have been encouraged to exhibit their treasures. In the middle of this festive disorder, small boys from notable Meccan families were circumcised, the soldiers fired their guns into the air, and in the evening there were fireworks, at which the skills of Egyptian specialists were much admired.[88]

The combination of fair and public festivity is not unique to the Meccan pilgrimage, but is characteristic of many festivities in the Ancient World.[89] It was the trade in luxury goods which set Mina apart from other fairs with a strongly festive component, most of which were oriented toward local consumption. The great Balkan fairs of the seventeenth and eighteenth centuries, which Ewliyā also admired very much, were not accompanied by major festivities.[90] Perhaps the closest parallel to what happened in Mina is the festival of the Egyptian saint Aḥmad Badawı of Ṭanṭa, where a great fair also formed part of the celebrations.[91] Ewliyā claims to have encountered Indian, Yemeni, Iranian and Arab traders in Ṭanṭa, who sold their wares in huts or tents serving as temporary shops. Some of these visitors also frequented the *khān*s of the city. Presumably the festive atmosphere in Mina, which the merchants enhanced by generous offerings of perfumes, also was good for business.[92] This atmosphere of generalized goodwill was all the more important as many of the buyers and sellers were not professionals.

Apart from the Indian textiles, aromatics and precious stones traded in Mecca and Mina, special attention should be paid to the coffee trade.[93] Ewliyā mentions the existence of coffee houses in Mina, where Abyssinian slave women sang and played their instruments. But coffee was also a commodity which down to the beginning of the eighteenth century was grown uniquely in the Yemen, and therefore available in the Hejaz more readily than elsewhere. Taking a load of coffee to Cairo or Istanbul could be a lucrative deal for a pilgrim with money to invest. In Ewliyā Čelebi's time, the consumption of coffee had reached a level which permitted the major merchants to compensate without any trouble for the loss of the transit trade in spices to Europe, which was one of the most important reasons for the seventeenth-century decline of Venice. Even in the eighteenth century, when coffee produced on the Caribbean islands had begun to compete with Yemeni coffee, the coffee dealers were among the wealthiest merchants of Cairo. The consumption of coffee in the Ottoman Empire was frequently forbidden, however, particularly in the reign of Murād IV (reigned 1623–40). In justifying the prohibition, the effects of coffee were said to be comparable to those of alcohol; but the decisive factor was probably the sociability of the coffee house, in which people talked to one another and what they said was not always readily controlled by the authorities. Prohibitions generally were effective for short periods only; and Ewliyā Čelebi did not fail to purchase several loads of coffee, which he took along to Cairo.[94]

As well as coffee, Chinese porcelain could be obtained in Mecca more easily than in other parts of the Ottoman Empire.[95] We have already encountered a sixteenth-century Sherif who gave away Chinese porcelain (or an Iranian imitation in fayence) as an official gift. This was not an exceptional circumstance; Ewliyā Čelebi, who probably was less impressed by this novelty than Pečewī, once remarked, not without irony, that the Sherif gave away 'cups and saucers'.[96] At the Ottoman court there were connoisseurs of porcelain, and the Sultans of the period built up a major collection of sixteenth- and seventeenth-century Chinese porcelain. Certain pieces were elaborately decorated at the Ottoman court with gold and jewellery, but, given the state of our sources, we cannot determine whether this decoration was intended to enhance a highly esteemed piece or to compensate for the low intrinsic value assigned to this material.[97]

METHODS OF BARGAINING: AN INDICATOR OF CULTURAL CONTACTS?

Among Meccan merchants, a special form of bargaining was current, which Ewliyā apparently encountered in this city for the first time and which he has described at some length.[98] A customer desiring to acquire a certain piece of goods negotiated the price with the seller by mutually holding hands under a piece of cloth. The offer was made and accepted or refused by manual signs, while the parties to the purchase neither looked at one another nor said a word. Thus an outsider had no way of knowing the price agreed upon, or indeed if a purchase had been made, even if the deal concerned very large sums, this secrecy was deemed such an advantage that the risk of misunderstandings was not a deterrent.

Ewliyā calls this method of doing business an auction. Why it thus appeared to him can be better understood with the help of an older description of a similar practice, which we find in the account of the Bolognese traveller Ludovico di Varthéma.[99] The latter had become a Mamluk and visited Mecca in 1503; later he continued his travels to India. In the city of Calicut, on the southwestern coast of India, the traveller observed a method of bargaining by manual signs; only, in this case, a broker also was involved. Seller and broker, or at a later stage buyer and broker, without speaking, counted 'from one ducat to a hundred thousand', thus indicating the range of prices considered appropriate for the goods in question. Again the fingers were hidden under a piece of fabric, and when the two partners came to an agreement, they indicated this fact to one another by a sign of the fingertips. Probably Ewliyā also knew that the method of bargaining he had seen involved counting, and this fact reminded him of an auction.

We cannot be sure whether this custom was Indian or Arab in origin; given the frequency of commercial relations between the two coasts, either one of the two is possible. However, an Indian origin seems more likely. Probably, merchants perceived a twofold advantage in this proceeding; on the one hand, traders with no common language could negotiate with one another, although the example described by Ludovico di Varthéma shows that brokers might be employed nonetheless. In addition, by keeping the deal secret from outsiders, the merchants in question affirmed their membership of an exclusive commercial fraternity, one of the trading communities so characteristic of early modern India. Established merchants of Mecca also may have wished to emphasize that they were 'different' from the many 'amateurs' who crowded into the city during the pilgrimage season.

'INVISIBLE' TRADE

Although Mecca and the nearby fair of Mina constituted major centres of international trade, the Ottoman central administration paid very little attention to what happened there. Provincial records located in Cairo are slightly more explicit but, even so, Ewliyā's account still constitutes by far the most usable source, one which sometimes permits us to make sense of certain vague allusions in the Ottoman documents. In the last few decades, economic historians of India have also concerned themselves with trade relations between the Indian subcontinent and the Arabian peninsula. But the material at their disposal is largely Portuguese, Dutch and later English, and its perspective is defined accordingly. Reconstructing this trade, therefore, is something of a jigsaw puzzle. We can only hope that a few more pieces will be located in the future.[100]

Ottoman archives contain so little evidence on the trade of Mecca and Mina because the documents of the time so often were financial in character, and the Ottoman state collected scarcely any taxes in the Hejaz. The fair of Mina owed its liveliness to its exemption from all taxes. If market dues were collected in Mecca proper – and at present we have no evidence that they were – they filled the coffers of the Sherif. Thus, even if everything went well, the Ottoman administration benefited from Hejazi trade only to the extent that it collected one half of the Jeddah customs. The archive materials of early modern states concentrated upon war and the collection of taxes, and the Ottoman state was no exception to this rule. Thus the war in Yemen and the conflicts with the Portuguese are fairly well documented, while trade relations which did not immediately benefit the state treasury were passed over in silence.

Moreover, artisans' guilds, which constituted an important means of taxation and control in the Ottoman core lands of Rumelia and Anatolia, due to the special conditions obtaining in the Hejaz either did not exist at all or at least did not function in the manner known elsewhere. This is another reason for the lack of trade-oriented documentation. In most Ottoman cities, on the other hand, the local *ḳāḍī* registers and the record books of the central administration contain a fair number of complaints concerning the quality and prices of goods manufactured by local craftsmen, including disputes with merchants. Moreover, the Sherifs, who dealt with many issues which elsewhere would have been the responsibility of the local governor, do not seem to have kept many written records. All these features underline the special character of Mecca as a city which lived by and for the pilgrims, and in which Ottoman government was exercised only within narrowly circumscribed limits.

Conclusion

It has been one of the main aims of this book to depict the manner in which the Ottoman political class, which for four centuries organized many of the more visible aspects of the pilgrimage, viewed and depicted its own role in the Hejaz.[1] An attempt certainly has been made to analyse Ottoman rule in the Holy Cities with the aid of categories used in contemporary political discourse, and not that of the sixteenth or seventeenth centuries. But at the centre of the story we have placed the Ottoman authorities and, wherever possible, the pilgrims themselves.

If we were dealing with a chapter of European history, this would not need any justification. We have accustomed ourselves to studying the Spanish Reconquista between the thirteenth and sixteenth centuries from a Spanish point of view, or to regarding the integration of formerly Ottoman Hungary into the eighteenth-century Habsburg Empire from a Viennese perspective. But when Middle Eastern history is dealt with in Europe or North America, such an 'internalist' perspective does not go without saying: quite the contrary. Somehow authors will assume, at least subconsciously, that events within the Ottoman Empire receive their significance mainly from the impact which they have upon developments in Europe. Yet this is a narrow and unrealistic view. Over the centuries, political and economic processes of major importance, such as the securing of food supplies for pilgrims and permanent inhabitants of the Hejaz, took place without European rulers or merchants having any share in the undertaking. It should be the aim of any historical work concerning the Middle East to counteract the unfortunate tendency of regarding European–American history as the only 'real' history, to which everything else is merely an adjunct.[2] Admittedly many historians do not see it that way, and even when an effort is made to present Middle Eastern history in its own terms, the attempt is not always successful.

INTERNAL VERSUS EXTERNAL PERSPECTIVES

There are other reasons why, in our imaginary travels through Istanbul, Damascus, Cairo and the Hejaz, we have taken for our guides not Richard Burton and John Lewis Burckhardt, but mainly the secretaries of the Sultan's Council, Ewliyā Čelebi and Süheylī. It is the principal task of historians to reconstruct the environments and historical processes of the past. But this is only possible if we familiarize ourselves with as many data from the relevant period as possible, so that, in a squeeze, we could have bought supplies at the fair of Muzayrib or participated in the festivities at Mina, without making undue fools of ourselves. To a somewhat lesser extent, this also applies to readers. Both sides will find their tasks easier if the writings of Ottoman authors are given priority. For if the account is built mainly on the observations of Burckhardt, Burton or Rutter, the danger of producing a variety of European social and intellectual history, instead of the Ottoman history we are aiming at, is very great indeed.

This statement has an affinity to historicist positions, and as such needs qualification.[3] For it should not be taken to mean that in explaining Ottoman hajj procedures, no categories should be used apart from those known to the participants themselves. That kind of an approach seems impractical, and to advocate it would be self-contradictory, as the key category of sultanic legitimation, upon which our entire account is constructed, was not employed by sixteenth- or seventeenth-century Ottomans. Moreover, in the minds of many historians, historicist positions are associated with a staunch political conservatism, and this connotation is certainly not intended either. Thus the position taken here is eclectic; reconstructions of human relationships connected with the hajj are undertaken on the basis of Ottoman material, and with a strong emphasis on the interpretations given to these events by the participants. But, at the same time, many crucial categories of analysis come from the arsenal of history writing in the late twentieth century.

The present study is conceived as a work of political and above all social history, which means that we focus upon changes within Ottoman society itself. Obviously, the pilgrimage could also be treated from totally different perspectives, a focus on religious practice constituting the most obvious alternative. Yet it seems that there is a strong explanatory force inherent in regarding ceremonies, buildings or literary texts as products of the societies in which they were created, and to explain what social and political needs were satisfied by putting up one kind of building rather than another, or by writing pilgrimage accounts and chronicles rather than novels or newspaper articles. This does not mean that we would advocate a reduction of all human activity to social and possibly even economic needs. Throughout the centuries, art, literature and religion have often developed in ways that owe as much to the internal dynamics of the field in question as to the social context, and the pilgrimage above everything else is a religious phenomenon which cannot be reduced (for instance) to commercial interests. But even though we admit that the history of religion, and thereby of the pilgrimage to Mecca, need to be studied on their own terms, that does not preclude close attention to the social and political context in which this phenomenon took place.

HISTORICAL CHANGE, RAPID OR SLOW-MOVING

Throughout the Ottoman period, the social and political structures which enabled pilgrims to get to the Holy Cities and back again, changed very slowly. Slow change does not mean no change at all. In the present study, we have attempted to show that the 'timeless Orient' of European travelogues and secondary studies is a construct with little relation to reality. In the course of our study, we have encountered a number of instances of historical change even in the Holy Cities, where existing arrangements often were legitimized by religious means, and change was correspondingly slow. Around the year 1600, the Ottoman administration in the face of appreciable local resistance attempted to impose its own ideas of what a well-organized pilgrimage city was supposed to look like. The attempt of Sultan Murād III to separate the Great Mosque from the surrounding urban tissue demonstrates the will of this ruler to impose new urban concepts upon the ancient city (see Chapter 5). It is therefore a grave methodological error to amalgamate data from the twelfth, sixteenth and nineteenth centuries, with the facile assumption that 'nothing changed much anyway'. For this proceeding renders invisible the slow but significant change the historian should try to track down.

The amalgamation of data specific to centuries far removed from one another at first sight may appear as mere sloppiness, but in reality it has a deeper significance.[4] Quite a few European and American students of the Ottoman Empire have tended to regard Ottoman state and society as the 'other' par excellence, incomprehensible and, moreover, scarcely repaying any effort at comprehension. To put it somewhat crudely, if European society has a history, the 'other', in this case the Ottoman, has none. In the political realm, however, the existence of change could not well be denied, and the most frequently used scheme of Ottoman history assumes a rapid 'rise' between about 1300 and 1520, a short period of 'florescence' (1520–1600), and a long period of decline from 1600 to the end of the empire in 1918–23. On the other hand, the society which *nolens volens* supported this state supposedly changed little if at all in the course of the centuries.[5] Agricultural techniques, religious notions, fashions and family structures remained all but immobile and, outside of the major cities, the changing tides of history had but a limited impact upon the lives of ordinary people.

During the last few decades, the work of Marc Bloch, Fernand Braudel and Emmanuel Le Roy Ladurie, in particular, has alerted historians to the importance of long-term, evenly paced secular change. If we transfer their insights into the Middle Eastern field – which unfortunately still happens but rarely – the notion that the social history of the Middle East was an area of 'slow' historical movement ceases to be usable as a feature by which to differentiate the history of this region from its European counterpart. Even in economically active regions of Europe such as northern and central Italy, certain aspects of feudal social structure survived even the Napoleonic period and, according to some authors, retained their vitality down to the middle of the twentieth century.[6] Where latecomers to industrialization such as the German territories are concerned, the survival of feudal structures and values into the twentieth century is not merely well-known to the specialist but forms part of general culture. We thus would do well to avoid the stereotype which contrasts a 'static Orient' and a 'dynamic Occident' and limit ourselves to the more modest statement that before the industrial revolution and its worldwide consequences, the pace of historical change throughout the world was a good deal slower than today.

The period covered by the present study may be considered 'medium length', amounting to somewhat less than two centuries. Long enough for historical change to occur, it allows us to point up the interplay between structural and conjunctural factors which constitutes the essence of social and economic history. At the same time it is still short enough to permit the researcher a reasonable grasp of the available sources. The relative brevity of the timespan from 1517 to 1683 also makes the problem of amalgamating, or not amalgamating, data from different periods somewhat easier to handle. While the use of historical evidence from different periods obscures intervening change, for periods where documentation is limited, we often are obliged to use texts from a previous or following decade, or even century, to make sense of the text we are trying to interpret. This contradiction can be held within manageable bounds most easily if the period studied is not too long.

When pointing out the dynamic aspects of Ottoman early modern social history we sometimes encounter the objection that this state was dynamic in its early days because it controlled the great international trade routes of the fifteenth and sixteenth centuries. When the Ottomans failed in their attempt to dislodge the Portuguese from the Indian Ocean, and when, in the early seventeenth century, the Dutch took over from the Portuguese as the principal European trading power in the Indian Ocean region, supposedly this dynamism was rapidly lost.[7] In this view, Ottoman dynamism is regarded as a result of a configuration basically external to the empire itself, and Ottoman–European trade relations in this context play an especially important role. But the present study has shown that the Ottoman administration of the sixteenth century made considerable efforts to change social arrangements in the Hejaz. As the Hejaz of this period was quite remote from European trade, and European political influence all but non-existent before the nineteenth century, it does not seem reasonable to link all change and dynamism in the area directly or indirectly to European intervention.

Initiatives originating with the Ottoman central administration were particularly visible in the built environment. The Great Mosque of Mecca was refashioned to conform to Ottoman models, and the attempt of Sultan Murād III (reigned 1574–95) to disengage the mosque from the surrounding houses may almost be regarded as a forerunner of twentieth-century urban solutions. Behind these initiatives, we discern the intention to impose a mode of behaviour in the sacred precinct which Ottoman bureaucrats considered appropriate, and which differed from the behaviour considered normal among the generality of pilgrims and townsmen. Unfortunately, the documentation unearthed to date does not permit us to figure out to what extent the Ottoman administration succeeded or failed in imposing its ideas in the long run.

If we try to set up an alternative model to the all but immobile society often referred to in the literature, it makes sense to imagine Ottoman state and society as a permanently growing complex of institutions and practices. This model implies that society, and particularly Ottoman society in the Hejaz, was not monolithic, so that not only consensus but also numerous contradictions existed between its different subsections.[8] A comparison of the Ottoman Empire after 1600 with *ancien régime* France seems appropriate; in both cases the creation of new institutions rarely involved the abrogation of the old ones, and the resulting complexity is often confusing to the outsider. A comparable overlay, only of even greater complexity, existed in the Hejaz; norms and social practices from the times of the Prophet Muḥammad and his immediate successors, buildings from the Abbasid period, a supply system which had assumed its most salient features in the period of the Mamluk Sultans, and Ottoman institutions for ensuring the security of the pilgrims all functioned at the very same time, and, as we have seen, friction resulting from this heterogeneity was not rare.

Political action in the Hejaz involved the reduction of this friction to manageable proportions at minimal cost to a remote central administration, usually hard pressed for funds. It would have been beyond the means of the Ottoman government to impose in this remote province, which largely lacked both a peasantry and urban artisans, the administrative structure characteristic of the 'core' provinces, with their tax grants, market tolls and craft guilds. There is no evidence that direct administration was ever considered. To mention a minor but characteristic example of this attitude: when Ewliyā Čelebi, after his adventurous travel to the Hejaz in 1672, expressed his annoyance at Sherif Sa′d who made life so difficult for the pilgrims, he did not say that he wished the Ottoman Sultan might punish his iniquities by fire and sword. This way of speaking, however, had come quite naturally to the pious and scholarly Ibn D̲jubayr, who in his time had felt wronged by a remote predecessor of Sherif Sa′d (see Chapter 1). Ewliyā limits himself to a gleeful enumeration of the humiliations to which the medieval Sherifs supposedly had been subjected by an irate Mamluk Sultan.[9] In Ewliyā's view, the Sherifs formed part of the inescapable political realities of the Hejaz, who might be manipulated at times, but who for the most part had to be endured.

This is all the more remarkable as, by the end of the First World War, the situation had changed completely. When amir Ibn Sa′ūd took power in the Hejaz in 1925, he no longer felt bound by the centuries-old custom that a suzerain might depose a Sherif, but had to replace him by another member of the same family. Certainly the length and bitterness of the struggle by which Ibn Sa′ūd had come to power explains this radical innovation, but only in part. In all probability the amir felt much less compelled to come to an agreement with the Sherifal family, as his Wahabi convictions allowed him more radical departures from established political practices than had been true of the nineteenth-century political class of the Ottoman Empire.[10] After all, the Wahabi variety of Islam aimed at reshaping political conditions as far as possible according to the practice of early Islam. Given this outlook, there was no further need to seek accommodation with the Sherifs, who, after all, had established themselves well after the Abbasid rise to power. Thus it is not merely due to short-range considerations that the end of Ottoman rule in the Hejaz also resulted in the eclipse of the Sherifal dynasty, after about a thousand years of rule.

RELIGION AND CHANGING TIMES

It is remarkable that a religious movement which took the early Islamic period for a model should have been so much inclined toward radical innovation in the political sphere. This should induce us to reflect anew on the role of religion in historical change. In Islam, religious scholars will attempt to solve problems occurring in the course of time by referring to the Koran and to the Sunna – that is, the practice of the Prophet Muḥammad as recorded in his sayings, some of them real and others attributed.[11] This gives the impression that religious practice is immutable and monolithic, particularly since the freedom of interpretation allowed religious scholars is strictly limited. Here again, experience of European history should guard us against hasty conclusions. Even though the dogma of the Catholic Church changed little from the Council of Trent (1545–9 and 1562–3) to the Second Vaticanum (1962–5), the piety and world view of, for example, Teilhard de Chardin, differs profoundly from that of Ignatius Loyola. Not only are beliefs and ritual significant: at least as important are the attitudes both of religious scholars and ordinary believers toward their faith. To give an example: all Muslims concur in the belief that the Prophet Muḥammad was a human being and in no way divine. But while Ottoman Sunnis of the seventeenth or nineteenth centuries did not feel that visits to the Prophet's grave in any way contradicted this belief, many Wahabis of the nineteenth and early twentieth centuries found it very difficult to tolerate this practice. In their view, visits to the Prophet's grave might tempt fallible human beings to place a human being at the side of God, and thereby commit the sin of idolatry. Other examples abound. Thus many non-Wahabi Muslims of past centuries, would not have regarded the existence of a corpus of legends concerning the Prophet as detracting in any way from the humanity of the Prophet, even though many twentieth-century Muslims may see the matter in a different light. Nor was the respect accorded the descendants of the Prophet, including the Sherifs of Mecca, regarded as a culpable narrowing of the distance between God and mankind.

In a more mundane sphere, it seems that not all pilgrims shared the views of sixteenth-century Ottoman administrations concerning a clear separation of the sacred and profane, as evinced in the quarrel concerning the Iranians and their 'cradles and mattresses' (see Chapter 5). Wealthy pilgrims of the sixteenth century, and of later times too, apparently could not be convinced that there was anything reprehensible about houses whose windows overlooked the Great Mosque. Quite to the contrary, nineteenth-century accounts of the city record the existence of such houses; unfortunately, at present we do not know from what time onwards they were rebuilt. Thus, even if the basic features of the faith remain unchanged, the practice of religion, like most other human activities, shows something we might call a period style. Because religion had a strong impact on the daily lives of the Hejazis, and this religion was based upon immutable texts, it is tempting to assume that the politics and lifestyle of the inhabitants of Mecca and Medina also remained immutable over the centuries. But this assumption would still be an error.[12]

THE PILGRIMAGE AS AN INTEGRATIVE FACTOR

Apart from the interplay of a continuity and socio-political change, the present study has focused upon the pilgrimage as an integrative factor within Ottoman society, and the role of pilgrim protection in the legitimation of the Ottoman Sultan. The integration of state territories, that is the increasing mutual involvement of cities, regions and social groups within a given territory, has been a favourite topic of many historians ever since the nineteenth century. This scholarly interest has been conditioned by practical considerations, as from the late eighteenth century onward, the major states and societies of Europe forced the pace of integration by the creation of national markets, a system of roads and canals, and, ultimately, national educational systems.[13] Moreover, in the second half of the twentieth century, at least in western Europe, a further spurt of integration has been experienced, not only on the inter-state level, but also in terms of social organization. Many professional associations, political movements and clubs, which often succeed in arousing strong loyalties in their members, function on a supra-national level. These experiences no doubt constitute an important reason why a late twentieth-century historian regards the integrative potential of the pilgrimage as something crucially important.

In the nineteenth century, the Ottoman political class also pursued the integration of its remaining territory by means of railway construction, administrative reform and a new-style educational system.[14] This task proved beyond the means of a multinational empire plagued by outside intervention and a severe shortage of capital. Nonetheless, the legacy it left to its successor states, particularly in the form of a trained bureaucracy, proved significant. This state of affairs encourages us to search for policies pursued by governments and factors operating in favour of integration within the major empires of the preindustrial period as well. These factors often differ in kind from those to which we are accustomed today. But this does not mean that political integration was not pursued in preindustrial empires, and that the latter were held together exclusively by military force. Military might was not unimportant on the level of the empire as a whole, but the Ottoman administration in the Hejaz disposed only of a very minor military force, and had to depend on political solutions. This was possible because a whole web of interests had been created which tied different sections of the Hejazi population to the Ottoman state. The Beduins could only expect to receive their subsidies if the central administration was both able and willing to pay. By demonstrations of their 'nuisance value', which in extreme cases might include major attacks upon the pilgrimage caravans, they might attempt to increase their subsidies. But a withdrawal of the Ottoman central government from this area would have been a disadvantage and not an advantage to most Hejazi Beduins.

The inhabitants of Mecca and Medina, too, were integrated into the Ottoman system by pious foundations and subsidies. Throughout the centuries the townsmen have provided essential goods and services to pilgrims, for which they demanded and received high prices. Many of them rented their houses, permitted the installation of temporary stalls in their porches, and provided the pilgrims with food and water. Many inhabitants of Mecca and Medina acted as guides to the pilgrims, showed them the proper execution of the relevant rituals and helped them organize their journeys to Mina, Muzdalifa and 'Arafat. Apart from gifts and payments on the part of individual pilgrims, the official donations received by the townsmen enabled them to survive, and presumably they demanded less from individual pilgrims than they would have done if no official support had been forthcoming. Thus the pious foundations of Egypt, by their remittances of grain and money, contributed not only to the integration of the Hejazis, but to that of the pilgrims as well.

As to the inhabitants of the numerous Ottoman towns with a number of foundations benefiting the Holy Cities, they were included in a wider geographical horizon by the mere existence of these foundations. In a time in which travel was difficult and expensive, it must have been of some significance to experience a concrete link with Mecca and Medina, even though we do not know whether some Rumelians and Anatolians did not react with a degree of hostility against the outflow of locally needed resources. Whatever the reaction, horizons were widened to include the remote cities of the Hejaz, which most of the people concerned could scarcely hope to see with their own eyes.

Apart from the economic interests of certain groups of the population, the integrative function of the pilgrimage routes themselves should be taken into consideration. The routes travelled by pilgrims also functioned as trade routes, partly because pilgrimage caravans were used by merchants (see Chapter 2), partly because many pilgrims did some trading on the side. Trade routes, on the other hand, were at the basis of the economic resilience which the Ottoman Empire showed down into the eighteenth century. Crises, which outside observers often presumed would destroy the state, time and again were overcome, and between 1700 and 1760 Ottoman trade and crafts even went through a period of expansion.[15] In his monumental work on capitalism and the economy in the early modern world, Fernand Braudel has connected this remarkable resilience of the Ottoman polity with the fact that, down to the beginning of the nineteenth century, the government continued to control the trade routes leading through its territory.[16] Braudel's judgment does not refer to the international transit routes: some of the latter, particularly the route leading from the silk-producing regions of western Iran to Izmir and Istanbul, at the beginning of the eighteenth century were in a state of profound crisis.[17] But internal trade continued to flourish down to the 1760s, when it fell victim to the exigencies of almost constant war.

Among Ottoman internal trade routes, the connection between Istanbul and the Hejaz by way of Damascus was of major importance, and the same thing can be said of the overland route from Cairo to Mecca and Medina and the Red Sea route. The commercial activity along these routes was due not only to the supply trade of the Holy Cities, but also to the trade in coffee, which from the sixteenth century onward became increasingly popular in the Ottoman Empire. Down into the fifteenth century, as we have seen, coffee had been all but unknown outside of Yemen.[18] But by the year 1500, it was being brought to Mecca by pilgrims and merchants from the Yemen, and rapidly caught on. In the seventeenth century the coffee trade even became so profitable that Cairo wholesalers recouped their losses from the transit trade in spices to Europe, now in the hands of the Dutch, and did not experience the profound commercial crisis the Venetians suffered after losing the transit trade. Thus the pilgrimage routes contributed to the development of a new branch of commerce, which permitted Cairene traders to hold their own against European competitors down into the eighteenth century.[19] Moreover, the Hejaz, where previously money could only be made in connection with the pilgrimage trade, now turned into a significant coffee entrepôt.

THE SULTAN AS THE SERVITOR OF MECCA AND MEDINA

In a number of different contexts, we have discussed the role of the Ottoman Sultan as the protector of pilgrims and permanent inhabitants of the Hejaz. This role no doubt legitimized the ruler in the eyes of the Ottoman political class, and possibly in the eyes of foreign pilgrims as well; on this latter aspect, however, we possess little evidence. Probably the demonstrative protection accorded Central Asian pilgrims was intended to mobilize support for the Ottoman Sultan at the Sunni courts of Transoxania, as the *khān*s of this region formed a counterweight to the Shi'i Shahs of Iran (see Chapter 6).[20] At the present stage of our knowledge, it is equally hard to determine whether the Ottoman political class envisaged legitimizing the Sultan in the eyes of ordinary Ottoman tax-payers, or whether the latter's opinions were regarded as insignificant.

Ottoman Sultans frequently used the title 'Servant of the two Holy Places' (*Khādim al-Ḥaramayn*), and this surely was a means of legitimizing the ruler as the protector of the pilgrimage. More explicit uses of the same motif can be found in sixteenth-century rescripts. Thus it was certainly not by chance that, in the second half of the sixteenth century, an Ottoman Sultan opposed the expansion of the Czars into the steppes of what is today southern Russia with the argument that the pilgrimage routes had to be kept open for Central Asian Sunnis.[21] The effectiveness of this rhetoric was surely enhanced by the fact that it contrasted the Ottoman Sultan as a Sunni Muslim ruler not only with the infidel Czar but also with the Shi'i Shah – who, after all, had also placed major impediments in the way of Central Asian pilgrims.

Ottoman Sultans affixed numerous inscriptions to buildings in the Holy Cities, in order to commemorate a variety of construction and repair projects. These texts could be read by educated pilgrims both from outside the empire and from within: almost certainly they were drafted in Arabic, as sixteenth-century epigraphic texts in Ottoman Turkish constituted something of a rarity. We have seen that the Ottoman administration was greatly concerned about the visibility and legibility of such inscriptions, and that the texts at times were drafted in Istanbul (see Chapter 5). Probably the central government wanted to make sure that the Sherif did not claim a greater share of merit than the Sultan and his Council were ready to concede to him. It was also considered important to describe the Sultan who had ordered this or that construction project as a worthy successor to the prophets and distinguished personalities of Muslim history who had also embellished the Great Mosque in the course of its history.

As the Ottoman dynasty as a whole was legitimated by construction projects, rather than any Sultan as an individual, the sisters, daughters, mothers and consorts of Ottoman rulers could take on major roles as benefactresses of the Muslim community. This role recently has begun to interest historians with a feminist commitment, who concern themselves with the opportunities for political action open to women of the Ottoman political class, and particularly to royal women. For the most part, researchers have concentrated upon Istanbul, which did in fact house the majority of the royal women's foundations.[22] Often, however, Mecca, Medina and the stopping points along the pilgrimage routes were selected by Ottoman princesses as sites of their largesse. Apart from Khurrem Sultan (Roxolana), there is her daughter Mihr-ü-māh (died in 1578). A sister of Süleymān the Magnificent also contributed to the repair of the pipes which supplied Mecca with water. The number of princesses who went on the pilgrimage also appears to have been more important than assumed by previous researchers. Since Sultans and princes practically never appeared in the Hejaz, the occasional presence of royal women took on a strong symbolic connotation.

Apart from public construction, the Ottoman dynasty could be legitimated by gifts which were exposed to the public of Istanbul, Cairo or Damascus before expeditions to the Hejaz. Aḥmed I (reigned 1603–17) appeared at a ceremonial showing of the newly fashioned support system for the Ka'aba and other decorative elements destined for the mosques of Mecca and Medina (see Chapter 5). At least in the eighteenth century, the remission of the Sultan's subsidies to the inhabitants of the Hejaz was celebrated by elaborate ceremonies.[23] As Sherifs, Beduin shaykhs and Meccan notables, by the acceptance of these gifts, admitted that they 'ate the bread of the Sultan', they also admitted the legitimacy of the ruler who had bestowed this bounty upon them.

Throughout the present study, we have emphasized the importance of negotiations which preceded the recognition of Ottoman legitimacy by the Sultan's more prominent Hejazi subjects. These negotiations were indispensable, as the distances involved, and Ottoman commitments in other parts of the empire, precluded the imposition of policies by military force alone. It would be a mistake, however, to assume that the Ottoman administration negotiated with the Hejazi notables merely because it had no other choice; for, after all, the Ottoman government was not necessarily obliged to commit itself heavily on the Rumelian and Iranian frontiers while establishing only a minor military presence on its southern borders. Therefore, the emphasis on negotiation should also be regarded as a political decision, and not merely a necessity imposed from outside.

It is necessary to emphasize these elementary truths because most twentieth-century historians dealing with the early modern Near East strongly emphasize the military dimension.[24] The *'ulemā* of this period, by accepting that even an unjust ruler was preferable to anarchy, supposedly capitulated *vis à vis* the power of any Sultan who might happen to stabilize his rule, so that there was no need for a special legitimating stance. But this view is scarcely applicable to the political situation of seventeenth-century Istanbul. Serious military defeats and a disadvantageous peace might destroy a Sultan's legitimacy and result in his deposition. To mention but a few examples: Meḥmed IV (reigned 1648–87) lost his throne after the failed siege of Vienna; Muṣṭafā II (reigned 1695–1703) was deposed after losing the battle of Zenta in 1697 and accepting the disastrous peace of Karlowitz in 1699.[25] Aḥmed III (reigned 1703–33) lost his throne due to further military failures, but also because, in the courtly celebrations of his time, the Ottoman elite indulged in the consumption of European-style luxuries in a manner that was all too provocative for many overtaxed Istanbul craftsmen, to say nothing of dissatisfied janissaries and *'ulemā*.[26] Ottoman Sultans therefore had every reason in the world to establish and confirm their legitimacy in a dialogue with those personages within and outside the court who could mount a challenge to their rule. The Hejazi elites belonged in this category, and their consent was actively sought.

PILGRIMS AND HISTORIANS

Thus we may hope the reader will conclude that there was nothing 'romantic' or 'exotic' about the pilgrimage, but that a great deal of hard work, sustained negotiations and complicated financial transactions went into its organization year after year. This more realistic perspective also coincides to some degree with that of sixteenth or seventeenth-century Ottoman officials, who corresponded at length about the political and financial ramifications of the pilgrimage. It must be admitted, however, that an interest in phenomena regarded in one way or another as 'exotic' was not completely alien to educated Ottomans of the early modern period. The accounts of an Ottoman ambassador who visited France in the early eighteenth century demonstrate this fact.[27] But the most obvious example is surely the travelogue of Ewliyā Čelebi, whose account of a visit to Vienna, and also his description of the Red Sea and its coast, suggest an interest in things that to an Istanbul gentleman appeared strange and yet not altogether unattractive.[28] The exotic is always in the eye of the beholder; it disappears when we reconstruct political and cultural processes by adopting, within certain limits, the perspective of the participants.

There is, however, no gainsaying that in this book the pilgrimage has been reconstructed by a rationalist historian of the late twentieth century, and that simple fact makes any attempt at an internalist perspective inherently problematic. For the tension between the vision of a sixteenth-century Ottoman pilgrim or bureaucrat and the view of a modern historian cannot be dissolved by even the most sophisticated form of historical analysis. But it is possible to keep this tension in mind and regard with respect the humanity of the people whom we have encountered at an often decisive stage of their lives. Historians are professionally tempted to misuse their advantage of hindsight, becoming authoritarian, domineering figures who claim to understand the authors of their sources better than the latter understood themselves. Another type of relationship is equally possible. Even while using the scholarly resources of our own age, we can and should take seriously the considerations which pilgrims and administrators had in mind when producing the texts on which we depend today. Better comprehension is the product of a permanent tension between immersion in the world of the sources and maintaining the critical distance of analysis.

Chronology

All dates refer to the Common Era (CE)

*c*570–632 CE	Life of the Prophet Muḥammad.
622	The Prophet Muḥammad and his companions leave Mecca and settle in Medina. This event, called the Hidjra, constitutes the beginning of the Muslim era.
630	The Muslims occupy Mecca; Islamization of the pilgrimage.
632	The Farewell Pilgrimage of the Prophet Muḥammad sets the standard for all future pilgrimages.
632–56	Medina the capital of the caliphal Empire. Conquest of Byzantine and Sassanian territory.
632–4	Caliphate of Abu Bakr.
634–44	Caliphate of 'Umar.
644–56	Caliphate of 'Uthmān.
656–61	Caliphate of 'Alī, the son-in-law of the Prophet.
661	Mu'āwiya establishes himself as the first caliph of the Ummayad dynasty.
680	Battle between Ḥusayn, son of 'Alī and grandson to the Prophet Muḥammad, and Ibn Sa'd, in the service of the Ummayad caliph Yazīd I. Ḥusayn's death in the battle of Karbalā takes on central religious significance in the belief system of Shi'i Muslims.

681–92	Caliphate of ʼAbd Allāh b. Zubayr (Ibn Zubayr) in Mecca. Restoration of the Kaʼaba.
692	Ibn Zubayr killed. Al-Ḥadjdjādj conquers Mecca for the Ummayad caliph ʼAbd al-Mālik. Destruction and reconstruction of the Kaʼaba.
747–50	Construction of a gallery in the Great Mosque of Mecca, some of whose elements remain visible today. An older gallery dating from 692–705 is no longer extant.
750	End of the Ummayad dynasty. The Abbasids establish themselves as caliphs in Baghdad.
after 777	Construction of the gallery of the Great Mosque of Mecca by the Abbasid caliph al-Mahdī (reigned 775–85) and his successors.
786–809	Caliphate of Hārūn al-Rashīd, who comes to Mecca several times as a pilgrim. His consort Zubayda has water conduits installed.
about 960	The Sherifs establish themselves as local rulers of Mecca.
before 929	Pilgrimage of Ibn ʼAbd Rabbih.
1047	First pilgrimage of Naṣīr-i Khosraw.
1175–93	Reign of Saladin (Ṣalāḥ al-Dīn Ayyūbī) in Egypt, Syria and Palestine.
1183	Pilgrimage of Ibn Djubayr.
about 1200	Within the Sherifal family, the Ḳatāda dynasty begins its period of rule.
1258	The last Abbasid caliph of Baghdad is murdered by the Mongols.
1260–1517	The Mamluk Sultans of Egypt and Syria control the Hejaz.
1468–96	Reign of Sultan Ḳāʼit Bāy in Egypt and Syria. Repairs to the Great Mosque of Medina after a fire, and construction of a theological school in Mecca.
1453	Conquest of Istanbul (Constantinople) by the Ottoman Sultan Meḥmed II (reigned 1451–81).
1481–1512	Reign of Sultan Bāyezīd II. Official gifts sent to Mecca and Medina.
about 1514	Jeddah threatened by the Portuguese.
1517	Ottoman conquest of Egypt by Sultan Selīm I (reigned 1512–20): the Hejaz enters the Ottoman realm.
1520–66	Reign of Süleymān the Lawgiver. Construction of soup kitchens in Mecca and Medina in the name

	of his consort K̲h̲urrem Sultan (Roxolana). Repair of the Meccan water conduits and construction of a seventh minaret to the Great Mosque.
1538	Unsuccessful campaign of K̲h̲ādim Süleymān Pasha against the Portuguese positions on the western coast of India.
1554–7	Exile of the Mughal prince Kāmrān in Mecca.
1566–74	Reign of Selīm II. Reshaping of the gallery of the Great Mosque of Mecca, which in many places is tantamount to a rebuilding from the foundations upward. Construction of domes over the gallery.
1574–82	Pilgrimage of Salīma and Gul-badan, consort and aunt to the Mughal ruler Akbar (reigned 1564–1605).
1574–95	Reign of Murād III. The town quarter adjacent to the mosque is torn down.
1585–90	A direct link is established from the eastern coast of India (Masulipatnam) to the Arabian peninsula.
1582	The pilgrimage of Mi'mar Sinān, the 'Ottoman Michelangelo'.
1611–12	The Ka'aba supported by iron braces. The architect responsible is Meḥmed Ag̲h̲a, who also built the Blue Mosque in Istanbul.
1630–31	Mutinying Ottoman troops occupy Mecca. They are defeated by the Mamluk amirs Ḳāsim and Riḍwān, operating in the name of Sultan Murād IV (reigned 1623–40). Destruction of the Ka'aba in a flash flood. Under the direction of Riḍwān Beg, the building is taken down stone by stone and largely rebuilt with the same materials
1632	Pilgrimage of 'Abd al-Raḥmān Ḥibrī.
1671	The Beduin chief Ibn Ras̲h̲īd attacks the pilgrimage caravan of Damascus. Sherif Sa'd rebels in Mecca.
1672	Sherif Sa'd deposed by the governor of Damascus Ṣarı Ḥüseyin Pasha. Pilgrimage of Ewliyā Čelebi.
1683–99	Ottoman–Habsburg war.

Notes

INTRODUCTION

1. Compare the article 'Ḥadjdj' in the *Encyclopedia of Islam*, 2nd edition (London, 1954–), henceforth *EI*. A good summary of early Islamic history is found in Hodgson (1974), vol. 1, pp. 3–230.
2. Ibn Djubayr's pilgrimage account has been translated into both English and French (see Bibliography for details). I have mainly worked with the French translation by Maurice Gaudefroy-Demombynes, and am grateful to Dr Doris Behrens-Abouseif who checked quotations against the original. The English translation contains a biography of Ibn Djubayr (p. 15 ff.).
3. Faroqhi (1992).
4. MD 6, p. 562, no. 1222 (972/1564–5).
5. De Planhol (1958), pp. 113–14.
6. On gold and silver ratios in early modern India see Subrahmanyam (1990), p. 83 ff.
7. Ashtor (1986).
8. Wüstenfeld (reprint, 1964), vol. 4, p. 302.
9. Faroqhi (forthcoming).
10. Faroqhi (1991).
11. Shaw (1962), p. 253 ff.
12. Faroqhi (1992), p. 319.
13. Compare the *ḳāḍī* register of the district of Çorum, dated 1595–7, today probably preserved in the Library of Çorum. I do not know whether, in the past few months, this register has been transferred to the National Library in Ankara: fol. 58b.
14. Naṣīr-i Khusraw (1881), pp. 162, 167.
15. Ibn Djubayr (1949–51), pp. 148–9. For the practical problems that might

ensue if a foreign ruler wished to make a donation, see Wüstenfeld (reprint, 1964), vol. 4, p. 248.
16. Shaw (1962), p. 249.
17. For an analysis of this situation in the eighteenth century, see Barbir (1980), p. 97 ff.
18. About 800 rescripts were located in the Mühimme Defterleri (henceforth MD), called Registers of Important Affairs in the text of this study. I checked registers 3–96, in addition to the series Mühimme Zeyli 1–10 (henceforth MZ). Mühimmes 1 and 2 do not contain usable documentation. Accounts were found in the section Maliyeden Müdevver (henceforth MM). An Egyptian provincial account has been published and translated into English: Shaw (1968). Inalcık (1973) contains a comprehensive introduction to sixteenth-century Ottoman history and institutions.
19. Evliya Çelebi (1896–1938), vol. 9, pp. 565–842.
20. Süheylī (Süheilî) Efendi, 'Tārīkh-i Mekke-i mükerrime' also called simply 'Risāle'. I used the manuscript in the Vienna National Library, Flügel (1865–7), vol. 2, p. 125.
21. Caʿfer Efendi, ed. Crane (1987).
22. Meḥmed Edīb wrote at the end of the seventeenth century. Of his account there exists an early French translation: El-Hadj Mehemmed Edib, tr. Bianchi (Paris, 1825).

CHAPTER 1

1. Hodgson (1974), vol. 1, pp. 241 ff., 473 ff.; vol. 2, pp. 12–52; vol. 3, p. 69 ff.
2. Naṣīr-i Khusraw (1881). See also his biography in *EI*.
3. Bulliet (1972), *passim*.
4. The pilgrimage account given on the next few pages is based principally on the descriptions of Ibn Djubayr. In order to limit the number of notes, only a selection of page references has been included.
5. Masson (1911), p. 401.
6. Hanna (1983), p. 16.
7. Ibn Jubayr, tr. Broadhurst (1952), p. 64.
8. *Ibid.*, p. 66.
9. *Ibid.*, pp. 72–3.
10. *EI*, article 'Ḥadjdj'.
11. Burton (reprint, 1964), vol. 1, p. 141.
12. Evliya Çelebi (1896–1938), vol. 9, p. 676.
13. Ibn Djubayr (1949–51), p. 92.
14. Al-Ḥarawī (1957).
15. Ibn Djubayr (1949–51), p. 109.
16. Hartmann (1975), p. 121.
17. Ibn Djubayr (1949–51), p. 194.
18. Ibn Djubayr (1949–51), p. 197.
19. Evliya Çelebi (1896–1938), vol. 9, p. 685 ff.

20. Ibn D̲j̲ubayr (1949–51), pp. 199–200.
21. Evliya Çelebi (1896–1938), vol. 9, p. 702.
22. Ibn D̲j̲ubayr (1949–51), p. 206.
23. *Ibid.*, p. 208.
24. *Ibid.*, p. 156.
25. *Ibid.*, p. 177 f.
26. *Ibid.*, p. 157.
27. *Ibid.*, p. 137.
28. Hodgson (1974), vol. 1, p. 200.
29. Naṣīr-i K̲h̲osraw ed. Schefer (1881), pp. 163–5.
30. Ibn 'Abd Rabbihi ed. Shafī (1973), pp. 416–38.
31. *Ibid.*, p. 433.
32. Wüstenfeld (1860) gives an abridged translation of Samhūdī's work. For a critical discussion of the sources concerning the Prophet's mosque, compare Sauvaget (1947).
33. Wüstenfeld (1860), p. 67.
34. On history and institutions of the Mamluk period, compare the relevant article in *EI*. Wüstenfeld (reprint, 1964), vol. 4, p. 287, claims that a covering for the Ka'aba by Timur's son S̲h̲āhruk̲h̲ was accepted, while Holt, in the *EI* article 'Mamluk', p. 324, expresses the contrary opinion.
35. Wüstenfeld (1964), vol. 4, p. 248.
36. *Ibid.*, vol. 4, p. 253 f.
37. *Ibid.*, vol. 4, p. 264 f.
38. *Ibid.*, vol. 4, p. 290 f.
39. *Ibid.*, vol. 4, p. 291 f.
40. Wüstenfeld (reprint, 1964), vol. 4, p. 292.
41. *Ibid.*, p. 302.
42. Mughul (1965), pp. 37–47.

CHAPTER 2

1. Jomier (1953), p. 85. However, this information concerns the early nineteenth century.
2. Compare the article 'Makka' in *EI* by A.J. Wensinck and C.E. Bosworth.
3. Al-D̲j̲azarī (1384/1964–5) p. 91 ff.
4. *Ibid.*, pp. 91–5.
5. *Ibid.*, p. 124.
6. MM 1645, p. 20. On the *sürre emīni*, compare d'Ohsson (1787–1824), vol. 3, p. 262 ff.
7. MM 927, p. 93, compare MD 28, p. 150, no. 351 (981/1573–4) on the duties of *ketk̲h̲üdā* and *mirāk̲h̲ōr*.
8. And (1982) clearly demonstrates the public character of many Ottoman celebrations.
9. Evliya Çelebi (1896–1938), vol. 10, p. 424 ff.
10. *Ibid.*, vol. 10, p. 442 f.
11. *Ibid.*, vol. 10, p. 432. On the *maḥmal* see Jomier (1953), *passim*.
12. Evliya Çelebi (1896–1938), vol. 10, p. 427.

13. Inalcık (1973), p. 77 ff.
14. Evliya Çelebi (1896–1938), vol. 9, p. 570 f.
15. *Ibid.*, vol. 10, p. 441 ff.
16. Ḥibrī (1975), pp. 111–28; (1976), pp. 55–72; (1978), pp. 147–62. Ḥibrī's itinerary in: *Tarih Enstitüsü Dergisi*, 6, pp. 124–8. Compare Mehemmed Edib (1825), pp. 81–169, Burckhardt (1822), pp. 656–61.
17. MM 4108.
18. Taeschner (1924–6), map at the end of vol. 1.
19. Evliya Çelebi (1896–1938), vol. 9, p. 582.
20. See map in Inalcık (1973), p. 122 f.
21. MM 927, p. 93.
22. Al-Djazarī (1384/1964–5), p. 103.
23. Evliya Çelebi (1896–1938), vol. 9, pp. 575, 599. See also Burckhardt (1822), p. 660.
24. MD 27, p. 158, no. 364 (988/1575–6). Compare Kātib Čelebi (1145/1732) fol. 512b.
25. MD 23, p. 32, no. 65 (981/1573–4). There were however complaints concerning the misuse of foundation revenues.
26. MD 42, p. 334, no. 1021 (988/1580–1).
27. MD 40, p. 164, no. 358 (987/1579–80); MD 35, p. 225, no. 560 (980/1578–9). Evliya Çelebi (1896–1938), vol. 9, p. 565 describes the *wādjib al-re'āyet* as regular members of the Pasha of Damascus's suite. But documents such as MD 53, p. 27, no. 68 show that, at least in the sixteenth century, this cannot have applied to all beneficiaries.
28. MD 7, p. 525 f., no. 1506 (975/1567–8). In sixteenth-century documents, the Damascus support caravan was called *istiḳbāl* and its members *ḳarshudju*. See MD 12, p. 168, no. 335 (978/1570–1); MD 7, p. 525 f., no. 1506 (975/1567–8); MD 12, p. 168, no. 355 (978/1570–1); MD 12, p. 445, no. 862 (979/1571–2); MD 24, p. 288, no. 781 (981/1573–4).
29. MD 12, p. 164, no. 348 (978/1570–1).
30. Evliya Çelebi (1896–1938), vol. 10, p. 438.
31. The Black Scribe and the Son of Djānbolāt were famous seventeenth-century rebels. See Griswold (1983).
32. MD 28, p. 142, no. 336 (984/1576–7).
33. MD 31, p. 256, no. 565 (985/1577–8).
34. MD 62, p. 256, no. 580 (996/1587–8).
35. Jomier (1953), p. 86.
36. *Ibid.*, p. 87. The anonymous source has been published by Hakluyt (1901), vol. 5, pp. 329–65. See also Beckingham (1977), pp. 75–80.
37. Jomier (1953), p. 87. On Ludovico di Varthéma, see Jones/Badger (1863), pp. 24, 37, 42. Compare also Anonymous (1901), p. 356.
38. Ali Bey (1814), vol. 2, p. 337.
39. Burckhardt (1829), vol. 2, p. 46.
40. MM 1003.
41. MM 1003, pp. 55, 57.
42. MD 28, p. 96, no. 225 (984/1576–7).

43. MD 40, p. 48, no. 103 (987/1579–80).
44. MM 4345, p. 65.
45. Bakhit (1982), pp. 53–68.
46. MD 26, p. 17, no. 48 (982/1574–5).
47. MD 14, p. 188, no. 269 (979/1571–2); MD 9, p. 24, no. 66 (977/1569–70). Compare also Bulliet (1975), pp. 165–178 and Faroqhi (1982), pp. 523–39.
48. MD 62, p. 52, no. 120 (995/1586–7).
49. MD 36, p. 23, no. 69 (986/1578–9).
50. MM 4345, pp. 16, 43 (1067/1656–7).
51. MD 5, p. 461, no. 1239 (973/1565–6); MD 36, p. 23, no. 69 (986/1578–9).
52. MD 36, p. 23, no. 69 (986/1578–9).
53. MD 7, p. 969, no. 2681 (976/1568–9).
54. MD 5, p. 206, no. 519 (973/1565–6).
55. MD 69, p. 15, no. 26 (1000/1591–2); MD 5, p. 208, no. 520 (973/1565–6).
56. Tresse (1937), p. 149 ff.
57. MD 29, p. 6, no. 12 (984/1576–7).
58. MD 69, p. 39, no. 76 (1000/1591–2).
59. MD 36, p. 23, no. 69 (986/1578–9).
60. MD 69, p. 69, no. 138 (1000/1591–2). On the official rate of exchange compare MD 73, p. 199, no. 462 (1003/1594–5).
61. Compare the unpublished paper of Anthony Greenwood, read at the annual convention of Middle East Studies Association, Chicago 1983. See also: Faroqhi (1984), p. 221 ff.; Mantran (1962), pp. 194–200; Cvetkova (1976), pp. 325–35.
62. Mantran (1962), p. 195, based upon Evliya Çelebi (1896–1938), vol. 1, p. 561 f.
63. See Kütükoğlu (1983) and the unpublished dissertation by Kafadar, 1986.
64. Tresse (1937), p. 149 ff.
65. MD 30, p. 28, no. 68 (985/1577–8); MD 9, p. 22, no. 58 (977/1569–70).
66. Rafeq (1970), pp. 53–9.

CHAPTER 3

1. Barkan (1953–4)(a), pp. 238–50. Majer (1982), pp. 40–63.
2. On Istanbul, see Sahillioğlu (1964), pp. 228–33. On Cairo, compare Raymond (1973–4), vol. 1, p. 17 ff. According to MD 73, p. 176, no. 413 (1003/1584–5), 1 gold piece (*altın*) equalled 120 *akče* and 1 ghurush 70 *akče*. Thus 1 *pāra* = 3 *akče*, but the rate of exchange was liable to fluctuation.
3. Shaw (1968), p. 158 ff.
4. Compare Başbakanlık Arşivi, Istanbul, Series Maliyeden Müdevver (MM): MM 5672, pp. 17 ff., 38 ff.; Shaw (1968), p. 165. MM 5672, p. 60 ff.; MM 5162, p. 14 ff.; MM 5658, p. 13 ff. According to MM 5162,

4,392,331 *pāra* equalled 44,851 *ḥasene* (gold pieces, *altın*) and 34 *pāra*. Compare also MM 5568, pp. 138 f., 146, 148 f., 151; MM 2520, p. 50; MM 86; MM 4901, pp. 2–6; MM 875.

5. Griswold (1983), p. 60 ff. Abu-Husayn (1985), pp. 67–128.
6. Sharon (1975), p. 26 ff.
7. MM 875.
8. Rafeq (1970), p. 55 ff. contains an extensive and most useful discussion of eighteenth-century pilgrimage problems as seen from Damascus.
9. Evliya Çelebi (1896–1938), vol. 9, pp. 565 ff. The editors claim, on p. 565, that Ewliyā visited Mecca in 1670–1. But that is highly improbable, as Ibn Rashīd's attack on the pilgrimage caravan occurred that year, and Ewliyā claims to have travelled a year later. See Rafeq (1970), p. 55 f. Cavit Baysun's biography of Ewliyā in *IA* also mentions 1082/1671–2 as the year of his pilgrimage. An edition of Ḥibrī's account can be found in: Ḥibrī (1975), pp. 111–28; (1976), pp. 55–72; (1978), pp. 147–62.
10. Shaw (1962), pp. 240–50.
11. MD 69, p. 34, no. 65 (1000/1591–2).
12. Al-Djazarī (1384/1964–5). I am grateful to Dr Humaydan for finding me a copy of this work.
13. Evliya Çelebi (1896–1938), vol. 9, p. 572 ff.
14. On the *maḥmal*, see Jomier (1953), *passim*.
15. Shaw (1962), p. 240. For a different opinion compare Holt (1961), p. 221. Holt believes that during the first ten years of Ottoman rule, Mamluks were appointed as commanders of the pilgrimage. According to MD 30, p. 275, no. 639 (985/1577–8) the commander was supposed to be one of the *ümerā* (see Shaw (1962), p. 199). But from MD 52, p. 297, no. 793 (992/1584) we learn that a wealthy Cairene merchant also might be awarded this honour.
16. MD 3, p. 525, no. 1553 (968/1560–1).
17. According to Shaw (1962), p. xxii an Egyptian 'purse' equalled 25,000 *pāra* or 60,000 *akče*. Later the Ottoman administration admitted that 16 purses were insufficient, and the commander was assigned 18 purses. Compare MD 12, p. 449, no. 868 (979/1571–2).
18. Concerning Özdemiroghlu, see Yavuz (1984), pp. 61, 99. MD 3, p. 525, no. 1553 (968/1560–1).
19. MD 14, p. 812 f., no. 1180 (978/1570–1); MD 30, p. 25, no. 90 (985/1577–8).
20. MD 43, p. 79, no. 161 (988/1580–1).
21. MD 14, p. 1149, no. 1692 (978/1570–1).
22. MD 61, p. 73, no. 190 (994/1585–6).
23. Yavuz (1984), p. 61.
24. Abu-Husayn (1985), p. 168 f.
25. *Ibid.*, pp. 164–71. On this milieu compare also Bakhit (1982) (b), *passim*.
26. See the article 'Adjlun' in *EI* (D. Sourdel).
27. MD 46, p. 1, no. 1 (989/1581).
28. Abu-Husayn (1985), p. 170.
29. MD 18, p. 28, no. 52 (979/1571–2); MD 24, p. 196, no. 522 (981/1573–4); MD 26, p. 156, no. 420 (982/1574–5).

30. Abu-Husayn (1985), *passim*.
31. In MD 47, p. 107, no. 272 (990/1582), Ḳānṣūh is referred to as a Beduin amir. On strife between the 'Reds' and the 'Whites', see Bakhit (1982), p. 214 and MD 14, p. 675, no. 973 (978/1570–1). Ḳānṣūh Beg's ties to the faction of the 'Reds' are alluded to; but not explicitly stated.
32. MD 14, p. 1023, no. 1515 (978/1570–1).
33. This version of the name is given by Bakhit (1982), p. 223. Hütteroth and Abdulfattah (1977), p. 169, refer to a tribe called 'Urbān Na'īm' living in the same area. It is thus not quite clear which group the rescript refers to. On the dispute between Ḳānṣūh and Nu'aym/Na'īm, see MD 14, p. 830, no. 1206 (978/1570–1).
34. Abu-Husayn (1985), p. 170 f. MD 64, p. 86 f., no. 252 (996/1587–8).
35. Rafeq (1970), p. 71.
36. The pilgrims were attacked while in the Great Mosque, unarmed and in pilgrims' garb – if Ewliyā's story is accurate. Even though the attack was instigated by the Sherif, the actual attackers were Beduins. Therefore this event may be regarded as another example of a Beduin raid against a pilgrimage caravan.
37. Barbir (1980), p. 10. On p. 200 f. there is a list of the most significant attacks upon the Syrian pilgrimage caravan. Between 1531 and 1671 no attacks are mentioned at all. However, Ibn Ṭūlūn and Ibn Ğum'a (1952), p. 198, refer to an attack in 1012/1603–4. See also Ca'fer Efendi, ed. Crane (1987), p. 39.
38. MD 3, p. 75, no. 189 (966/1558–9).
39. MD 29, p. 6, no. 11 (984/1576–7).
40. For the Ottoman realm, a good survey can be found in the article 'Hil'at' by Fuat Köprülü in *IA*.
41. Barbir (1980), pp. 99, 105. Bakhit (1982), pp. 200–4. MD 28, p. 17, no. 26 (984/1576–7).
42. On the role of Riḍwān Beg, see Holt (1959), pp. 225–9. Compare Raymond (1973–4), vol. 1, pp. 5–7, 264 and Holt (1961) p. 243 ff.
43. On the last years of Ottoman rule, compare Wüstenfeld (1884), pp. 52–6 and Uzunçarşılı (1972), pp. 80–4.
44. This campaign was commanded by Riḍwān Beg and his superior, Ḳāsim Beg.
45. Ḥibrī (1976), p. 58. On Ḥibrī's account of contemporary political difficulties, see p. 60 f.
46. *Ibid.*, p. 58.
47. Compare the article 'Murād IV' in *IA* (Cavit Baysun).
48. Al-Nābulsī (1986), pp. 316–26.
49. Uzunçarşılı (1972), p. 86 f.
50. Evliya Çelebi (1896–1938), vol. 9, p. 602.
51. Ca'fer Efendi (1987).
52. *Ibid.*, p. 9 f. For a listing of the Ottoman governors of Damascus, see Laoust (1952). The list contains two Pashas named K͟husrew. The first officiated in 946/1539–40 and 970/1562–3, the second in 1004/1595–6 and 1007/1598–9 (pp. 183, 186, 194, 196). Probably our text

refers to the second Khusrew Pasha, but the second term of the earlier personage also constitutes a possibility.

53. Ca'fer Efendi (1987), p. 7.
54. *Ibid.*, p. 38 f.
55. *Ibid.*, p. 41.
56. Ibn Djubayr (1949–51), p. 156.
57. See Barbir (1979–80), pp. 68–81 for an overview of the problem.
58. MM 2520, p. 20; MM 932, p. 51 (1056/1646–7).
59. Hakluyt (1901), vol. 5, p. 342.
60. Heyd (1960), p. 82 f.
61. MD 3, p. 122, no. 317 (966/1558–9); MD 12, p. 478, no. 918 (979/1571–2).
62. Jomier (1953), p. 80 ff.
63. MD 7, p. 278, no. 786 (975/1567–8).
64. MD 14, p. 997, no. 1483 (979/1571–2).
65. MD 62, p. 255, no. 579 (996/1587–8).
66. MD 3, p. 370, no. 1094 (967/1559–60).
67. MD 52, p. 105, no. 258 (991/1583). It also happened that the soldiers occupied the water reservoirs and allowed the pilgrims access only after payment of a fee: MD 14, p. 540, no. 828 (978/1570–1).
68. Muṣṭafā 'Ālī (1975), p. 55 f.
69. Evliya Çelebi (1896–1938), vol. 9, p. 801. See also MD 78, p. 297, no. 778 (1018/1609–10). In this rescript the Egyptian caravan is forbidden to stay in Medina for over three days.
70. An account of life in a desert fort in the year 1876 is found in Doughty (1979), vol. 1, p. 160 ff; vol. 1, pp. 1–255 contains a detailed description of the pilgrimage route from Damascus to the stopping point of Madā' in Ṣāliḥ.
71. Evliya Çelebi (1896–1938), vol. 9, p. 602.
72. MD 3, p. 203, no. 563 (967/1559–60); MD 23, p. 210, no. 443 (981/1573–4).
73. MD 46, p. 183, no. 380 (989/1581).
74. Evliya Çelebi (1896–1938), vol. 9, p. 590.
75. Mehemmed Edib (1825), pp. 128–32.
76. Evliya Çelebi (1896–1938), vol. 9, p. 776; MM 4345, p. 65. See also Barbir (1980), pp. 176–7.
77. Compare Sharon (1975), p. 18.

CHAPTER 4

1. Fleischer (1986), p. 253 ff.
2. Inalcık (1954), pp. 104–29.
3. Hodgson (1974), vol. 1, pp. 198–221, 320–6.
4. Wüstenfeld (1964), vol. 4, *passim*.
5. Ibn Djubayr (1949–51), p. 146, mentions subsidies distributed to the Beduins by the vizier of the ruler of Mosul, but there is no mention of grants to the inhabitants of the Holy Cities.

6. Uzluk (1958), p. 54 f., Konyalı (1970), p. 401 ff.
7. Gökbilgin (1952), pp. 234 f., 317.
8. Published by Barkan (1979), pp. 1–380 as 'Defter-i müsevvedât-ı in'âm ve tasaddukaat ve teşrifât ve irsâliyât ve 'âdet ve nukeriye ve gayruhu vâcib-i sene . . . (909) (26. VI. 1503–13. VI. 1504). Location and call number of the document are missing. The edition begins on p. 296.
9. D'Ohsson (1787–1824), vol. 3, p. 258.
10. In Sunni Islam there are four recognized schools of law, which differ in certain points of law and ritual, but are all considered equally orthodox. Believers are free to choose their school of law, but in different regions of the Muslim world, one or the other predominates. In the Ottoman Empire as in modern Turkey, the Ḥanefīs constituted the dominant school.
11. Budgets of the Ottoman central government have been published: Barkan (1953–4), pp. 251–329; (1957–8), pp. 219–76; (1957–8), pp. 277–332; (1955–6), pp. 304–47; (1955–6), pp. 225–303. Compare also Barkan (1953–4), pp. 239–50 and Majer (1982), pp. 40–63.
12. Kafadar (1986, 1989). On the *eshrefiye* see Artuk and Artuk (1971, 1974), vol. 2, pp. 494–504. When compiling the table, the *eshrefiye* has been counted as 50 *akče* throughout, even though in the early part of Bāyezīd's reign, 45 *akče* would have been more appropriate.
13. Shaw (1962), p. 5.
14. Shaw (1968), p. 155 ff.
15. Muṣṭafā 'Ālī (1975), p. 82 f.
16. MM 5672, p. 17 ff.; MM 5672, p. 38 ff.; MM 5162, p. 14 ff.; MM 5658, p. 13 ff.
17. Ca'fer Efendi (1987), p. 47 ff.
18. Shaw (1962), p. 269.
19. The term *deshishe* originally signified 'porridge'.
20. Shaw (1962), p. 21.
21. Wüstenfeld (1964), vol. 4, p. 302.
22. MM 12784.
23. MD 70, p. 159, no. 312 (1001/1592–3).
24. MM 1806, p. 2.
25. On house prices, see Faroqhi (1987), pp. 116–46. On bread and chickens, see Kütükoğlu (1978), p. 22 f.
26. MM 1806, p. 5.
27. MM 1806, p. 9. On coins, see Artuk and Artuk (1971, 1974), vol. 2, pp. 494, 556.
28. MM 1806, p. 11.
29. MM 1806, p. 18.
30. In the Syrian provincial budgets we find very few data concerning the food supply of Mecca and Medina; the pilgrimage caravan definitely occupied centre stage. Foundations for the benefit of the Holy Cities seem to have been insignificant. In 1657–8, 169 inhabitants of Mecca and Medina received salaries or pensions from the Syrian budget. These payments totalled less than 600,000 *pāra*, while Beduin subsidies and other expenses connected with the pilgrimage amounted to almost nine

million *pāra*. It is difficult to estimate even roughly the amount of money which flowed from the Syrian exchequer in the direction of Mecca and Medina, but at least maximal (150,000 gold pieces) and minimal (55,000 gold pieces) figures can be suggested. However, in 1657–8, for reasons which remain unknown, about 220,000 gold pieces were spent (MM 956, p. 6 ff.). All these figures are dubious because, in cases of emergency, the caravan commanders borrowed substantial sums, which were only repaid much later, if at all. Thus expenditures were redistributed over the years, and the figures we possess give only a distorted picture of reality.

31. See Flügel (1865–7), vol. 2, no. 895, p. 123 f. This is a slightly abridged and updated Ottoman version of Ḳuṭb al-Dīn's chronicle, composed probably by the poet Bāḳī at the behest of the Grand Vizier Soḳollu Meḥmed Pasha (died 1579). The sections referred to here are on fols 223–5. For a German summary see Wüstenfeld (reprint, 1964), vol. 4, pp. 314–23.
32. MD 39, p. 115, no. 278 (987/1579–80).
33. MD 73, p. 460, no. 1015 (1003/1594–5).
34. MD 89, p. 26, no. 68 (1052/1642–3).
35. The Sherif received subsidies not merely for himself, but for his Beduin allies as well.
36. This impression is based on the Mühimme Registers of this period. But due to numerous gaps in our documentation, it may well be an optical illusion.
37. MD 43, p. 266, no. 490 (988/1580–1). On Meccan participation in the mid-nineteenth century pilgrimage compare Burton (reprint, 1964), vol. 2, p. 188.
38. MD 48, p. 318, no. 938 (991/1583).
39. Anonymous and Gölpınarlı (1958), p. 56, mentions a good example from Anatolia.
40. Sahillioğlu (1978), p. 10.
41. MD 49, p. 71, no. 249 (991/1583).
42. Masters (1988), pp. 147–51, discusses the results of a money famine in Aleppo.
43. MD 49, p. 71, no. 249 (991/1583).
44. MD 58, p. 277, no. 707 (993/1585); MD 60, p. 128, no. 308 (994/1585–6).
45. MD 75, pp. 8–9, no. 20 (1012/1603–4).
46. On the Ḥusaynīs of Medina (mid-nineteenth century) compare Burton (reprint, 1964), vol. 2, p. 3. The descendants of Ḥasan, the Prophet's other grandson, were Sunnis and often hostile to the Ḥusaynīs. Compare MD 47, p. 241, no. 578 (990/1582). On the Ḥusaynīs in general see MD 47, p. 241, no. 578 (990/1582); MD 39, p. 115, no. 278 (987/1579–80); MD 31, p. 267, no. 589 (985/1577–8); MD 6, p. 190, no. 409 (972/1564–5); MD 46, p. 100, no. 189 (989/1581).
47. MM 5672, p. 38 (1010–11/1601–3).
48. MD 73, p. 460, no. 1015 (1003/1594–5). It is hard to determine the equivalent of the *irdeb* or *ardeb*, because this measure varied from one

locality to the next. In early eighteenth-century Cairo, 1 *irdeb* corresponded to 6 *kile* of Istanbul, or 153.9 kg. See Shaw (1962), p. 79.

49. Compare the individual items mentioned by Shaw (1968), p. 154 ff. These were added, and the total (in *pāras*) then converted into gold pieces. From the document published by Shaw we learn that 1 gold piece then equalled 40 *pāra*. For the higher estimate compare Shaw (1962), p. 268. When converting *pāra* into gold pieces, the same exchange rate was again applied.
50. Finkel (1988), Appendix 10. On rates of exchange, see Sahillioğlu (1964), p. 233: in 1605, 1 gold piece was equivalent to 120 *akče*.
51. Compare the Syrian provincial account of 1075/1664–5 (MM 2394, pp. 5–9). Many later budgets show a similar tendency.
52. MD 75, p. 178, no. 350 (1013/1604–5). Sultan Aḥmed I reigned 1603–17. His deceased predecessor therefore was Meḥmed III reigned 1595–1603 .

CHAPTER 5

1. On the construction history of the Great Mosque in pre-Ottoman times see Gaudefroy-Demombynes (1923), pp. 26–154.
2. Ibn Djubayr (1949–51), p. 107.
3. Burton (reprint, 1964), vol. 2, p. 295.
4. On empire-wide practice, see Barkan (1962–3), pp. 239–96.
5. Kuran (1987), pp. 268–86.
6. Necipoğlu Kafadar (1986), p. 99.
7. Barkan (1972, 1979), vol. 1, pp. 386–93. MD 10, p. 253, no. 391 (979/1571–2).
8. MD 26, p. 297, no. 864 (982/1574–5); MD 27, p. 166, no. 381 (983/1575–6).
9. Compare Barkan (1972, 1979), vol. 1, pp. 361–80.
10. MD 23, p. 5, no. 7 (981/1573–4).
11. MD 23, p. 297, no. 644 (981/1573–4).
12. Ca'fer Efendi (1987), p. 57. At this time, golden keys for the Prophet's mausoleum also were remitted to the Hejaz.
13. 'Zübdet al-Tewā-rikh' by Muṣṭafā b. Ibrāhīm. The relevant section has been translated by Howard Crane in Ca'fer Efendi (1987), p. 57.
14. MD 28, p. 96, no. 226 (984/1576–7).
15. Evliya Çelebi (1896–1938), vol. 9, p. 779.
16. Snouck Hurgronje (1931), p. 11 ff.
17. MD 31, p. 369, no. 820 (985/1577–8).
18. MD 6, p. 604, no. 1332 (972/1564–5); MD 21, p. 205, no. 488 (980/1572–3).
19. MM 7222. For an interpretation of this text see Faroqhi (1986b), pp. 111–26.
20. Barkan (1972, 1979), vol. 1, pp. 132–7, points out that slave labour was rarely employed on the Süleymāniye construction site.
21. MD 7, p. 343, no. 200 (975/1567–8).

22. Barkan (1972, 1979), vol. 2, p. 292.
23. MD 5, p. 545, no. 1493 (973/1565–6).
24. MD 10, p. 253, no. 391 (979/1571–2).
25. MD 7, p. 314, no. 899 (975/1567–8).
26. MD 58, p. 277, no. 706 (993/1585).
27. MD 6, p. 45, no. 91 (972/1564–5).
28. MD 14, p. 954 ff., no. 1416 (978/1570–1). For construction costs of the Süleymāniye, see Barkan (1972, 1979), vol. 1, p. 41; for those of the Sultan Aḥmed Mosque, vol. 2, p. 276.
29. Ca'fer Efendi (1987), p. 33 ff.
30. Necipoğlu Kafadar (1986), p. 99.
31. Ca'fer Efendi (1987), p. 58.
32. Necipoğlu Kafadar (1986), p. 107.
33. Ca'fer Efendi (1987), p. 55.
34. Necipoğlu Kafadar (1986), p. 111 ff.
35. Ḳuṭb al-Dīn Muḥammad b. Aḥmad al-Makkī, 'Al-i'lām be-'alām balad Allāh al-ḥarām', tr. by Bāḳī (?) 1006/1597–8. See Flügel (1865–7), vol. 2, p. 123 f., fol. 225B.
36. MD 53, p. 172, no. 502 (992/1584).
37. MD 7, p. 169, no. 442 (975/1567–8). See also Wüstenfeld (reprint, 1964), vol, p. 314 ff. MD 26, p. 217, no. 616 (982/1574–5).
38. Barkan (1972, 1979), vol. 1, map facing p. 1.
39. Evliya Çelebi (1896–1938), vol. 9, p. 782.
40. MD 14, p. 412, no. 579 (978/1570–1).
41. Ḳuṭb al-Dīn, tr. by Bāḳī, fol. 254A ff. See also Wüstenfeld (reprint, 1964), vol. 4, p. 319.
42. *Ibid.*, fol. 255A. Esin (1985) gives an account of events according to Ḳuṭb al-Dīn's chronicle.
43. MD 23, p. 2, no. 6 (981/1573–4).
44. For a discussion of building types and their possible meanings, see Necipoğlu Kafadar (1986).
45. MD 10, p. 253, no. 391 (979/1571–2).
46. MD 12, p. 438, no. 849 (979/1571–2).
47. MD 21, p. 231, no. 553 (980/1572–3).
48. MD 22, p. 313, no. 624 (981/1573–4). See also Wüstenfeld (reprint, 1964), vol. 4, p. 316.
49. MD 22, p. 296, no. 587 (981/1573–4).
50. MD 21, p. 231, no. 553 (980/1572–3), Burton (reprint, 1964), vol. 2, p. 264.
51. MD 33, p. 1, no. 1 (985/1577–8).
52. MD 28, p. 188, no. 438 (984/1576–7).
53. MD 31, p. 386, no. 858 (985/1577–8).
54. MD 6, p. 48, no. 95 (972/1564–5).
55. For the equivalent of the standard Ottoman *vuḳiye* or *okka* see Hinz (1955), p. 24.
56. MD 7, p. 332, no. 955 (975/1567–8).
57. MD 6, p. 44, no. 90 (972/1564–5).

58. MD 9, p. 63, no. 169 (977/1569–70).
59. Uzunçarşılı (1972), pp. 65–7.
60. MD 16, p. 211, no. 407 (979/1571–2).
61. MD 33, p. 39, no. 82 (985/1577–8); MD 30, p. 17, no. 41 (985/1577–8).
62. MD 7, p. 874, no. 2400 (976/1568–9); MD 69, p. 130, no. 262 (1001/1592–3).
63. MD 7, p. 313, no. 896 (975/1567–8); MD 7, p. 169, no. 442 (975/1567–8).
64. MD 73, p. 282, no. 646 (1003/1594–5).
65. MD 26, p. 242, no. 693 (982/1574–5).
66. MD 29, p. 143, no. 352 (985/1577–8); MD 64, p. 217, no. 557 (997/1588–9).
67. MD 96, p. 59, no. 309; p. 60, no. 311; p. 60, no. 312 (1089/1678–9); MZ 2, p. 43 (date probably 982/1574–5).
68. MD 92, p. 22, no. 106 (1067/1656–7); MD 89, p. 86, no. 213 (1053/1643–4).
69. The Süleymāniye and Sultan Aḥmed Mosques are good examples of this type of spatial structure. However, in Mecca, the open space was soon filled up by the temporary shelters of poor people: Wüstenfeld (reprint, 1964), vol. 4, p. 321.
70. Sultan Murād himself owned a house in this area: MD 26, p. 241, no. 693 (980/1572–3).
71. MD 30, p. 5, no. 14 (985/1577–8).
72. MD 39, p. 229, no. 458 (988/1580–1).
73. MD 6, p. 213, no. 456 (972/1564–5).
74. MD 14, pp. 954–6, no. 1416 (978/1570–1).
75. MD 43, p. 184, no. 336 (988/1580–1).
76. MD 22, p. 273, no. 535 (981/1573–4).
77. MD 23, p. 84, no. 173 (981/1573–4).
78. MD 7, p. 343, no. 990 (975/1567–8).
79. MD 28, p. 14, no. 30 (984/1576–7); MD 96, p. 60, no. 312 (1089/1678–9).
80. MD 58, p. 275, no. 699 (993/1585).
81. MD 42, p. 44, no. 244, (989/1581).
82. MD 40, p. 88, no. 200 (probably 987/1579–80). A *ḳurna* is a wash basin used in baths.
83. MD 43, p. 264, no. 503 (989/1581).
84. MD 23, p. 112, no. 227 (981/1573–4).
85. MD 3, p. 368, no. 1088 (936/1555–6). It is possible that the expression *Ḥaram-ı sherīf* ('Noble Sanctuary') refers to the territory of Mecca as a whole. But more probably, the Great Mosque is intended. Who is meant by the 'deceased princess' also is open to debate. Süleymān's consort Roxolana and his daughter Mihr-ü-māh can be excluded, even though both established foundations in Mecca. Roxolana died in 1558, while Mihr-ü-māh survived until 1578.
86. MD 28, p. 1, no. 2 (984/1576–7).
87. MD 31, p. 334, no. 744 (985/1577–8).

88. MD 26, p. 241, no. 693 (980/1572–3).
89. MD 26, p. 241, no. 693 (980/1572–3).
90. Delumeau (1977), p. 175 ff.
91. MD 64, p. 16, no. 44 (996/1587–8).
92. MD 35, p. 80, no. 194 (986/1578–9).
93. MD 33, p. 169, no. 339 (985/1577–8).
94. Ca'fer Efendi (1987), p. 54.
95. *Ibid.*, p. 57.
96. Süheylī (Suheilî) Efendi, 'Tārīkh-i Mekke-i mükerrime', also called 'Risāle'. The manuscript used here belongs to the Vienna National Library, see Flügel (1865–7), vol. 2, p. 125. An overview of Meccan inundations is found on fols 66A ff. According to Burckhardt (1829), vol. 1, p. 244, the flood which caused the collapse of the Ka'aba took place in 1626. An excellent account of the rebuilding of the Ka'aba, largely based on Süheylī but using official documents as well, can be found in Eyyüb Ṣabrī (1301–6/1883–9), vol. 1, pp. 514–60. On page 560 ff. a number of relevant documents have been published. I am grateful to Dr Christoph Neumann for pointing this out to me. On the water pipes of Mecca there is also an extensive account by Eyyüb Ṣabrī, *ibid.*, p. 738 ff.
97. Süheylī, 'Risāle', fol. 30A.
98. *Ibid.*, fols 30B–31A.
99. *Ibid.*, fol. 31A.
100. *Ibid.*, fol. 31B. A *müftī* is an official who profers opinions on the conformity of judicial measures with Islamic law.
101. Probably this is the same Riḍwān Beg who from 1631 to his death in 1656 commanded the Cairo pilgrimage caravan. His fame rests on the town quarter he founded in Cairo, the Ḳaṣaba Riḍwān. On his biography see Holt (1959), pp. 221–30 and Raymond (1973–4), vol. 1, pp. 5–7, 264. Strangely enough Süheylī does not call him commander of the pilgrimage, but it is hard to believe that two Riḍwān Begs should have held responsible positions in Mecca at the same time. The rescript from Istanbul ordering the renovation of the Ka'aba has been published: Feridūn Beg (1275/1858–9), vol. 2, p. 101.

    When translating the text cited here, we are confronted with the problem that the word '*hidjdjān*' can mean both 'noble' and 'dromedary'. The context permits both translations. But in any case, messengers were sent to Cairo, and I have thus avoided taking sides in this thorny little problem of interpretation.
102. Süheylī, 'Risāle', fol. 32B ff. Apparently there was a dispute between Istanbul and Cairo officials, reflected in the chronicle of Muṣṭafā Na'īmā, which however was composed almost seventy years after the events discussed here. In his very extensive account, Na'īmā fails to mention Riḍwān Beg by name, although an anonymous official is probably identical with the celebrated Mamluk commander. On the other hand, a certain Seyyid Meḥmed, elder and controller of the Prophet's descendants, is mentioned as the person in charge of the Ka'aba restoration by Na'īmā, while Suheylī makes no mention of him.

It is improbable that these discrepancies are due to lack of information or negligence, particularly on Na'īmā's part, since the latter in his official position as imperial chronicler possessed the means for collecting an extensive documentation. It is much more likely that tensions between the Mamluks and the central power, which in Na'īmā's time were very much on the agenda, induced the latter to play down Riḍwān Beg's participation. Compare Muṣṭafā Na'īmā (n.d.), vol. 3, p. 44 f. On the circumstances of Na'īmā's history-writing, see Thomas (1972).

103. *Ibid.*, fol. 37A.
104. *Ibid.*, fol. 35B.
105. *Ibid.*, fol. 42A.
106. On Sinān, see Saî Çelebi (1988). On Meḥmed Agha, Ca'fer Efendi (1987), pp. 33–76. Sinān's year of birth is disputed, see Kuran (1987), p. 24.
107. Süheylī, 'Risāle', fols 60–64A.
108. *Ibid.*, fol. 41A.
109. *Ibid.*, fol. 45B. For the equivalents, see Hinz (1955), supplement 1, 1, p. 16.
110. Süheylī, 'Risāle', fol. 53A.
111. *Ibid.*, fols 49A, 50A.
112. *Ibid.*, fol. 6A ff. For historical information see *EI*, article 'Ka'ba' (A.J. Wensick, J. Jomier).
113. See Uzunçarşılı (1948), pp. 120–6.
114. In the Ottoman context, the *muḥtesib* mentioned here was in charge of policing the market and often farmed his office. See the relevant article in *EI* by Robert Mantran.
115. Süheylī, 'Risāle', fol. 54A.
116. *Ibid.*, fols 45A, 51A, 55A, 59A and many other examples.
117. Ca'fer Efendi (1987), p. 67.
118. Süheylī, 'Risāle', fols 46B, 48A, 54B.
119. *Ibid.*, fol. 38A.
120. *Ibid.*, fols 58B–59A.
121. *Ibid.*, fol. 62B.
122. *Ibid.*, fols 59A, 60A. Necipoğlu Kafadar (1986), p. 100.
123. MD 27, p. 174, no. 397 (983/1575–6).
124. MD 43, p. 70, no. 143 (988/1580).
125. MD 58, p. 277, no. 706 (993/1585); M23, p. 317 (984/1576–7).
126. MD 60, p. 25, no. 59 (993/1585).
127. MD 60, p. 297, no. 674 (994/1585–6).
128. MD 62, p. 236, no. 527 (996/1587–8).
129. MD 62, p. 236, no. 527 (996/1587–8).
130. MD 64, p. 4, no. 14 (997/1588–9).
131. MD 64, p. 45, no. 124 (997/1588–9).
132. MD 73, p. 394, no. 862 (1003/1594–5).
133. MD 31, p. 83, no. 212 (985/1577–8); MZ 3, p. 265 (984/1576–7).
134. MD 73, p. 562, no. 1226 (1003/1594–5).
135. MD 58, p. 277, no. 706 (993/1585).

136. MD 73, p. 368, no. 806 (1003/1594–5).
137. MD 64, p. 205, no. 524 (997/1588–9).
138. MZ 3, p. 333 (984/1576–7).
139. MD 7, p. 273, no. 772 (975/1567–8).
140. MD 35, p. 97, no. 941 (986/1578–9).
141. MD 36, p. 295, no. 782 (987/1579–80).
142. MD 60, p. 297, no. 674 (994/1585–6).
143. Evliya Çelebi (1896–1938), vol. 9, p. 643; MD 60, p. 279, no. 643 (994/1585–6).
144. MD 76, p. 118, no. 304 (1016/1607–8).
145. MD 96, p. 110, no. 552; p 108, no. 542 (1089/1678–9).
146. MD 96, p. 107, no. 536 (1089/1678–9).
147. Evliya Çelebi (1896–1938), vol. 9, p. 656 f.
148. MD 73, p. 214, no. 500 (1003/1594–5).
149. MZ 3, p. 316 (984/1576–7); Evliya Çelebi (1896–1938), vol. 9, p. 656.
150. For an illustrated document to demonstrate the completion of a pilgrimage, see Esin (1984), p. 179 ff.
151. Meḥmed Yemīnī, 'Kitāb-ı Faḍā'il-i Mekke-i mu'aẓẓama', manuscript in the Vienna National Library, see Flügel (1865–7), vol. 2, p. 125 f., where the text is described as anonymous.
152. As an example, compare Evliya Çelebi (1896–1938), vol. 9, p. 750.
153. Nayır (1975), pp. 135–7.

CHAPTER 6

There is a distinguished study by Naimur Rahman Farooqi, 'Mughal–Ottoman Relations: A Study of Political and Diplomatic Relations between Mughal India and the Ottoman Empire, 1556–1748', PhD dissertation, Madison, Wisconsin 1986, now also available as a book. I owe a great deal to this work, but unfortunately I was not able to see it in its published form.

1. Evliya Çelebi (1896–1938), vol. 9, p. 682, seems to feel that the interests of the pilgrims were much more important than the deference to be accorded the Sherifs as the descendants of the Prophet. A Sultan might therefore earn his respect if he aided the pilgrims at the expense of the Sherifs.
2. MD 6, p. 17, no. 39 (972/1564–5).
3. Düzdağ (1972), pp. 109–11.
4. MD 6, p. 17, no. 39 (972/1564–5).
5. Compare MD 7, p. 271, no. 748 (975/1567–8); MD 7, p. 241, no. 671 (975/1567–8).
6. Thus in several sixteenth-century Balkan towns the slaughter of sheep was forbidden, so as not to endanger the meat supply of Istanbul.
7. MD 30, p. 182, no. 428 (985/1577–8) concerns the pilgrims of Fez and Marrakesh.
8. MD 6, p. 313, no. 665 (972/1564–5).
9. Compare the introduction by Annette Beveridge to Gulbadan und

Beveridge (reprint, 1972), p. 69 f. See also Abū al-Faḍl (1898–1939), vol. 3, p. 570f.
10. On Djem, see the relevant article in *EI* by Halil Inalcık.
11. Alderson (1956), p. 125 f. for the fifteenth and eighteenth centuries mentions several princesses who went on the pilgrimage, but gives no information for the sixteenth and seventeenth. On Shāh Sultan, see MD 19, p. 203 f, nos 419–21 (980/1572–3).
12. Ibn Djubayr (1949–51), p. 211 ff.
13. MD 6, p. 313, no. 665 (972/1564–5).
14. MD 16, p. 375, no. 657 (979/1571–2); MD 75, p. 165, no. 304 (1013/1604–5). We learn that the envoy of the ruler of Bukhara intended to visit Egypt, Mecca and Yemen on his way home.
15. Ottoman officials on pilgrimage enjoyed similar privileges: MD 19, p. 203 f., nos 419–21 (980/1572–3).
16. Badāōnī (reprint, 1973), vol. 1, p. 443.
17. Riazul-Islam (1971/1982), vol. 2, p. 295 ff. Farooqi (1986), p. 27 is of the same opinion.
18. Badāōnī (reprint, 1973), vol. 2, pp. 217, 246.
19. Evliya Çelebi (1896–1938), vol. 9, pp. 772–3.
20. Badāōnī (reprint, 1973), vol. 2, p. 246.
21. *Ibid.*, p. 321 f.
22. See the article 'Kāmrān' in *EI* by H. Beveridge.
23. MD 39, p. 238, no. 471 (988/1580–1). For an extensive interpretation of this visit and its ramifications see Farooqi (1986), p. 35.
24. MD 35, p. 292, no. 740 (986/1578–9); MD 43, p. 54, no. 107 (988/1580–1); MD 43, p. 184, no. 336 (988/1580–1); MD 58, p. 260, no. 659 (993/1585). According to Farooqi (1986), p. 36, Akbar after this dispute broke off all relations with the Ottoman Sultans.
25. This whole section is based upon Farooqi (1988), pp. 198–220, who also discusses previous work on the subject. According to Farooqi (1986), p. 251 Princess Gul-badan had to turn over a village to the Portuguese to receive her safe conduct.
26. MD 7, p. 410, no. 1180 (975/1567–8); p. 910, no. 2491 (976/1568–9); p. 913, no. 1502 (976/1568–9), see also: Kütükoğlu (1962), pp. 11, 200, Kütükoğlu (1975), pp. 128–45. MD 7, p. 725, no. 1988 (978/1570–1).
27. MD 6, p. 355, no. 761 (972/1564–5).
28. On Ottoman influence in the Persian Gulf region compare Orhonlu (1967), Mandaville (1970), Orhonlu (1970), Özbaran (1971), Özbaran (1972), Özbaran (1977).
29. MD 14, p. 385, no. 542 (978/1570–1).
30. MD 23, p. 163, no. 341 (981/1573–4).
31. Hammer-Purgstall (1963), vol. 4, p. 52 ff.
32. MD 27, p. 115, no. 271 (983/1575–6); MD 31, p. 45, no. 115 (985/1577–8).
33. MD 42, p. 175, no. 553 (988/1580–1).
34. MD 43, p. 114, no. 211 (988/1580–1); MD 42, p. 176, no. 554 (988/1580–1); p. 282, no. 868 (989/1581).
35. Evliya Çelebi (1896–1938), vol. 9, p. 702.

36. MD 7, p. 980, no. 2717 (976/1568–9).
37. MD 6, p. 313, no. 665 (972/1564–5).
38. MD 6, p. 17, no. 39 (972/1564–5).
39. Niewohner-Eberhard (1975), pp. 103–27. In this context, the regulations concerning the burial of Iranian Shi'is near the mausolea of the Caliph 'Alī and Imām Ḥusayn, issued by the Ottoman administration in 1564–5 and 1570–1, are also of interest. Before the Ottoman conquest of Iraq it had apparently been customary to bury certain Shi'is in the courtyards of the two sanctuaries; this was prohibited by the Ottoman administration. The argument in favour of this new ruling was religious and not political: supposedly ordinary mortals could never have acquired sufficient merit to justify burial in the proximity of the great saints of Islam. Outside of the sanctuary court, burials remained permissible. But only important personalities, such as members of the Shah's family, were conceded such a privilege; in such cases, the relatives of the deceased could acquire a piece of land suitable for the construction of a mausoleum (MD 6, p. 17, no. 39). However, cemeteries and mausolea were to be located at a considerable distance from the sanctuaries (MD 12, p. 217, no. 450).
40. MD 30, p. 191, no. 449 (985/1577–8).
41. MD 26, p. 241, no. 693 (980/1572–3).
42. MD 24, p. 44, no. 124 (981/1573–4).
43. MD 24, p. 88, no. 234 (981/1573–4).
44. MD 24, p. 44, no. 124 (981/1573–4).
45. Riazul-Islam (1971/1982), vol. 2, p. 310 f. On Transoxania see Ott (1974). Sometimes Iranian pilgrims to Mecca also used the steppe route to the Black Sea. Compare Inalcık (1979–80), p. 464.
46. MD 7, p. 240, no. 667 (975/1567–8); p. 295, no. 838 (975/1567–8).
47. MD 7, p. 241, no. 671 (975/1567–8).
48. MD 27, p. 56, no. 142 (983/1575–6).
49. MD 24, p. 142, no. 389 (987/1579–80). On the Nogay, see Inalcık (1948), pp. 349–402, 360. See also Kurat (1966), *passim*. Inalcık (1948) also contains background information on Ottoman–Tatar relations. On the Nogay, consult also Benningsen, Lemercier-Quelquejay (1976), pp. 203–36. Inalcık assumes that in sixteenth-century Istanbul there was a well-developed 'northern policy', while Benningsen and Lemercier-Quelquejay assume that the Ottoman Sultans were little interested in Kazan and the Nogays. For a more recent restatement of Inalcık's opinions, see Inalcık (1979–80), p. 458 f.
50. Inalcık (1948), p. 368 f.
51. Inalcık (*ibid.*, pp. 391–5) discusses the preparations for a second Astrakhan campaign, which were broken off due to a disagreement with the Tatars. MD 7, p. 984, no. 2722 (about 976/1568–9) is an official letter of the Sultan to the Khan, which advocates a campaign against Astrakhan. The letter insists on the need to keep open the pilgrimage routes. Compare also MD 7, p. 295, no. 838 (975/1568–9). For the interpretation of this important text, see Inalcık (1948), p. 373.
52. MD 7, p. 271, no. 748 (975/1567–8).
53. MD 49, p. 72, no. 250 (991/1583).

54. MD 31, p. 192, no. 431 (985/1577–8).
55. On caravans traversing North Africa, see Raymond (1973–4), vol. 2, p. 470 ff.
56. Compare Hess (1978), p. 96 f.
57. MD 30, p. 182, no. 428 (985/1577–8).
58. MD 30, p. 219, no. 505 (985/1577–8). A safe conduct for all Moroccan pilgrims is found on p. 182 of the same register (no. 428).
59. MD 27, p. 56, no. 142 (983/1575–6).
60. Niewohner-Eberhard (1975), p. 116.
61. Compare MD 6, p. 17, no. 39 (972/1564–5). Niewohner-Eberhard (1975), p. 116.

CHAPTER 7

1. See the article 'Mamlūk' in *EI* by P.M. Holt.
2. Mughul (1965), p. 46.
3. Wüstenfeld (reprint, 1964), vol. 4, p. 300. Mughul (1965), p. 39.
4. Uzunçarşılı (1972), p. 17.
5. *Ibid.*, p. 26. Orhonlu (1974), p. 129 ff.
6. MD 73, p. 12, no. 27 (1003/1594–5).
7. Fleischer (1986), pp. 180, 184–5.
8. MD 23, p. 286, no. 615 (981/1575–6); MD 23, p. 287, no. 616 (981/1575–6).
9. Uzunçarşılı (1972), p. 19 ff.
10. MD 58, p. 201, no. 527 (993/1585).
11. Evliya Çelebi (1896–1938), vol. 9, p. 679.
12. Uzunçarşılı (1972), p. 87.
13. MD 27, p. 403, no. 965 (983/1575–6).
14. MD 75, p. 308, no. 645 (1013/1604–5).
15. MD 14, p. 440, no. 623 (987/1570–1); MD 7, p. 215, no. 595 (975/1567–8).
16. MD 39, p. 51, no. 119 (987/1579–80).
17. Uzunçarşılı (1965), pp. 95–100.
18. Barkan (1980), p. 316.
19. Faroqhi (1973), p. 211.
20. MD 64, p. 11, no. 30 (996/1587–8).
21. MD 91, p. 141, no. 447 (1056/1646–7).
22. MD 58, p. 279, no. 709 (993/1585).
23. MD 60, p. 294, no. 681 (994/1585–6).
24. MD 9, p. 80, no. 210 (972/1564–5).
25. MD 31, p. 245, no. 539 (985/1577–8).
26. MD 58, p. 23, no. 69 (993/1585).
27. MD 24, p. 119, no. 328 (981/1573–4).
28. MD 29, p. 224, no. 513 (984/1576–7).
29. MD 7, p. 81, no. 219 (975/1567–8).
30. MD 92, p. 51, no. 227 (1068/1657–8).
31. MD 17, p. 8, no. 13 (979/1571–2).

32. Uzunçarşılı (1972), p. 23.
33. Peçevî (1980), vol. 1, p. 484 f.
34. MD 27, p. 20, no. 60 (983/1575–6).
35. Braudel (1966), vol. 1, p. 495 ff.
36. Compare Faroqhi (forthcoming).
37. Inalcık (1979–80), pp. 1–66.
38. Arasaratnam (1986), p. 268 f.
39. Das Gupta (1988), p. 110 f.
40. Aghassian, Kévonian (1988), p. 166.
41. Serjeant (1988a), p. 72.
42. Farooqi (1986), pp. 205–9.
43. Subrahmanyam (1988), pp. 503–30.
44. Subrahmanyam (1988), p. 509.
45. Das Gupta (1988), p. 109 f.
46. Serjeant (1988b), p. 149 f.
47. Bouchon (1988), p. 53.
48. Subrahmanyam (1988), p. 510 ff.
49. Thomaz (1988), p. 42.
50. Arasaratnam (1986), p. 294 ff.
51. Sahillioğlu (1978), p. 13 f.
52. Masters (1988), p. 192.
53. The expression 'provisionism' for one of the basic components of Ottoman economic thinking was employed by Mehmet Genç at a lecture before the Congress for Turkish Social and Economic History, Munich, 1986. On 'provisionism' in late eighteenth-century France compare Vovelle (1980), p. 228 ff.
54. On the interpretation of this text see Inalcık (1970), pp. 207–18 and Masters (1988), p. 192 ff.
55. MD 47, p. 122, no. 308 (990/1582); MD 27, p. 20, no. 60 (983/1575).
56. MD 47, p. 123, no. 309 (990/1582).
57. MD 67, p. 111, no. 298 (999/1590–1).
58. MD 67, p. 113, no. 305 (999/1590–1).
59. Braudel (1966), vol. 1, pp. 383–421. On taxes collected in Yemeni ports, compare Sahillioğlu (1985), pp. 287–319.
60. MD 67, p. 131, no. 352 (999/1590–1).
61. Masters (1988), p. 194.
62. MD 70, p. 68, no. 141 (1001/1592–3).
63. Peçevî (1980), vol. 1, p. 484 f.
64. Subrahmanyam (1988), p. 505.
65. MD 6, p. 122, no. 256 (972/1564–5).
66. Shaw (1962), p. 253.
67. MZ 3, p. 179 (984/1576–7).
68. Shaw (1962), p. 261 ff.
69. Ibn D̲j̲ubayr (1949–51), p. 79 f., Burton, vol. 1 (reprint, 1964), p. 209.
70. MD 6, p. 128, no. 269 (972/1564–5).
71. MM 5310 (1015–16/1606–8).
72. MD 58, p. 158, no. 418 (993/1585).

73. Faroqhi (forthcoming) contains a further discussion of Red Sea transportation.
74. MD 30, p. 299, no. 691 (985/1577–8).
75. Arasaratnam (1988), p. 534.
76. Evliya Çelebi (1896–1938), vol. 9, p. 716.
77. *Ibid.*, p. 966.
78. On sixteenth-century Muzayrib compare Bakhit (1982), p. 113. MD 88, p. 52, no. 123 (1047/1637–8). According to our text, buyer and seller both had to pay 15 *aḳče* for goods worth 1 ghurush, or a total of 30 *aḳče*. According to Sahillioğlu (1964), p. 229, in 1637–8 the Galata exchange rate was 120 *aḳče* to 1 *riyāl ghurush*. The equivalent for Damascus is unknown, so that we have used the Galata exchange rate: 30:120 equals 25 per cent.
79. Ochsenwald (1980), p. 22.
80. Ḥibri (1975), pp. 111–28; (1976), pp. 55–72; (1978), pp. 147–62. See particularly (1975), p. 125.
81. Evliya Çelebi (1896–1938), vol. 9, p. 554.
82. *Ibid.*, p. 570.
83. Mehemmed Edib (1825), p. 122.
84. Evliya Çelebi (1896–1938), vol. 9, pp. 779, 782. He also notes that Meccan women performed few household duties (p. 782).
85. *Ibid.*, p. 776.
86. *Ibid.*, p. 712.
87. *Ibid.*, p. 713.
88. *Ibid.*, p. 714 f.
89. Vryonis (1981), pp. 196–226.
90. Evliya Çelebi (1896–1938), vol. 9, p. 186. Mehlan (1938), pp. 10–49.
91. Evliya Çelebi (1896–1938), vol. 10, p. 612.
92. Evliya Çelebi (1896–1938), vol. 9, p. 713.
93. *Ibid.*, p. 713. Kissling (1975), pp. 342–55 and Hattox (1985).
94. Hattox (1985), p. 102 and Evliya Çelebi (1896–1938), vol. 9, p. 796.
95. Rogers, Ward (1988), p. 140 ff.
96. Evliya Çelebi (1896–1938), vol. 10, p. 445.
97. Rogers, Ward (1988), p. 140.
98. Evliya Çelebi (1896–1938), vol. 9, p. 776.
99. Pearson (1988), p. 462.
100. For the problems of foreign trade in general, compare Curtin (1984), Mehta (1974), Habib (1990).

CONCLUSION

1. A stimulating discussion of the problems touched upon here is İslamoğlu-İnan (1987), pp. 1–26.
2. This section owes a good deal to Said (1979). When reading Said's book, however, one may easily come to the conclusion that racism and ethnocentrism are inherent characteristics of European and American studies on 'the Orient', and that all attempts to escape this paradigm are

doomed in advance. The present author is less pessimistic in her assumptions, whether with justification or not is hard to judge at present. But if Said's assessment is totally correct, European/American historians and philologists dealing with the Middle East, who do not wish to comport themselves as racists and ethnocentrists, would be well advised to change their area of specialization. In any case, Said's work is a necessary corrective against naive assumptions about steadily progressing and 'value-free' scholarship.

3. This section owes a great deal to discussions with Halil Berktay.
4. Strangely enough, quite a few Turkish scholars, particularly of the older generation, seem to share these views. Compare Uzunçarşılı (1948), still a basic work of reference.
5. As one among many studies based on these assumptions, see Ward and Rustow (eds.) (1964).
6. An admittedly extreme example of this tendency is Romano (1980), pp. 22–75. See also Weber (1976).
7. For a coherent statement of these views, see Lewis (1968), p. 28. Lewis's statements are based on the work of Halil Inalcık, Fuat Köprülü and Sabri Ülgener.
8. I am grateful to Engin Akarlı for a stimulating discussion of these matters. See also Labrousse *et alii* (1970), vol. 2, particularly pp. 119–60 and 567–600; these sections are the work of Pierre Goubert. On the *ancien régime* in the Ottoman Empire see Cezar (1986).
9. On these issues compare Kortepeter (1979), pp. 229–46.
10. Rutter (1928) provides a vivid description of the transition from Sherifian to Sa'udi rule in Mecca.
11. Hodgson (1974), vol. 1, pp. 365–92.
12. Ochsenwald (1984) defends the view that in the Hejaz 'religion' determined 'politics'. However he strictly limits his claims to the seventy-odd years covered by his study.
13. For a recent treatment of this problem in a French context, compare Braudel (1986).
14. Shaw (1976–7), vol. 2, pp. 226–30.
15. Genç, 49/4 (1984), pp. 52–61, 50/5 (1984), pp. 86–93.
16. Braudel (1979), vol. 2, pp. 402–16. On the economic importance of the pilgrimage routes compare also Raymond (1985), p. 48.
17. Erim (1984, 1991). I thank the author for allowing me to read her unpublished dissertation.
18. Hattox (1985), Faroqhi (1986) (a).
19. Raymond (1973–4), vol. 1, pp. 143–6.
20. Farooqi (1988), pp. 198–220.
21. Inalcık (1948), pp. 349–402.
22. Dengler (1978), pp. 229–44; Bates (1978), pp. 245–60; Peirce (1988), pp. 43–82.
23. Uzunçarşılı (1945), p. 181 ff.
24. See Lapidus (1984), pp. 77 f. and 131. The author discusses the Mamluk period in Egypt and Syria; he does not, however, conclude that

the Mamluk rulers had no need for legitimation beyond the claim that their rule averted anarchy.

25. Abou-El-Haj (1974), pp. 131–7.
26. Aktepe (1958), p. 41 ff.
27. Göçek (1987).
28. Kreutel (1948–52); Faroqhi (1991).

Bibliography

ARCHIVAL SOURCES

The documentation used in this book has been taken largely from the Başbakanlık Arşivi in Istanbul, also known as the Osmanlı Arşivi. The principal sections used were the Mühimme Defterleri (Registers of Important Affairs) and Maliyeden Müdevver ('Transferred from the Financial Office'). In the MDs all sultanic rescripts issued by the Sultan's Council (*diwān-ı humāyūn*) were entered; the members of this council were the viziers, the head of the Finance Office (*defterdār*) and the Chancellor (*nis͟hāndjı*). The series of extant registers begins in the middle of the sixteenth century, although a few isolated specimens have been preserved from the first half of the century as well. These registers are richest for the late sixteenth and early seventeenth centuries, although even within this period, certain years are amply documented and the records of others must have been lost.

About 800 documents from the MDs were informative enough to merit a closer analysis. Almost all this material relates to the period 1565 to 1605. Remarkably enough, the restoration projects of Aḥmed I (reigned 1603–17) and Murād III (reigned 1623–40), which must have been the subject of ample correspondence, are passed over in almost total silence. Presumably from the seventeenth century onwards, more and more special purpose registers were created. Public construction was in all probability documented in a separate series, which later either was lost or may yet emerge in the course of future cataloguing. But even as things stand now, the documentation is so ample that only a small part of the rescripts consulted could be mentioned in the notes.

Among the financial records of Maliyeden Müdevver, about 50 registers yielded usable data for our purposes. Most useful were the Syrian and Egyptian provincial accounts, also known as 'Budgets'. The Egyptian sources all concern the years around 1600, while the Syrian accounts are distributed over the entire seventeenth century. In both instances the accounts record only the money paid out for the 'official' sector of the caravan, that is for officers and men in addition to horses, camels and ammunition. Beduin subsidies have also been included. We also find several documents concerning foundations whose aim it was to succour the inhabitants of the Holy Cities. There is additional information on these foundations in the tax registers of the sixteenth century (section Tapu Tahrir of the Başbakanlık Arşivi in Istanbul). The foundation descriptions contained in these registers include information on beneficiaries, and the 1546 register of Istanbul foundations published by Barkan and Ayverdi (Istanbul, 1970) is especially rich in this respect.

The *ḳāḍī* registers of Balkan and Anatolian cities, by contrast, contain few court cases directly relevant to the pilgrimage. The court registers of Cairo and Damascus contain large quantities of hitherto unused information; unfortunately nothing is known of the whereabouts of the registers of Mecca and Medina.

Başbakanlık Arşivi, Mühimme Defterleri (MD): 3, 5, 6, 7, 9, 10, 12, 14, 16, 17, 18, 19, 21, 22, 23, 24, 26, 27, 28, 29, 30, 31, 33, 34, 35, 36, 39, 40, 42, 43, 46, 47, 48, 49, 51, 52, 53, 55, 58, 60, 61, 62, 64, 67, 68, 69, 70, 71, 73, 74, 75, 76, 78, 80, 81, 82, 85, 86, 88, 89, 90, 91, 92, 93, 94, 95, 96

Başbakanlık Arşivi, Mühimme Zeyli (MZ): 1, 2, 3, 4, 5, 6, 9

Başbakanlık Arşivi, Maliyeden Müdevver (MM): 7056, 5671, 5672, 5162, 5658, 5672, 3651, 6005, 5592, 1806, 7603, 4108, 2521, 1653, 1003, 2520, 5568, 880, 2916, 1308, 1286, 1290, 4895, 926, 927, 872, 86, 876, 2525, 932, 1647, 2530, 1644, 2459, 2535, 4345, 1645, 4345, 956, 2394, 2396, 952, 943, 1011, 4901, 941, 1007, 4475, 875, 4901, 241

Ḳāḍīregister, Çorum Belediye Kütüphanesi, Çorum: Register No 1741–2 (Çorum)

PRIMARY SOURCES

['Abd al-Karīm], *The Memoirs of Khojeh Abdulkurreem, A Cashmerian of Distinction*, trans. by Francis Gladwin (London, 1793)

[Abū al-Faḍl], *The Akbar Nama of Abu-l-Fazl*, trans. by Henry Beveridge, Bibliotheca Indica, 3 vols (Calcutta, 1898–1939)

Muṣṭafā 'Ālī's *Description of Cairo of 1599, Text, Transliteration, Translation, Notes*, trans. and ed. by Andreas Tietze, Österr. Akademie der Wissenschaften, Philosophisch-hist. Klasse, Denkschriften, vol. 120, Forschungen zur islamischen Philologie und Kulturgeschichte vol. V (Vienna, 1975)

Ali Bey [Domingo Badia y Leblich], *Voyages d'Ali Bey El-Abbasi en Afrique et en Asie pendant les années 1803–1807*, 2 vols (Paris, 1814)

Anonymous author, *Manakıb-ı Hacı Bektâş-ı Veli 'Vilâyet-nâme'*, ed. by Abdülbaki Gölpınarlı (Istanbul, 1958)

—— 'A description of the yeerely voyage or pilgrimage of the Mahumitans, Turkes and Moores unto Mecca in Arabia', in *The Principal Navigations, Voyages, Traffiques and Discoveries of the English Nation*, ed. by Richard Hakluyt, 12 vols (reprint, Glasgow, 1901), vol. 5, pp. 329–65

—— *Das Vilâyet-nâme des Hâdschim Sultan, Eine türkische Heiligenlegende*, ed. and trans. by Rudolf Tschudi (Berlin, 1914)

Mohamed Arkoun, Ezzedine Guellouz, Abdelaziz Frikha, *Pèlerinage à la Mecque* (Lausanne, Paris and Tunis, 1977)

'Abdu-l-qādir Ibni Mulūk Shāh, called al-Badāōnī, *Muntakhabut-tawārikh*, trans. by George S.A. Ranking *et al.*, A.D. Oriental Series, 3 vols., (reprint, Delhi, 1973)

Ömer Lütfi Barkan, '933–934 (M 1527–1528) Malî Yılına Ait bir Bütçe Örneği', *IFM*, 15, 1–4 (1953–4), 251–329

—— '1079–1080 (1669–1670) Malî Yılına Ait bir Osmanlı Bütçesi ve Ekleri', *IFM*, 17, 1–4 (1955–6), 225–303

—— 974–975 (M 1567–1568) Malî Yılına Ait bır Osmanlı Bütçesi', *IFM*, 19, 1–4 (1957–8), 277–332

—— '1070–1071 (1660–1661) Tarihi Osmanlı Bütçesi ve bir Mukayese', *IFM*, 17 (1955–6), 304–47

—— '954–955 (1547–1548) Malî Yılına Ait bir Osmanlı Bütçesi', *IFM*, 19 (1957–8), 219–76

—— 'Istanbul Saraylarına ait Muhasebe Defterleri', *Belgeler, Türk Tarih Belgeleri Dergisi*, IX, 13 (1979), 1–380: 'Defter-i müsevvedât-ı in'âm ve tasaddukaat ve teşrifât ve irsâliyât ve adet ve nukeriye ve gayruhu vâcib-i sene tis'a ve tis'a mie (909), (26.VI. 1503–13. VI. 1504), p. 296 ff.

Ömer Lütfi Barkan, Ekrem Hakkı Ayverdi, *Istanbul Vakıfları Tahrîr Defteri, 953 (1546) Târîhli*, Istanbul Fetih Cemiyeti Istanbul Enstitüsü 61 (Istanbul, 1970)

John Lewis Burckhardt, *Travels to Syria and the Holy Land* (London, 1822)

—— *Travels in Arabia, Comprehending an Account of those Territories in Hedjaz which the Mohammedans regard as Sacred*, 2 vols. (London, 1829)

Richard Burton, *Personal Narrative of a Pilgrimage to al-Madinah & Mecca*, 2 vols. (reprint, New York, 1964)

[Ogier Ghiselin von Busbeck], *Vier Briefe aus der Türkei von Oghier Ghiselin von Busbeck*, trans. and comm. by Wolfram von den Steinen (Erlangen, 1926)

[Ca'fer Efendi], *Risāle-i Mi'māriyye, An Early Seventeenth-Century Treatise on Architecture*, ed. by Howard Crane (Leiden, 1987)

Caïd ben Chérif, *Aux villes saintes de l'Islam* (Paris, 1919)

el-Hadj Nacir ed dine E. Dinet and el-Hadj Sliman ben Ibrahim Baâmer, *Le pèlerinage de la Maison sacrée d'Allah*, 2 vols (Paris, 1962)

'Abd al-Kādir al-Djazarī, *Durar al-fawā'id al-munaẓẓama fī akhbār alḥādjdj ve ṭarīḳ Makka al-mu'aẓẓama*, (Mecca, 1384/1964–5)

Charles Doughty, *Travels in Arabia Deserta*, introduced by T.E. Lawrence, 2 vols. (reprint, New York, 1979)

M. Ertuğrul Düzdağ, *Şeyhülislâm Ebusuûd Efendi Fetvaları Isığında 16. Asır Türk Hayatı* (Istanbul, 1972)

Esat Efendi, introduced by Yavuz Ercan, '(Her yıl gelenek haline gelmiş olan) Sürre-i Hümayun Gönderme Töreni', *Tarih ve Toplum*, 3 (1985), 377–80

Evliya Çelebi, *Seyahatnamesi*, 10 vols. (Istanbul, 1314/1896–1938)

—— *Im Reiche des Goldenen Apfels, Des türkischen Weltenbummlers Evliya Çelebi denkwürdige Reise in das Giaurenland und in die Stadt und Festung Wien, anno 1665*, trans. and introduced by Richard Kreutel (Graz, Vienna and Cologne, 1957)

Ferīdūn Beg, *Medjmū'a-ı münshe'at-ı selāṭīn*, 2 vols. (Istanbul, 1275/1858–9)

Giovanni Finati, *Narrative of the Life and Adventures of Giovanni Finati, Native of Ferrara*, trans. and ed. by William John Banks Esq., 2 vols. (London, 1830)

[Gul-badan Begam], *The History of Humāyūn (Humāyūn-nāma) by Gulbadan begam (Princess Rose-body)*, trans. and introduced by Annette S. Beveridge (reprint, Delhi, 1972)

Abū'l-Ḥasan'Alī b. Abī Bakr al-Ḥarawī, *Guide des lieux du pèlerinage*, trans. by Janine Sourdel-Thomime (Damascus, 1957)

Hassan Mohammed El-Hawary and Gaston Wiet, *Matériaux pour un Corpus Inscriptionum Arabicarum, Quatrième partie: Arabie, Inscriptions et Monuments de la Mecque, Haram et Ka'ba*, vol. 1, fasc. 1, revised by Nikita Elisséef (Cairo, 1985)

Colin Heywood, 'The Red Sea Trade and Ottoman Wakf Support for the Population of Mecca and Medina in the Later Seventeenth Century', in *La vie sociale dans les provinces arabes à l'époque ottomane*, ed. by Abdeljelil Temimi, 3 vols (Zaghouan, 1988), vol. 3, pp. 165–84

['Abd al-Raḥmān Ḥibrī], 'Menasik-i mesalik', ed. by Sevim Ilgürel, *Tarih Enstitüsü Dergisi*, 6 (1975), 111–28, *Tarih Dergisi*, 30 (1976), 55–72, *Tarih Dergisi*, 31 (1978), 147–62

[Ibn 'Abd Rabbih], 'A Description of the Two Sanctuaries of Islam by Ibn 'Abd Rabbihi (†940)', trans. and comm. by Muḥammad Shafí', in *'Adjabnāme, A Volume of Oriental Studies presented to Edward G. Browne*, ed. by T.W. Arnold and Reynold A. Nicholson (reprint, Amsterdam, 1973), pp. 416–38

[Ibn Djubayr], *Les voyages d'Ibn Jobair*, trans. by Maurice Gaudefroy-Demombynes (Paris, 1949–51)

[Ibn Djubayr], *The Travels of Ibn Jubayr*, trans. by R.C. Broadhurst (London, 1952)

[Ibn Malīḥ], *Labsal dessen, der bei Tag und bei Nacht reist, Ibn Mālīḥs (sic) Uns as-sārī was-sārib, Ein marokkanisches Pilgerbuch des frühen 17. Jahrhunderts*, trans. and comm. by Sabine Schupp, Islamkundliche Untersuchungen, vol. 106 (Berlin, 1985)

Ibn Ṭūlūn and Ibn Ǧum'a, *Les gouverneurs de Damas sous les Mamlouks et les premiers Ottomans (658–1156/1260–1744)*, trans. by Henri Laoust (Damascus, 1952)

Cassim Izzeddine, *Organisation et réformes sanitaires au Hedjaz et le Pèlerinage de 1329 (1911–12)* (Constantinople, 1913)

—— *Les epidémies de choléra au Hedjaz* (Constantinople, 1918)

Kātib Čelebi, Djihānnumā (Istanbul, 1145/1732)

—— *Fedhleke*, 2 vols. (Istanbul, 1286–7/1869–71)

H. Kazem Zadeh, 'Relation d'un pèlerinage à la Mecque en 1910–11', *Revue du monde musulman*, 6, 19 (1912), 144–227

T.C. Keane (Hajj Mohammed Amin), *Six Months in Mecca: An Account of the Mohammedan Pilgrimage to Meccah, Recently Accomplished by an Englishman Professing Mohammedanism* (London, 1881)

Ḳuṭb al-Dīn Muḥammad b. Aḥmad al-Makkī, 'Al-i'lām be-'alām balad Allāh al-ḥarām', trans. by Bāḳī (?) in 1006/1597–8. Compare Gustav Flügel, *Die arabischen, persischen und türkischen Handschriften der kaiserlich-königlichen Hofbibliothek zu Wien*, 3 vols. (Vienna, 1865–7), vol. 2, p. 123 f, No. 895

T.E. Lawrence, *Seven Pillars of Wisdom, a Triumph* (London and Toronto, 1935)

Vincent le Blanc, *Les voyages fameux du Sieur Vincent le Blanc, marseillois* (Paris, 1658)

Heinrich von Maltzan, *Meine Wallfahrt nach Mekka*, ed. by Gernot Giertz (reprint, Tübingen, 1982)

Henry Maundrell, *A Journey from Aleppo to Jerusalem in 1697*, introduced by David Howell (reprint, Beirut, 1963)

El-Hadj Mehemmed Edib ben Mehemmed, derviche, 'Itineraire de Constantinople à la Mecque (Extrait de l'ouvrage turc intitulé Kitab Menassik el-Hadj), trans. by M. Bianchi, in *Recueil de Mémoires de la Société de Géographie* (Paris, 1825), pp. 81–169

'Abd al-Ghānī al-Nābulsī, *Al-ḥaḳīḳa wa'l-madjāz fī'l-riḥla ilā bilād al-Shām wa Miṣr* (Cairo, 1986)

Na'īmā, *Tarīkh-i Na'īmā*, 6 vols. (n.p. [Istanbul], n.d.)

[Naṣīr-i Khosraw], *Sefernameh, Le voyage de Nassiri Khosrau, en Syrie, en Palestine, en Egypte, en Arabie et en Perse*, trans. by Charles Schefer (Paris, 1881)

Gérard de Nerval, *Reise in den Orient*, ed. by Norbert Miller and Friedhelm Kemp, trans. by Anjuta Aigner-Dünnwald, introduced by Christoph Kunze (Munich, 1986)

Carsten Niebuhr, *Reisebeschreibung nach Arabien und andern umliegenden Ländern* (Copenhagen, 1772)

—— *Description de l'Arabie, faite sur des observations propres et des airs recueillis dans les lieux mêmes* (Amsterdam, 1774–80)

Mouradgea d'Ohsson, *Tableau général de l'Empire Ottoman, divisée en deux parties, Dont l'une comprend la Législation Mahometane; l'autre l'Histoire de l'Empire Ottoman*, 7 vols. (Paris, 1787–1824)

Halit Ongan, *Ankara'nın İki Numaralı Şer'iye Sicili*, Türk Tarih Kurumu Yayınları, 14, 4 (Ankara, 1974)

Peçevî Ibrahim Efendi, *Tarîh-i Peçevî*, introduced by Fahri Ç. Derin and Vahit Çabuk, 2 vols. (reprint, Istanbul, 1980)

[Joseph Pitts], 'An Account by Joseph Pitts of his Journey from Algiers to Mecca and Medina and back', in *The Red Sea and Adjacent Countries at the Close of the Seventeenth Century, as described by Joseph Pitts, William Daniel and Charles Jacques Poncet*, ed. by Sir William Foster CIE (London, 1949), pp. 3–49

H. St John [Abdullah] Philby, *Forty Years in the Wilderness* (London, 1957)

Richard Pococke, *A Description of the East and Some Other Countries*, 2 (London, 1743), vol. 1 *Observations on Egypt*

Meḥmed Rāshid, *Tārīkh-i Rāshid*, 5 vols. (Istanbul, 1282/1865–6)

Riazul-Islam, *A Calendar of Documents on Indo–Persian Relations (1500–1750)*, 2 vols. (Teheran and Karachi, 1971, 1982)
Ibrāhīm Rifa'at Pascha, *Mir'at al-Ḥaramayn*, 2 vols. (Cairo, 1344/1925)
Léon Roches, *Trente-deux ans à travers l'Islam (1832–1864)*, 2 vols. (Paris, 1887), vol. 2 *Mission à La Mecque, Le maréchal Bugeaud en Afrique*
Eldon Rutter, *The Holy Cities of Arabia*, 2 vols. (London, 1928)
Eyyüb Ṣabrī, *Mir'at al-Ḥarmeyn*, 3 vols. (Istanbul, 1301–6/1883–9)
Sa'd al-Dīn, *Tādj al-tewārīkh* (Istanbul, 1279/1862–3)
Saî Çelebi, *Tezkiretü'l Bünyan, Mimar Sinan'ın Kendi Ağzından Hayat ve Eserleri*, ed. by Sadık Erdem (Istanbul, 1988)
Ulrich Jasper Seetzen, *Reisen durch Syrien, Palästina, Phönicien, die Transjordan-Länder, Arabia Petraea und Unter-Aegypten*, ed. and comm. by Fr. Kruse (Berlin, 1854)
Stanford Shaw, *The Budget of Ottoman Egypt 1005–1006/1596–97)* (The Hague and Paris, 1968)
Azmat Sheikh, *The Holy Mecca and Medina – Saudi Arabia* (Lahore, 1980)
Silaḥdār Fındıḳlılı Meḥmed Agha, *Silaḥdār Tārīkhi*, ed. by Ahmed Refik, 2 vols. (Istanbul, 1928)
C. Snouck Hurgronje, *Mekka in the Latter Part of the 19th Century, Daily Life, Customs and Learning, The Moslims of the Eastern Archipelago*, trans. by J.H. Monahan (London and Leiden, 1931)
Süheylī (Suheilî) Efendi, 'Tārīkh-i Mekke-i mükerrime', see Flügel, *Handschriften Wien*, vol. 2, p. 125, No. 896
Sultan Jahan Begam, The Nawab, *The Story of a Pilgrimage to Hijaz* (Calcutta, 1909)
Ṭashköprüzāde, *Eš-Šaqâ'iq en-no'mânijje von Ṭašköprüzâde, enthaltend die Biographien der türkischen und im osmanischen Reiche wirkenden Gelehrten, Derwisch-Scheihs und Ärzte von der Regierung Sultan Otmān's bis zu der Sülaimân's des Grossen*, trans. and comm. by Osman Rescher (Istanbul, 1927)
Jean Thévenot, *Voyage du Levant*, ed. and introduced by Stéphane Yérasimos (Paris, 1980)
Abdel Magid Turki, Hadj Rabah Souami, *Récits de pèlerinage à la Mecque, Étude analytique, Journal d'un pélerin*, introduced by Lakhdar Souami (Paris, 1979)
Feridun Nafız Uzluk, *Fatih Devrinde Karaman Eyâleti Vakıfları Fihristi, Tapu ve Kadastro Umum Müdürlüğü Arşivindeki Deftere Göre*, Vakıflar Umum Müdürlüğü Neşriyatı (Ankara, 1958)
Ludovico di Varthéma, *The Travels of Ludovico di Varthéma*, ed. by

John Winter Jones, Georges Percy Badger, Hakluyt Society, I. Series No. XXXII (New York, 1863)

A[rchibald] J.B. Wavell, *A Modern Pilgrim in Mecca and a Siege in Sanaa* (London, 1912)

Johann Wild, *Reysbeschreibung eines gefangenen Christen Anno 1604*, trans. and introduced by Georg A. Narciss and Karl Teply (Stuttgart, 1964)

Meḥmed Yemīnī, 'Kitāb-ı Faḍā'il-i Mekke-i mu'aẓẓama', see Flügel, *Handschriften Wien*, vol. 2, p. 125 f., No. 897, who describes this work as anonymous.

SECONDARY SOURCES (MECCA, MEDINA, THE PILGRIMAGE)

A. 'Ankawi, 'The Pilgrimage to Mecca in Mamluk Times', *Arabian Studies*, I (1974), 146–70.

C.F. Beckingham, 'The Date of Pitts's Pilgrimage to Mecca', *Journal of the Royal Asiatic Society*, (1950), p. 112 f.

—— 'Hakluyt's Description of the Ḥajj', *Arabian Studies*, IV (1977), 75–80

Mustafa Bilge, 'Arabia in the Work of Awliya Chalaby (The XVIIth Century Turkish Muslim Traveller)', in *Sources for the History of Arabia*, vol. I, part 2, ed. by Abdelgadir Mahmoud Abdalla, Sami Al-Sakkar, Richard T. Mortel, Abd Al-Rahman, T. Al-Ansari (Riyad, 1979), pp. 213–27

Mohammed Jamil Brownson, 'Mecca: The Socio-Economic Dynamics of the Sacred City', in *Hajj Studies*, vol. 1, ed. by Ziauddin Sarkar and M. Zaki Badawi (London, n.d.), pp. 117–36

Adil A. Bushnak, 'The Hajj Transportation System', in *Hajj Studies*, vol. 1, ed. by Ziauddin Sarkar and M. Zaki Badawi (London, n.d.), pp. 87–116

Dr Firmin Duguet, *Le pélerinage de la Mecque* (Paris, 1932)

Kurt Erdmann, 'Ka'bah-Fliesen', *Ars Orientalis*, 3 (1959), 192–7

Emel Esin, *Mekka und Medina*, trans. by Eva Bornemann, photographs by Haluk Doğanbey (Frankfurt, 1963)

—— 'Un manuscrit illustré representant les sanctuaires de la Mecque et Médine et le dome du Mi-Radj, à l'époque des Sultans turcs Selim et Süleyman Ier (H.922–74/1516–66)', in *Les provinces arabes et leurs sources documentaires à l'époque ottomane, partie française et anglaise*, ed. by Abdeljelil Temimi (Tunis, 1984), pp. 175–90

—— 'The Renovations Effected, in the Ka'bah Mosque, by the

Ottoman Sultan Selim II (H.974–82/1566–74)', *Revue d'histoire maghrébine*, 12, 39–40 (1985), 225–33

Richard Ettinghausen, 'Die bildliche Darstellung der Ka'aba im Islamischen Kulturkreis', *Zeitschrift der Deutschen Morgenländischen Gesellschaft*, 86–7 (NF 11–12) (1932–4) 111–37

—— 'Mughal–Ottoman Relations: A Study of Political and Diplomatic Relations between Mughal India and the Ottoman Empire 1556–1748', PhD dissertation, Madison, Wisconsin, 1986

Naim R. Farooqi, 'Moguls, Ottomans and Pilgrims: Protecting the Routes to Mecca in the Sixteenth and Seventeenth Centuries', *The International History Review*, X, 2 (1988), 198–220

Suraiya Faroqhi, 'Ottoman Documents concerning the Hajj during the Sixteenth and Seventeenth centuries', in *La vie sociale dans les provinces arabes à l'époque ottomane*, ed. by Abdeljelil Temimi, 3 vols. (Zaghouan, 1988), vol. 3, pp. 151–64

—— 'Anatolian Townsmen as Pilgrims to Mecca: Some Evidence from the Sixteenth–Seventeenth Centuries', in *Rencontres de L'Ecole du Louvre, Süleyman le Magnifique et son temps*, ed. Gilles Veinstein (Paris, 1992), pp. 309–26

Zaki M.A. Farsi, *Makkah al mukarramah, City and Hajj Guide* (Jeddah, 1408/1987–8)

—— *Map and guide of Almadinah almunawwarah* (Jeddah, n.d.)

Carol G. Fisher and Alan Fisher, 'Illustrations of Mecca and Medina in Islamic Manuscripts', in *Islamic Art from Michigan Collections*, ed. by Carol G. Fisher and Alan Fisher (East Lansing, Michigan, 1982), pp. 40–7

Maurice Gaudefroy-Demombynes, *Contribution à l'étude du Pèlerinage de la Mecque (Note d'histoire religieuse)*, PhD thesis, *l'Université de Paris* (Paris, 1923)

Gerald de Gaury, *Rulers of Mecca* (London, 1951)

Nejat Göyünc, 'Some documents concerning the Ka'aba in the 16th century', in *Studies in the History of Arabia*, vol. 1, 2, *Sources for the History of Arabia*, ed. by Abdelgadir Mahmoud Abdalla *et al.* (Riyad, 1979), pp. 177–81

Jacques Jomier OP, *Le maḥmal et la caravane égyptienne des pèlerins de la Mecque (XIIIe–XXe siècles)*, Publications de l'Institut Français d'Archéologie Orientale, XX (Cairo, 1953)

—— 'Le Maḥmal du sultan Qānṣūh al-Ghūrī (Début XVIe siècle)', *Annales Islamologiques*, XI (1972), 183–8

C.M. Kortepeter, 'A Source for the History of Ottoman–Hijaz Relations: The *Seyahatnâme* of Awliya Chalaby and the Rebellion of *Sharif* Sa'd b. Zayd in the Years 1671–72/1081–82', in: *Sources for the History of Arabia*, vol. 1, parts 1, 2, ed. by Abdelgadir Mahmoud Abdalla *et al.* (Riyad, 1979) pp. 229–46

David Edwin Long, *The Hajj Today, A Survey of the Contemporary Makkah Pilgrimage* (Albany, NY, 1979)

Ghazy Abdul Wahed Makky, 'Pilgrim Accommodation in Mecca: Spatial Structures, Costs and National Origins', in *Hajj Studies*, vol. 1, ed. by Ziauddin Sarkar and M.A. Zaki Badawi (London, n.d.), pp. 59–72

—— *Mecca, The Pilgrimage City, A Study of Pilgrim Accommodation* (London, 1978)

Ayyub Malik, 'Developments in Historic and Modern Islamic Cities', in *Hajj Studies*, vol. 1, ed. by Ziauddin Sarkar and M.A. Zaki Badawi (London, n.d.), pp. 137–61

Sulaiman Mousa, 'T.E. Lawrence and his Arab Contemporaries', *Arabian Studies*, VII (1985), 7–22

William Ochsenwald, *The Hijaz Railroad* (Charlottesville, Virginia, 1980)

—— *Religion, Society and the State in Arabia, The Hijaz under Ottoman Control 1840–1908* (Columbus, Ohio, 1984)

Francis E. Peters, *Jerusalem and Mecca. The Typology of the Holy City in the Near East*, New York University Studies in Near Eastern Civilization, No. 11 (New York, 1986)

A. Popovic, 'Le pèlerinage à la Mecque des musulmans des régions yougoslaves', in *Mélanges d'islamologie dédiés à la mémoire de A. Abel*, 2 vols. (Brussels, n.d., probably 1974), vol. 2, Correspondance d'Orient, No. 13, Publications du Centre pour l'Etude des Problèmes du Monde musulman contemporain, pp. 335–63

Abdul Karim Rafeq, *The Province of Damascus 1723–1783* (Beirut, 1970)

—— 'New Light on the Transportation of the Damascene Pilgrimage During the Ottoman Period', in *Islamic and Middle Eastern Societies*, ed. by Robert Olson (Brattleboro, Vermont, 1987), pp. 127–36

Augustus Ralli, *Christians at Mecca* (London, 1909)

William R. Roff, 'Sanitation and Security. The Imperial Powers and the Nineteenth Century Hajj', *Arabian Studies*, VI (1982), 143–60

Jean Sauvaget, 'Les caravansérails syriens du ḥadjdj de Constantinople', *Ars Islamica*, IV (1937), 98–121

—— *La mosquée omeyyade de Médine. Etude sur les origines architecturales de la mosquée et de la basilique* (Paris, 1947)

Stanford J. Shaw, *The Financial and Administrative Organization and Development of Ottoman Egypt, 1517–1798* (Princeton, 1962)

Christian Snouck Hurgronje, 'Een mekkaansch gezantschap naar

Atjeh in 1683', in *Verspreide Geschriften*, 7 vols. (Bonn and Leipzig, 1923), vol. 3, pp. 139–47

Sanjay Subrahmanyam, 'Persians, Pilgrims and Portuguese: The Travails of Masulipatnam Shipping in the Western Indian Ocean, 1590–1665', *Modern Asian Studies*, 22, 3 (1988), 503–30

René Tresse, *Le pèlerinage syrien au villes saintes de l'Islam*, PhD thesis, *Université de Paris* (Paris, 1937)

Ismail Hakkı Uzunçarşılı, *Mekke-i mükerreme Emirleri*, Türk Tarih Kurumu Yayınlarından VIII, 59 (Ankara, 1972)

Gilles Veinstein, 'Les pèlerins de la Mecque à travers quelques inventaires après décès ottomans (XVIIe–XVIIIe siècles)', *Revue de l'Occident musulman et de la Méditerranée*, 31, 1 (1981), 63–71

—— 'Les pèlerins de la Mecque à travers quelques actes du Qâdî de Sarajevo (1557–1558)', *Turcica*, XXI–XXIII (1991), *Mélanges Irène Mélikoff*, 473–94.

Ferdinand Wüstenfeld, *Geschichte der Stadt Medina, Im Auszug aus dem Arabischen des Samhūdī, Abhandlungen der historisch-philologischen Klasse der königlichen Gesellschaft der Wissenschaften zu Göttingen*, vol. 9 (Göttingen, 1860)

—— *Geschichte der Stadt Mekka nach den arabischen Chroniken*, 4 vols. (reprint, Beirut, 1964)

OTHER SECONDARY SOURCES

Rifa'at Abou-El-Haj, 'Ottoman Attitudes toward Peace Making: The Karlowitz Case', *Der Islam*, 51, 1 (1974), 131–7

—— 'The Social Uses of the Past: Recent Arab Historiography of Ottoman Rule', *International Journal of Middle East Studies*, 14 (1982), 185–201

—— *The 1703 Rebellion and the Structure of Ottoman Politics* (Leiden, 1984)

Abdul-Rahim Abu-Husayn, *Provincial Leaderships in Syria 1575–1650* (Beirut, 1985)

Doris Behrens-Abouseif, *Fêtes populaires dans le Caire du moyen-age*, Quaderni dell'Instituto Italiano di Cultura per la RAE (Cairo, 1982)

Michel Aghassian, Kéram Kévonian, 'Le commerce arménien dans l'Océan Indien aux 17e et 18e siècles', in *Marchands et hommes d'affaires asiatiques dans l'Océan Indien et la Mer de Chine 13e–20e siècles*, ed. by Denys Lombard and Jean Aubin (Paris, 1988), pp. 155–82

Münir Aktepe, *Patrona Isyanı (1730)*, Istanbul Üniversitesi Edebiyat Fakültesi Yayınları No. 808 (Istanbul, 1958)
Anthony D. Alderson, *The Structure of the Ottoman Dynasty* (Oxford, 1956)
Metin And, *Osmanlı Şenliklerinde Türk Sanatları*, Kültür ve Turizm Bakanlığı Yayınları: 529, Sanat Eserleri Dizisi 2 (Ankara, 1982)
Metin And, *Osmanlı Şenliklerinde Türk Sanatları* (Ankara, 1982).
Sinnappah Arasaratnam, *Merchants, Companies and Commerce on the Coromandel Coast 1650–1740* (Delhi, 1986)
—— 'The Rice Trade in Eastern India 1650–1740', *Modern Asian Studies*, 22, 3 (1988), 531–49
Ibrahim and Cevriye Artuk, *Istanbul Arkeoloji Müzeleri Teşhirdeki Islâmî Sikkeler Kataloğu*, 2 vols., TC Başbakanlık Kültür Yayınları III, 7 (Istanbul 1971, 1974)
Eliyahu Ashtor, 'The Wheat Supply of the Mamluk Kingdom', in *East–West Trade in the Medieval Mediterranean*, ed. Benjamin Kedar (London, 1986), pp. 283–95
Franz Babinger, *Die Geschichtsschreiber der Osmanen und ihre Werke* (Leipzig, 1927)
—— *Mehmed der Eroberer und seine Zeit, Weltenstürmer einer Zeitwende* (Munich, 1953)
—— *Osmanlı Tarih Yazarları ve Eserleri*, trans. and comm. by Coşkun Üçok, Doğumunun 100. Yılında Atatürk Yayınları 44 (Ankara, 1982)
M. Adnan Bakhit, 'Sidon in Mamluk and Early Ottoman Times', *Osmanlı Araştırmaları, The Journal of Ottoman Studies*, III (1982), 53–68 (a)
—— *The Ottoman Province of Damascus in the Sixteenth Century* (Beirut, 1982) (b)
Karl Barbir, 'From Pasha to Efendi: The Assimilation of Ottomans into Damascene Society, 1516–1783', *International Journal of Turkish Studies*, 1, 1 (1979–80), 68–83
—— *Ottoman Rule in Damascus, 1708–1758* (Princeton, NJ, 1980)
Ömer Lütfi Barkan, 'Osmanlı Imparatorluğu 'Bütçe'lerine Dair Notlar', *IFM*, 15, 1–4 (1953–4), pp. 238–50 (a)
—— 'Şehirlerin teşekkül ve inkışafı tarihi bakımından Osmanlı İmparatorluğunda İmâret sitelerinin kuruluş ve işleyiş tarzına âit araştırmalar', *İFM*, 23, 1–2 (1962–3), pp. 239–96.
—— 'Türk Toprak Hukuku Tarihinde Tanzimat ve 1274 (1858) Tarihli Arazi Kanunnamesi', in *Türkiye'de Toprak Meselesi, Toplu Eserler*, 1, ed. Abidin Nesimi *et al.* (Istanbul, 1980), pp. 291–375

Ülkü Ü. Bates, 'Women as Patrons of Architecture in Turkey', in *Women in the Muslim World*, ed. by Lois Beck and Nikki Keddie (Cambridge, Mass., 1978), pp. 245–60

Cavit Baysun, 'Evliya Çelebi', in *IA*, vol. 4, pp. 400–12

—— 'Evliya Çelebi'ye dair Notlar', *Türkiyat Mecmuası*, XII (1955), pp. 257–64

Alexandre Benningsen, Chantal Lemercier-Quelquejay, 'La Moscovie, la Horde Nogay et le problème des communications entre l'Empire Ottoman et l'Asie centrale en 1552–1556', *Turcica,* VIII, 2 (1976), pp. 203–36

Robin Bidwell, *Travellers in Arabia* (London, 1976)

J. Richard Blackburn, 'The Collapse of Ottoman Authority in Yemen, 968/1560–976/1568', *Die Welt des Islams*, XIX, 1–4 (1979), pp. 119–76

Geneviève Bouchon, 'Un microcosme: Calicut au 16e siècle', in *Marchands et hommes d'affaires asiatiques dans l'Océan Indien et la Mer de Chine, 13e–20e siècles*, ed. by Denys Lombard and Jean Aubin (Paris, 1988), pp. 49–58

Fernand Braudel, *La Méditerranée et le monde méditerranéen à l'époque de Philippe II*, 2 vols. (Paris, 1966)

—— *Civilization matérielle, économie et capitalisme, XVe–XVIIIe siècle*, 3 vols. (Paris, 1979)

—— *L'identité de la France*, 3 vols. (Paris, 1986)

Fernand Braudel, Ernest Labrousse *et al.*, *Histoire économique et sociale de la France*, 4 vols. (Paris, 1970), vol. II, *Des derniers temps de l'age seigneurial aux préludes de l'âge industriel (1660–1789)*

Martin van Bruinessen and Hendrik Boeschoten, *Evliya Çelebi in Diyarbekir, The relevant section of the Seyahatname edited with translation, commentary and introduction* (Leiden and New York, 1988)

Richard W. Bulliet, *The Patricians of Nishapur, A Study in Medieval Islamic Social History* (Cambridge, Mass., 1972)

—— *The Camel and the Wheel* (Cambridge, Mass., 1975)

Yavuz Cezar, *Osmanlı Maliyesinde Bunalim ve Değişim Dönemi (XVIIIyy dan Tanzimat'a Mali Tarih*) (Istanbul, 1986)

Philip D. Curtin, *Cross-Cultural Trade in World History* (Cambridge, 1984)

Bistra Cvetkova, 'Les registres des *celepkeşan* en tant que sources pour l'histoire de la Bulgarie et des pays balkaniques', in *Hungaro–Turcica, Studies in Honour of Julius Nemeth* (Budapest, 1976), pp. 325–35

Ashin Das Gupta, 'A Note on the Shipowning Merchants of Surat c. 1700', in *Marchands et hommes d'affaires asiatiques dans l'Océan Indien et la Mer de Chine, 13e–20e siècles*, ed. by Denys Lombard and Jean Aubin (Paris, 1988), pp. 109–16

Jean Delumeau, *Catholicism Between Luther and Voltaire: A New View of the Counter-Reformation*, trans. by Jeremy Moiser, introduced by John Bossy (London and Philadelphia, 1977)

Ian C. Dengler, 'Turkish Women in the Ottoman Empire: The Classical Age', in *Women in the Muslim World*, ed. by Lois Beck and Nikki Keddie (Cambridge, Mass., 1978), pp. 229–44

Michael W. Dols, *The Black Death in the Middle East* (Princeton, NJ, 1977)

Ross Dunn, *The Adventures of Ibn Battuta, A Muslim Traveler of the 14th Century* (Berkeley and Los Angeles, 1986)

Meşkure Eren, *Evliya Çelebi Seyahatnamesi Birinci Cildinin Kaynakları Üzerinde Bir Araştırma* (Istanbul, 1960)

Neşe Erim, 'Onsekizinci Yüzyılda Erzurum Gümrüğü', PhD dissertation, Istanbul, 1984

—— 'Trade, Traders and the State in Eighteenth-Century Erzurum', *New Perspectives on Turkey*, 5–6 (1991), pp. 123–50

Faḍlallāh b. Rūzbihān, *Transoxanien und Turkestan zu Beginn des 16. Jahrhunderts, Das Mihmān-nāma-yi Buhara des Faḍlallāh b. Rūzbihān Hunǧi*, trans. and comm. by Ursula Ott, Islâmkundliche Untersuchungen, vol. 25 (Freiburg, 1974)

Suraiya Faroqhi, 'Social mobility among Ottoman *'ulemā* in the late sixteenth century', *International Journal of Middle East Studies*, 4 (1973), pp. 204–18.

—— 'Camels, Wagons, and the Ottoman State', *International Journal of Middle East Studies*, 14 (1982), pp. 523–39

—— *Towns and Townsmen of Ottoman Anatolia, Trade, Crafts and Food Production in an Urban Setting* (Cambridge, 1984)

—— 'Coffee and Spices: Official Ottoman Reactions to Egyptian Trade in the Later Sixteenth Century', *Wiener Zeitschrift für die Kunde des Morgenlandes*, 76 (1986), *Festschrift Andreas Tietze* . . . pp. 87–93 (a)

—— 'Long-Term Change and the Ottoman Construction Site: A Study of Builders, Wages and Iron Prices', in *Raiyyet Rüsûmu, Essays Presented to Halil Inalcık* . . ., ed. by Bernard Lewis *et al.* (Cambridge, Mass., 1986), pp. 111–26 (b)

—— *Men of Modest Substance, House Owners and House Property in Seventeenth Century Ankara and Kayseri* (Cambridge, 1987)

—— 'Red Sea Trade and Communications as Observed by Evliya Çelebi', *New Perspectives on Turkey*, 5–6 (1991), pp. 87–106

—— 'Ottoman Trade Controls and Supply Policies in the Red Sea Area (1550–1600)' in *The Reign of Süleyman the Magnificent*, ed. Cemal Kafadar (Istanbul, forthcoming)

Caroline Finkel, *The Administration of Warfare: The Ottoman Military Campaigns in Hungary, 1593–1606*, 2 vols., Beihefte zur Zeitschrift für die Kunde des Morgenlandes, vol. 14 (Vienna, 1988)

Cornell Fleischer, *Bureaucrat and Intellectual in the Ottoman Empire, The Historian Mustafa Âli (1541–1600)* (Princeton, NJ, 1986)

Gustav Flügel, *Die arabischen, persischen und türkischen Handschriften der kaiserlich-königlichen Hofbibliothek zu Wien*, 3 vols. (Vienna, 1865–7)

Mehmet Genç, 'XVIII Yüzyılda Osmanlı Ekonomisi ve Savaş', *Yapıt* 49/4 (1984), 52–61, 50/5 (1984), 86–93

Fatma Müge Göçek, *East Encounters West; France and the Ottoman Empire in the Eighteenth Century* (New York and Oxford, 1987)

Tayyib Gökbilgin, *XV–XVI Asırlarda Edirne ve Paşa Livası, Mülkler, Mukataaler*, Istanbul Üniversitesi Edebiyat Fakültesi Yayınlarından 508 (Istanbul, 1952)

Christina Phelps Grant, *The Syrian Desert, Caravans, Travel, Exploration* (London, 1937)

William Griswold, *The Great Anatolian Rebellion 1000–1020/1591–1611* (Berlin, 1983)

Ulrich Haarmann, 'Murtaḍā b. 'Ali b. 'Alawan's Journey through Arabia in 1121/1709', in *Sources for the History of Arabia*, vol. I, part 2, ed. by Abdelgadir Mahmoud Abdallah *et al.* (Riyad, 1979), pp. 247–51

Irfan Habib, 'Merchant Communities in Precolonial India', in *The Rise of Merchant Empires, Long-Distance Trade in the Early Modern World 1350–1750* (Cambridge, 1990), pp. 371–99

Joseph von Hammer-Purgstall, *Geschichte des Osmanischen Reiches grossentheils aus bisher unbenützten Handschriften und Archiven*, 10 vols. (reprint, Vienna, 1963)

Nelly Hanna, *An Urban History of Būlāq in the Mamluk and Ottoman Periods*, Supplément aux Annales Islamologiques (Cairo, 1983)

Angelika Hartmann, *an Nāṣir li-Dīn Allāh (1180–1225) – Politik, Religion und Kultur der späten Abbasidenzeit*, Studien zur Sprache, Geschichte und Kultur des Islamischen Orients (Berlin and New York, 1975)

Ralph Hattox, *Coffee and Coffeehouses, The Origins of a Social Beverage in the Medieval Near East*, University of Washington, Near Eastern Studies No. 3 (Seattle and London, 1985)

Andrew Hess, *The Forgotten Frontier, A History of the Sixteenth-Century Ibero–African Frontier* (Chicago and London, 1978)

Uriel Heyd, *Ottoman Documents on Palestine 1552–1615. A Study of the Firman according to the Mühimme Defteri* (Oxford, 1960)

Walther Hinz, *Islamische Masse und Gewichte, umgerechnet ins metrische System*, in *Handbuch der Orientalistik*, ed. by Berthold Spuler, suppl. vol. 1, 1 (Leiden, 1955)

Marshall Hodgson, *The Venture of Islam, Conscience and History in a World Civilization*, 3 vols. (Chicago, 1974)

David George Hogarth, *The Penetration of Arabia, A Record of the Development of Western Knowledge Concerning the Arabian Peninsula* (New York, 1904)

Sabine Höllmann, 'Ägyptisches Alltagsleben im 17. Jahrhundert: J.M. Wanslebens Reisenotizen als ethnologische Quelle', unpublished MA thesis, Munich, 1987

P.M. Holt, 'The Exalted Lineage of Riḍwān Beğ', *Bulletin of the School of Oriental and African Studies*, XII, 2 (1959), 221–30

—— 'The Beylicate in Ottoman Egypt during the Seventeenth Century', *Bulletin of the School of Oriental and African Studies*, XXIV, 2 (1961), 214–48

Wolf-Dieter Hütteroth, Kamal Abdulfattah, *Historical Geography of Palestine, Transjordan and Southern Syria in the Late 16th Century*, Erlanger Geographische Arbeiten (Erlangen, 1977)

Halil Inalcık, 'Osmanlı-Rus Rekabetinin Menşei ve Don-Volga Kanalı Teşebbüsü (1569)', *Belleten*, XII, 46 (1948), 349–402

—— 'Ottoman Methods of Conquest', *Studia Islamica*, II (1954), 104–29

—— 'The Ottoman Economic Mind and Aspects of the Ottoman Economy', in *Studies in the Economic History of the Middle East*, ed. by M.A. Cook (London, 1970), pp. 207–18

—— *The Ottoman Empire, The Classical Age 1300–1600*, trans. by Norman Itzkowitz and Colin Imber (London, 1973)

—— 'The Khan and the Tribal Aristocracy: The Crimean Khanate under Sahib Giray I.', *Harvard Ukranian Studies*, III, IV (1979–80), pp. 445–66

—— 'Osmanlı Pamuklu Pazarı, Hindistan ve İngiltere: Pazar Rekabetinde Emek Maliyetinin Rolü', *Türkiye İktisat Tarihi Üzerine Araştırmalar*, II, *ODTÜ Gelişme Dergisi*, (1979–80), pp. 1–65

Huri İslamoğlu-İnan, 'Introduction: Oriental despotism in world system perspective', in *The Ottoman Empire and the World Economy*, ed. by Huri Islamoğlu-İnan (Cambridge and Paris, 1987), pp. 1–26

Fahir Iz, 'Evliya Çelebi ve Seyahatnamesi', *Boğazici Üniversitesi Dergisi*, VII (1979), pp. 61–79

Cemal Kafadar, 'When Coins Turned into Drops of Dew and Bankers Became Robbers of Shadows; The Boundaries of Ottoman Economic Imagination at the End of the Sixteenth Century', PhD dissertation, McGill University, Montreal, 1986

—— 'Self and Others: The Diary of a Dervish in Seventeenth-Century Istanbul and First-Person Narratives in Ottoman Literature', *Studia Islamica 69* (1989), 121–50

Albert Kammerer, *La mer Rouge, l'Abyssinie et l'Arabie aux XVIe et XVIIe siècles et la cartographie des portulans du monde oriental, Étude d'histoire et de géographie historique, Mémoires de la Société royale de géographie d'Egypte*, vol. XVII (Cairo, 1947), part 1, *Abyssins et portugais devant l'Islam*

R.H. Kiermann, *L'exploration de l'Arabie, Depuis les temps anciens jusqu'à nos jours*, trans. by Charles Mourey (London, 1938)

Hans-Joachim Kissling, *Beiträge zur Kenntnis Thrakiens im 17. Jahrhundert*, Abhandlungen für die Kunde des Morgenlandes XXXII, 3 (Wiesbaden, 1956)

—— 'Zur Geschichte der Rausch- und Genussgifte im Osmanischen Reiche', *Südost-Forschungen*, XVI (1975) 342–56

Ibrahim Hakkı Konyalı, *Abide ve Kitâbeleri ile Ereğli Tarihi* (Istanbul, 1970)

Fuat Köprulü, 'Türk Halk Hikayeciliğine ait Maddeler, Meddahlar', in *Edebiyat Araştırmaları*, Türk Tarih Kurumu Yayınlarından VII, 47 (Ankara, 1966), 361–412

Klaus Kreisner, 'Zur inneren Gliederung der osmanischen Stadt', in: *XVIII. deutschen Orientalistentag . . . 1972, Vorträge*, ed. by W. Voigt, *Zeitschrift der Deutschen Morgenländischen Gesellschaft*, Supplement II (1974), 198–212

—— *Edirne im 17. Jahrhundert nach Evliya Çelebi. Ein Beitrag zur Kenntnis der osmanischen Stadt*, Islamkundliche Untersuchungen vol. 33 (Freiburg, 1975)

Richard Kreutel, 'Evliya Çelebis Bericht über die türkische Grossbotschaft des Jahres 1665 in Wien. Ein Vergleich mit zeitgenössischen türkischen und österreichischen Quellen', *Wiener Zeitschrift für die Kunde des Morgenlandes*, 51 (1948–52), 188–242

—— 'Neues zur Evliya Çelebi-Forschung', *Der Islam*, 48 (1972), 269–79

Aptullah Kuran, *Sinan, The Grand Old Master of Ottoman Architecture* (Washington, DC, and Istanbul, 1987).

Bekir Kütükoğlu, *Osmanlı-Iran Siyası Münasebetleri*, I (1578–1590), Istanbul Üniversitesi Edebiyat Fakültesi Yayınları No. 888 (Istanbul, 1962)

—— 'Les relations entre l'Empire Ottoman et l'Iran dans la seconde moitié du XVIe siècle', *Turcica*, VI (1975), 128–45

Mübahat Kütükoğlu, '1009 (1600) tarihli Narh Defterine göre Istanbul'da çeşidli eşya ve hizmet fiatları', *Tarih Enstitüsü Dergisi*, 9 (1978), 1–86

—— *Osmanlılarda Narh Müessesesi ve 1640 Tarihli Narh Defteri* (Istanbul, 1983)

Akdes Nimet Kurat, *Türkiye ve İdil Boyu (1569 Astarhan Seferi, Ten-İdil Kanalı ve XVI–XVII. Yüzyıl Osmanlı-Rus Münasebetleri*), Ankara Üniversitesi Dil ve Tarih Coğrafya Fakültesi Sa 151 (Ankara, 1966)

Ernest Labrousse *et alii, Histoire économique et sociale de la France*, vol. 2, *Des derniers temps de l'age seigneurial aux préludes de l'age industriel (1660–1789)* (Paris, 1970).

Ira Lapidus, *Muslim Cities in the Later Middle Ages* (Cambridge, 1984)

Emmanuel Le Roy Ladurie, 'A Concept: The Unification of the Globe by Disease (Fourteenth to Seventeenth Centuries)', in *The Mind and Method of the Historian*, trans. by Siân Reynolds and Ben Reynolds (Chicago, 1984), pp. 28–83

Bernard Lewis, *The Emergence of Modern Turkey*, 2nd edn. (London, 1968)

Pierre MacKay, 'The Manuscripts of the Seyahatname of Evliya Çelebi', *Der Islam*, 52 (1975), 278–98

Hans Georg Majer, 'Ein Osmanisches Budget aus der Zeit Meḥmed des Eroberers', *Der Islam*, 59, 1 (1982), 40–63

Jon S. Mandaville, 'The Ottoman Province of al-Ḥasā in the Sixteenth and Seventeenth Centuries', *Journal of the American Oriental Society*, 90, 3 (1970), 486–513

Robert Mantran, *Istanbul dans la seconde moitié du XVIIe siècle, Essai d'histoire institutionelle, économique et sociale*, Bibliothèque archéologique et historique de l'Institut Français d'Archéologie d'Istanbul, XII (Paris, 1962)

Paul Masson, *Histoire du commerce français dans le Levant au XVIIIe siècle* (Paris, 1911)

Bruce Masters, *The Origins of Western Economic Dominance in the Middle East, Mercantilism and the Islamic Economy in Aleppo, 1600–*

1750, New York University Studies in Near Eastern Civilization No. 12 (New York, 1988)

Arno Mehlan, 'Die grossen Balkanmessen zur Türkenzeit', *Vierteljahresschrift für Sozial- und Wirtschaftsgeschichte*, XXI, 1 (1938), 10–49

M.J. Mehta, 'Some Aspects of Surat as a Trading Centre in the Seventeenth Century', *Indian Historical Review*, 1, 2 (1974), 247–61

M. Yakub Mughul, 'Portekizli'lerle Kızıldeniz'de Mücadele ve Hicaz' da Osmanlı Hâkimiyetinin Yerleşmesi Hakkında bir Vesika', *Belgeler*, II, 3–4 (1965), 37–47

Alois Musil, *The Northern Heğâz, A topographical itinerary*, American Oriental Society, Oriental Studies and Explorations No. 1 (New York, 1926)

Zeynep Nayır, *Osmanlı Mimarlığında Sultan Ahmet Külliyesi ve Sonrası (1609–1690)* (Istanbul, 1975)

Gülru Necipoğlu Kafadar, 'The Süleymaniye Complex in Istanbul: An Interpretation', *Mukarnas*, 3 (1986), 92–117

Elke Niewohner-Eberhard, 'Machtpolitische Aspekte des osmanisch-safavidischen Kampfes um Bagdad im 16.–17. Jahrhundert', *Turcica*, VI (1975), 103–27

Cengiz Orhonlu, '1559 Bahreyn Seferine Âid bir Rapor', *Tarih Dergisi*, XVII, 22 (1967), 1–16

—— 'Hint Kaptanlığı ve Pirî Reis', *Belleten*, XXXIV, 134 (1970), 235–54

—— *Osmanlı İmparatorluğunum Güney Siyaseti, Habeş Eyaleti*, Istanbul Üniversitesi Edebiyat Fakültesi Yayınları No. 1856 (Istanbul, 1974)

Salih Özbaran, 'XVI. Yüzyılda Basra Körfezi Sahillerinde Osmanlılar: Basra Beylerbeyliğinin Kuruluşu', *Tarih Dergisi*, 25 (1971), 51–72

—— 'The Ottoman Turks and the Portuguese in the Persian Gulf, 1534–1581', *Journal of Asian History*, 6, 1 (1972), 45–87

—— 'Osmanlı İmparatorluğu ve Hindistan Yolu, Onaltıncı Yüzyılda Ticâret Yolları Üzerinde Türk-Portekiz Rekâbet ve Ilişkileri', *Tarih Dergisi*, 31 (1977), 65–146

—— 'A Turkish Report on the Red Sea and the Portuguese in the Indian Ocean (1525)', *Arabian Studies*, IV (1978), 81–8

Daniel Panzac, *La peste dans l'Empire Ottoman 1700–1850* (Louvain, 1985)

M.N. Pearson, 'Brokers in Western Indian Port Cities, Their Role in Servicing Foreign Merchants', *Modern Asian Studies*, 22, 3 (1988), 455–72

Leslie Peirce, 'Shifting Boundaries: Images of Ottoman Royal

Women in the 16th and 17th Centuries', *Critical Matrix, Princeton Working Papers in Womens' Studies*, 4 (1988), 43–82

Xavier de Planhol, *De la plaine pamphylienne aux lacs pisidiens, nomadisme et vie paysanne*. (Paris, 1958)

Ishwari Prasad, *The Life and Times of Humayun* (Bombay, Calcutta and Madras, 1956)

Donald Quataert, *Social Disintegration and Popular Resistance in the Ottoman Empire, 1881–1908, Reactions to European Economic Penetration*, New York University Studies in Near Eastern Civilization, No. 9 (New York and London, 1983)

Abdul-Karim Rafeq, 'The Law-Court Registers of Damascus, with Special Reference to Craft Corporations During the First Half of the Eighteenth Century', in *Les Arabes par leurs archives (XVIe–XXe siècles)*, ed. by Jacques Berque and Dominique Chevalier (Paris, 1976), pp. 141–59

André Raymond, *Artisans et commerçants au Caire au XVIIIe siècle*, 2 vols. (Damascus, 1973–4)

—— 'La conquête ottomane et le développement des grandes villes arabes. Le cas du Caire, de Damas et de Alep', *Revue de l'Occident musulman et de la Méditerrannée*, 1 (1979), 115–34

—— *The Great Arab Cities in the 16th–18th Centuries. An Introduction* (New York and London, 1984)

—— *Grandes villes arabes à l'époque ottomane* (Paris, 1985)

Saiyid Athar Abbas Rizvi, *Muslim Revivalist Movements in Northern India in the Sixteenth and Seventeenth Centuries* (Agra, 1965)

Saiyid Abbas Rizvi, Vincent J. Adams Flynn, *Fatḥpur-Sīkrī* (Bombay, 1975)

J.M. Rogers, R.M. Ward, *Süleyman the Magnificent* (London, 1988)

Ruggiero Romano, 'Versuch einer ökonomischen Typologie', in Ruggiero Romano ed., *Die Gleichzeitigkeit des Ungleichzeitigen, Studien zur Geschichte Italiens*, trans. and introduced by Eva Maek-Gérard (Frankfurt, 1980), pp. 22–75

Halil Sahillioğlu, 'XVII Asrın Ilk Yarısında Istanbul'da Tedavüldeki Sikkelerin Raici', *Belgeler*, 1, 1–2 (1964), 228–33

—— 'Osmanlı Para Tarihinde Dünya Para ve Maden Hareketinin Yeri', *Türkiye Iktisat Tarihi Üzerine Araştırmalar, ODTÜ Gelişme Dergisi*, special issue (1978), 1–38

—— 'Yemen'in 1599–1600 Yılı Bütçesi', in *Yusuf Hikmet Bayur Armağanı* (Ankara, 1985), pp. 287–319

Edward W. Said, *Orientalism* (New York, 1979)

Jean Sauvaget, *Alep, Essai sur le développement d'une grande ville syrienne, des origines au milieu du XIXe siècle*, Haut Commissariat de l'État Français en Syrie et au Liban, Service des Antiquités, Bibliothèque archéologique et historique, vol. XXXVI, 2 vols. (Paris, 1941)

Afaf Lutfi al-Sayyid Marsot, *Egypt in the Reign of Muhammad Ali* (Cambridge, 1984)

James C. Scott, *Weapons of the Weak, Everyday Forms of Peasant Resistance* (New Haven and London, 1985)

Robert B. Serjeant, (a) 'Yemeni Merchants and Trade in Yemen, 13th–16th Centuries', in *Marchands et hommes d'affaires asiatiques dans l'Océan Indien et dans la Mer de Chine, 13e–20e siècles*, ed. by Denys Lombard and Jean Aubin (Paris, 1988), pp. 61–82

—— (b)'The Ḥaḍramī Network', in *Marchands et hommes d'affaires asiatiques dans l'Océan Indien et la Mer de Chine, 13e–20e siècles*, ed. by Denys Lombard and Jean Aubin (Paris, 1988), pp. 147–54

Moshe Sharon, 'The Political Role of the Bedouins in Palestine during the Sixteenth and Seventeenth Centuries', in *Studies on Palestine during the Ottoman Period*, ed. by Moshe Ma'oz (Jerusalem, 1975), pp. 11–30

Stanford J. Shaw, *Between Old and New, The Ottoman Empire under Sultan Selim III 1789–1807* (Cambridge, Mass., 1971)

—— *History of the Ottoman Empire and Modern Turkey*, 2 vols. (Cambridge, 1976–77), vol. 2 with Ezel Kural Shaw, *Reform, Revolution and Republic, The Rise of Modern Turkey 1808–1975*

Ashirbadi Lal Srivastava, *Akbar the Great*, 2 vols. (Agra, 1962, 1967)

Sanjay Subrahmanyam, *The Political Economy of Commerce: Southern India, 1500–1650* (Cambridge, 1990)

Franz Taeschner, *Das anatolische Wegenetz nach osmanischen Quellen*, Türkische Bibliothek, vol. 23, 2 parts (Leipzig, 1924–6)

Karl Teply, 'Evliya Çelebi in Wien', *Der Islam*, 52 (1975), 125–31

Lewis V. Thomas, *A Study of Naima*, ed. by Norman Itzkowitz, New York University Studies in Near Eastern Civilization No. 4 (New York, 1972)

Luis Filipe F.R. Thomaz, 'Malaka et ses communautés marchandes au tournant du 16e siècle', in *Marchands et hommes d'affaires asiatiques dans l'Océan Indien et la Mer de Chine, 13e–20e siècles*, ed. by Denys Lombard and Jean Aubin (Paris, 1988), pp. 31–48

Ismail Hakkı Uzunçarşılı, *Osmanlı Devletinin Saray Teşkilâtı*, Türk Tarih Kurumu Yayınlarından VIII, 15 (Ankara, 1945)

—— *Osmanlı Devletinin Merkez ve Bahriye Teşkilâtı*, Türk Tarih Kurumu Yayınlarından VIII, 6 (Ankara, 1948)

Ismail Hakkı Uzunçarşılı, *Osmanlı Devletinin İlmiye Teşkilâtı* (Ankara, 1965).

Michel Vovelle, *Ville et campagne au 18e siècle (Chartres et la Beauce)* (Paris, 1980)

Spyros Vryonis, 'The *Panēgyris* of the Byzantine Saint. A Study in the Nature of a Medieval Institution, its Origins and Fate', in *The Byzantine Saint*, ed. by Sergei Hacke (London, 1981), pp. 196–226

Robert E. Ward and Dankwart A. Rustow (eds.), *Political Modernization in Japan and Turkey*, Studies in Political Development, 3 (Princeton, NJ, 1964)

Eugen Weber, *Peasants into Frenchmen, the Modernization of Rural France 1870–1914* (Stanford, Cal., 1976)

Ferdinand Wüstenfeld, *Jemen im XI. (XVII.) Jahrhundert. Die Kriege der Türken, die arabischen Imame und die Gelehrten* (Göttingen, 1884)

Hulûsi Yavuz, *Kâbe ve Haremeyn için Yemen'de Osmanlı Hâkimiyeti (1517–1571)* (Istanbul, 1984)

Index

Ābār 'Alī 18
'Abbās gate of the Great Mosque 103
Abbasids 7, 33, 74f, 92f, 99, 105, 117, 179f
'Abd al-Ghafūr 158
'Abd al-Ghānī al-Nābulusī 67
'Abd al-Ḳādir al-Djazarī 33ff, 41f, 46, 52, 59, 70
'Abd al-Ḳādir al-Djīlānī 144
'Abd al-Ḳahhār 'Ulvī 142
'Abd al-Malik, Moroccan sultan 142
'Abd al-Raḥmān III, caliph 26
'Abd al-Raḥmān Ḥibrī 58, 66ff, 69, 167
'Abd ül-Medjīd, sultan 28
Abraham (Ibrāhīm) 1, 19f, 22, 25, 72, 92, 112
Abū Bakr 26, 137
Abū Ḳubays 150
Abū Numayy *see* Sherif Abū Numayy
Abū Sa'īd, Ilchanid 28
Abyssinia(n) (Ḥabeshistān) 22, 148, 170
Adana 32
Aden 22, 159
'Ādiliya 39
'Adjlūn, fortress 62ff, 65
'Adjrūd 34
Adriatic coast 41
Aegean 96
Afghanistan 14
Afghans 47
Africa(n) 5, 13, 24, 96, 127, 182
Agra 159
Aḥmad Badawī 169
Aḥmad b. Ṭurabāy 58
Aḥmad-ı Yasawī 141
Aḥmed I 12, 20, 80, 95, 99, 105, 113, 116, 120, 122f, 125, 139, 151, 185, 201
Aḥmed III 186
Aḥmed Beg 59
'A'isha 27, 39
Akbar 129, 131–3, 139, 207
Akili, Aḳlu (the Whites) 64
al-'Arīsh 72
al-Djazarī *see* 'Abd al-Ḳādir al-Djazarī
Aleppo 41, 70, 122, 130
Alexandria 16f, 32
Algeria(n) 16
al-Hādī, caliph 92
al-Ḥadjdjādj 19, 92, 115
al-Harawī 19f
al-Ḥasā *see* Laḥsā
'Alī Beg 46, 61f
'Alī b. Shams al-Dīn 114
al-Khalīl *see* Khalīl al-Raḥmān
al-Mahdī, caliph 92, 100
al-Manṣūr, caliph 92, 100
Almohads *see* Muwahhidun

alms 36, 43, 88, 91, 138, 142f, 155f, 159, 166
al-Mudjāhid, sultan 29f
al-Nadjaf 137f
al-Nāṣir 130
al-Nāṣir li-Dīn Allāh 20
al-Samhūdī 27f, 193
al-'Ulā 43f, 67
Amasya 84
Amīr al-'Arab, Mamluk title 66
Anatolia(n) 3, 5, 13, 22, 32f, 41, 48, 51, 74, 76, 82ff, 89, 94, 96, 102, 107, 134f, 140, 146, 165, 172, 182
'Anaza 56
Andalusia(n) 17, 24
'Aqaba 16
Arabia(n) 54, 66f, 133, 144, 151, 158–63, 169, 171f
Arabian Gulf 133, 136
Arabic 69
'Arafāt 2, 9, 18, 21f, 29, 46, 59, 61, 86, 98, 108, 168, 182
Armenia(n) 159
arsenal 94
artillery 34, 37, 69
artisans 84, 95–7, 103, 167–9, 172, 179, 183, 186
Ashrafiya 30
Asia Minor 30; *see also* Anatolia
assemblies of notables 102, 114f
Astrachan 139–41, 208
Aydhāb, port 16f
Ayyubids 74, 76
Azak (Asov) 140

Bāb al-Nisā 121
Bāb al-Salām 121
Bāb Nāṣir 38
Bābur Khān 131
Badāōnī 131
Baghdad 15–17, 27, 76, 83f, 135, 138, 144, 147
Bahrain 24, 135, 137
Bāḳī, cemetery 122
Bāḳī, poet 101, 200
Balıklagu (Balaklava) 94
Balkans 4, 13, 51, 67f, 74, 76, 84, 206
Balkh 14
Banū Ḥusayn 56, 87f
Banū Shayba 118f
baraka 25
Barsbāy, sultan 28
Basra 23, 33, 54, 135–7, 144f
bath, public 83, 94, 107, 109, 111, 123
Baybars, sultan 39
Bāyezīd II 74, 76, 83, 129, 147
beduins 4, 6, 11, 22, 25, 29, 34f, 48, 54ff, 58ff, 62, 64ff, 69, 71–3, 76, 79, 86, 90, 134, 136, 146, 149–51, 182, 185, 200
beduin attacks on pilgrims 7, 9, 22f, 43, 54, 65ff, 68ff, 72, 143, 182, 197
beg (title) 114, 119
beg of Jeddah 148
beglerbegi of Egypt 148
beglerbeglik 136
Behrām Shaykh 11, 68
Belgrade 74
berāt 155
Bijapur 159f
Bilbays 41
biographical dictionary 15
Bi'r 'Alī 18
Birkat al-Ḥadjdj 38, 40
Black Sea 94f, 139–41, 165, 208
'Black Scribe' *see* Kara Yazıdjı
blacksmiths 97, 109, 121
Blue Mosque 67
bookbinder 96
Bosnia 107
Braudel, Fernand 177, 183
broker 171
'budgets' (accounts which record official expenses related to the caravan) 35, 55, 58, 76, 78ff, 88f
building experts and surveyors 115, 117
Bukhara 139, 141, 207
Bulgaria 95
Burckhardt, John Lewis 46, 175
Bursa 83f, 107, 126
Burton, Richard 17, 93, 165, 175
burying of implements and timber 120

Cairo 3f, 8, 14, 16, 29, 31ff, 37ff, 44f, 52, 60f, 69, 71, 76f, 94, 105, 108, 114, 135, 142, 147f, 152, 162,

164, 167f, 170, 172, 175, 185, 200, 204
Cairo caravan 42, 45f, 58, 61, 69, 142, 198, 204
Cairo, notables of 38
Čaḳmaḳ 80, 106
Čāldırān, battle 134
Calicut 160, 163, 171
calligraphers 103
camels 2, 9, 35f, 42–4, 46, 48ff, 55, 64, 69, 80, 141, 167
camel entrepreneurs 48ff, 64
canons 67, 69
caravan commander 2, 34ff, 37ff, 43f, 49, 51–3, 58ff, 65f, 70f, 79, 129, 130, 196, 200, 204
caravan *ḳāḍī* 34, 36, 45
caravans, auxiliary 44
carpenters 116, 118
cash supplies 34
Caspian Sea 139
Central Asian pilgrims 139–42, 144
Ceuta 16
China 127, 158
Chingiz Khan 13, 140f
Chinese porcelain 157, 170
Cochin 159
coffee 169f, 183
commander's secretary 34
construction workers 96
Cordoba 27
cotton textiles 160
couriers on official business 128
courier routes 41f
Crimean Tatars 140
crusaders 122
Čūbān, Amīr 28f
customs 156–8, 161–3, 171
Cyprus 83f, 94, 133
Cyprus war 94, 101

Daḥlān, Sayyid Aḥmad 156
Damascus 13, 32f, 35ff, 40ff, 49f, 52, 59, 65f, 68f, 87, 94, 130, 135, 137, 140, 149, 152, 167f, 175, 183, 185, 194, 196, 198
Damascus caravan 35ff, 43ff, 58–60, 65f, 68f, 71, 89, 137, 140, 197
Damascus market 168
dāni<u>sh</u>mend 123
dār al-ḥadī<u>th</u> 100, 121
Dead Sea 29
Delhi 139, 159
derwish shaykhs 39, 77
derwishes, Central Asian 141f, 144
desert forts 41, 43, 71ff, 90
'desert pilots' 34
De<u>sh</u>ī<u>sh</u>e (foundation) 80ff, 83, 87, 89, 91
devaluation of the currency 78, 83f, 89
dew<u>sh</u>irme (levy of boys) 68
<u>Dh</u>ū al-Ḥi<u>dj</u>dja 18, 21f
<u>Dh</u>ū al-Ḥulayfa 18
Dīn-i Ilāhī 131
Diu 148
diwan-i humayūn 50
Diyārbakır 83f
<u>Dj</u>abal al-Raḥmat 22
<u>Dj</u>a'fer Efendi 11, 68f, 73, 99, 102, 118
<u>Dj</u>ānbulādo<u>gh</u>lu 'Alī 44, 57
<u>Dj</u>nbulāt, mosque of 39
<u>Dj</u>ānībeg, Mamluk amir 106
djeleb 51f
<u>Dj</u>um'a Kāsib 68
dome(d) 97, 100–102, 120, 124, 126
Drinking water room of 'Abbās 116
Dutch 133, 159f, 172, 178, 183

Ebūssu'ūd Efendi 127
Edirne 66, 83f, 94, 107, 126, 167, 172
Edirne Kapı 95
Egypt(ian) 5f, 9f, 14, 16f, 27–30, 37, 42, 50, 58, 60, 70, 72–4, 76, 78–81, 87, 89f, 95f, 98, 103, 106–9, 114–16, 121–4, 142, 147f, 151, 156f, 164–9, 207
Egyptian caravan *see* Cairo caravan
Egyptian foundations 123, 165, 182
elementary school 94
endowments *see* foundation, pious
England, English 133, 142, 151, 158, 160f, 172
Ereğli 76
esedī <u>gh</u>urū<u>sh</u> 48

eshrefiye coins 83
Estado da India 159f
eunuchs (*aghāwāt*) 153
Ewliyā Čelebi 5, 11f, 18, 22ff, 37ff, 41, 43f, 51, 58f, 65, 67, 71–3, 96, 100, 123–5, 131, 137, 150, 166–72, 179, 186, 196

fair of Mina 169f
Fakhr al-Dīn ʿAlī II 53, 57f, 65
Fāṭima 137
Fatimids, caliphs 14f
Ferdosi, poet 13
fireworks 38, 52
flag of the Prophet 37
floods 59, 111, 113, 116, 204
foodstuffs, food supply 128, 141, 146, 161, 164–7, 174, 182, 199
food prices 97, 165
foundation
  benefiting the poor of Mecca and Medina 4, 76ff, 80ff, 82ff, 84, 87, 156, 182, 199
  pious 7, 10, 29, 48, 50, 93f, 106f, 108f, 122f, 125f, 165, 182, 194
  public 5f, 32, 34, 79
  see also deshīshe
France, French 142, 158, 161, 178, 186

Ghāzī Evrenos, descendants of 84
Gaza 41, 59
gifts, of the sultan to the population of Mecca and Medina 36–8, 59f, 76ff, 85
gifts, to the poor of Medina 75, 85
gifts, to the Sherifs of the Holy Cities 76
gifts to the beduins 8, 143; *see also ṣürre*
Goa 133
Golconda 159f, 166
gold(en) 5, 28, 49, 56, 70, 77, 79, 83–5, 87, 89f, 96, 99, 104, 119, 122, 155f, 170
gold and silver 4f, 58, 113, 116, 133, 161, 191
Golden Horde 140
governor of Damascus 44, 47, 52f, 59, 61f, 64f, 69, 71, 129, 133, 149, 166f, 197
governor of Egypt 37ff, 60, 72, 114, 118f, 123, 164
governor of Gaza 61f
governor of Ḥabeshistān (Ethiopia) 148
governor of Jeddah 146, 148–50, 152, 163f
governor of Jerusalem 61
governor of Yemen 60, 162
governors 128, 154, 156, 173
grain 98, 123f, 149, 154–6, 165f, 182
grain supply for Holy Cities 5f, 32, 79, 81ff, 86, 88f, 106, 147
Granada 15
grave of the Prophet Muḥammad 2, 26, 28, 67, 99, 121f, 153, 180
Greek Christians 22
Gujarat 159
Gulbadan Bēgam 129, 132, 207

Ḥabeshistān (Ethiopia) 148
Habsburg 129, 174
Habsburg–Ottoman war 53, 67, 79, 89
Hadramaut 160
ḥadīth 15
Hagar (Ḥadjar) 20, 112
Ḥanbalī 100
Ḥarb Beduins 67
Hārūn al-Rashīd 8, 22, 33, 57
Ḥawrān 68
Hebron *see* Khalīl al-Raḥmān
heirs 45, 88, 143
Ḥekīmoghlu Aḥmed 51f
horses 151, 167
hospices, in Mecca 15, 30f, 98, 131
hospitals 98, 106
hostels 108, 110f, 123
Humāyūn 131
Ḥunayn 28
Hungary 41, 174
Hurgronje *see* Snouck Hurgronje
Ḥusayn, king *see* Sherif Ḥusayn
Ḥusaynī 154
Ḥüseyin al-Kürdī 148
Ḥüseyin Pasha 71, 166

Ibn ʿAbd Rabbih 26f

Ibn al-Zamin 30
Ibn al-Zubayr 19, 92, 113
Ibn Djubayr 3, 15ff, 24ff, 69, 76, 93, 130, 165, 179, 191f
Ibn Farrukh 66
Ibn Sa'īd 62ff
Ibn Sa'ūd 179
Ibrāhīm, official in charge of the Meccan water supply 103f
Ibrāhīm Pasha 48f
Ibrāhīm Pečewī *see* Pečewī
iḥrām 17f, 21, 23, 197
'ilmiyye 6
Imām 103
Imām 'Alī 137–9, 144, 207
Imām Ḥusayn 137–9, 144, 207
India(n) 30, 42, 46, 94, 109, 127, 129, 131–4, 144, 147f, 154, 157–63, 165f, 169–72
Indian cotton 158, 160
Indian Ocean 133, 157, 159f, 178
Indian pilgrims 13, 131–4
Indian traders 5, 137, 146, 158–63
inscriptions 103, 105, 119f, 125f
intercession of the Prophet 28
Iran(ian) 13, 29, 74, 86, 111, 118, 127–30, 133–6, 138f, 144, 152f, 157f, 160f, 169, 181f, 186, 207
Iranian pilgrims 128, 134–6, 138, 208
Iraq(i) 14, 22f, 26, 46, 137–9, 144, 207
irdeb 86, 88
iron 94f, 113, 116
Ismā'īl, son of Hagar 20
Ismā'īl, prince *see* Shah Ismā'īl II
Istanbul 3, 9f, 32, 36, 40–43, 51f, 54, 58, 60–62, 66f, 72, 76f, 83–5, 87, 90, 94–100, 102f, 105–7, 114f, 121, 125f, 130, 132, 138–42, 144, 146, 147–9, 151f, 154–6, 162, 164, 166, 170, 175, 182, 184–7, 200, 204, 206
Italy 177
Ivan IV, Czar 140
Izmir 41, 182

Jacobo of Verona 46
janissaries 37, 51, 54, 69ff, 146, 153, 186
Jeddah 8f, 17f, 42, 86, 89f, 100, 103f, 110, 114, 146–8, 150f, 156–8, 160, 162f, 165, 172
Jerusalem 1, 29, 41, 72, 129, 152

ḳāḍī 6, 47, 52, 87, 97, 123, 128
ḳāḍī'asker of Rumelia 153
Ḳāḍī Ḥüseyin 104, 109, 120, 142f, 157
Ḳāḍī Ḥüseyin Mālikī 106
ḳāḍī of Cairo 152
ḳāḍī of Damascus 87, 152, 155
ḳāḍī of Istanbul 152f
ḳāḍī of Jerusalem 152
ḳāḍī of Mecca 21ff, 30, 42, 77, 102–4, 109, 111f, 121, 146, 152f
ḳāḍī of Medina 42, 77, 123, 146, 152
ḳāḍī register 7, 104, 172, 191
Ḳā'it Bāy 28, 30f, 33, 75, 80, 106, 122
Ḳal'at al-'Azlam 44
Kāmrān 131
Ḳānṣūh al-Ghūrī 33, 43, 106, 147
Ḳānṣūh Beg 61ff, 66, 68
Karak-Shaubak 63f
Ḳara Shāhīn Muṣṭafā Pasha 60
Ḳarāmān 83
Karamanids 76, 84
Ḳara Meydān 37f
Ḳara Yazıdjı 44, 194
Karbalā' 137f
Karlowitz, peace of 186
kaṣr see pavilion
ḳaṭār 34
Ḳāṭırdjıoghlu 4
Kays 64
Kayseri 84
Kefe (Kaffa, now Feodosiya) 94, 139, 142
ketkhüdā 36f
Khādim al-ḥaramayn 184
Khalīl al-Raḥmān (Hebron) 29, 41, 72
khān (building) 86, 90, 94, 169, 184
Khān of Khiva 141
Khān of Tashkent 130
Khān of the Uzbeks 139
Khaybar, oasis 149
Khodja Minas 159
Khorāsān(īs) 23f

Khurrem Sultan (Roxolana) 8, 80, 98, 106, 185, 203
Khusrev Pasha 68, 197
Ḳırḳkilīse 69
Ḳızılbash 136
Ḳızıllu (the Reds) 63f
Konya 32, 76, 140
Konya Ereğlisi 84
Ḳubā' 124
ḳul 40
Ḳuraysh 19
Ḳuṭb al-Dīn, Indian scholar 5, 30, 81, 85, 101, 114, 200

Laḥsā (al-Ḥasā) 135–7
larder, the Sultan's 42, 50
libraries 94, 107, 121
Library of Ashrafiya in Mecca 30
Library attached to the Prophet's Mosque 96
lodge (*tekke*) 107, 124
Ludovico di Varthéma 46, 171
lunatic asylum 106, 122
Luṭfullāh 121

madrasa (*medrese*) 15, 77, 87, 94, 97f, 100, 107, 122f, 150, 152
Mafāridja Beduins 64, 66
Maghribi(s) 6, 21, 23, 33
maḥmal (palanquin) 37ff, 59, 61
Maḥmūd of Ghazni 13
Maḥmūd Shāh 42
Maḳām al-'Umra 18
Malabar 158
Malaya 127, 157
Malika Khātūn 130
Mālikī medrese 106
Mamluk(s) 5f, 8, 27–9, 32–4, 39f, 59–62, 66, 69, 74f, 78, 80, 90, 94, 102, 106, 109, 114f, 117, 119, 122, 124, 126, 129, 146f, 164, 171, 179, 193, 196, 204, 212
Mar'ash 83
marble 20, 30f, 93f, 102f
Marwa 15, 20, 30, 106, 112
Masulipatnam 159f, 163
Ma'ṣūm Beg, Safawid vizier 134f
masons 97, 116, 118, 121
Mediterranean 94, 133, 162
Meḥmed Agha (head of Black Eunuchs) 11, 122f
Meḥmed Agha (Mi'mar) 67ff, 95, 99, 102, 116, 124f
Meḥmed b. Aḥmed 84
Meḥmed Čāvush 102
Meḥmed the Conqueror 28, 74, 76
Meḥmed Edīb 72, 168, 192
Meḥmed Pasha 114
Meḥmed II *see* Meḥmed the Conqueror
Meḥmed III 201
Meḥmed IV 186
Meḥmed Yemenī 124
merchants *see* traders
merchants of Mecca and Medina 85, 112, 171
messenger(s) 36f
Mewlewī derwishes 107
mewlewiyet (provincial *ḳāḍī*ship) 152
Mihr-ü-māh 185, 203
military prebends 49f, 54, 70f
Mi'mār Meḥmed Agha *see* Meḥmed Agha
Mina 22–4, 168–70, 172, 175, 182
minaret 27, 92, 100f
mīrākhōr (master of the stables) 36
Mīrzā Makhdūm 152f
Mocha 158
Moldavia and Wallachia 41
Mongols 13, 27, 62, 74
Morocco, Moroccan 142f
Moscow 140
Mosul 84
Mouradjea d'Ohsson 76
Mu'āwiya 26
Mu'aẓẓama, fort 72
müdjāwir 85
muezzin 36, 100
müftī 114, 117, 127, 204
Mughal 127, 129, 131–4, 139, 143, 159f
Muḥammad *see* Prophet Muḥammad
Mühimme Defterleri (Registers of Important Affairs) 10, 42, 52, 59, 66, 119, 128, 192, 200
muḳawwim see camel entrepreneurs
mülāzemet 156

Munā *see* Mina
Murād III 48, 80, 82, 85, 87f, 96f, 101, 105–8, 119, 122–4, 132, 176, 178
Murād IV 11, 20, 67, 107, 118–20, 170
musicians 36
muskets 69
Muṣliḥ al-Dīn, amir 85
Muṣṭafā ʿAlī 71, 79, 94, 98, 149, 157
Muṣṭafā Pasha 70
Muṣṭafā II 186
Muwaḥḥidūn, Spanish Sunni dynasty 17
Muzayrib 40, 43, 49, 167f, 175
Muzdalifa 22f, 182

Naʿīmā 161
naḳḳāshbāshı 120f
Naḳshbendī derwishes 107
Nāṣir-i Khosraw, poet 14f, 26
nāẓır (supervisor) 36
Nedjd 136
Neyshapur 15
Niger 127
Nogay princes 140f, 208
Nuʿaym 57
Nuʿaymoghlu, the Mafāridja Shaykh
Nuʿaymoghulları 64
Nūr al-Dīn Shahīd 122, 130

ʿörf 152
Ottoman–Iranian war 137, 139
Ottoman–Wahabi war 122
Özdemiroghlu ʿOthmān Pasha 60
Özü (Ochakow) 139

palanquin *see maḥmal*
pavilion (*ḳaṣr*) 98
Pečewi 157, 163, 170
pensions 86, 155f; *see also* subsidies
Perīkhān princess 139
Persia(n) *see* Iran(ian)
Persian Gulf 133, 135, 160, 207
pilgrimage guides (books) 14
pilgrimage guides (persons) 128, 182
pilgrims' accounts 14ff, 24ff, 26ff
pilgrims' garb *see iḥrām*
pirates 133, 147, 160, 163
Poland 41
poor, among the pilgrims 98, 102, 108, 110, 123, 131f
poor of the Holy Cities 155f, 160
population of Mecca and Medina 85ff
porcelain *see* Chinese porcelain
Portuguese 132f, 135f, 145, 147f, 157, 159f 172, 178, 207
Portuguese anonymous author 46
Portuguese attacks 31, 133, 147, 151, 156, 160, 163
poursuivants 36
prayer for the Sultan's soul 107, 118
preacher's chair of the Prophet Muḥammad 26f
Prophet's descendants 144, 180
Prophet Muḥammad 1, 7, 14, 17, 19, 21, 25f, 67, 74f, 87, 141, 144, 179f

rainpipe of Kaʿaba 99, 113
Ramaḍān 25, 114
Ramla 41
Rawḍa 26, 121
Red Sea 5, 9f, 14, 16, 29, 31, 34, 73, 133, 147f, 157–9, 161f, 164f, 183, 187
Registers of Important Affairs *see Mühimme Defterleri*
Rhodes 32
ribāṭ 123
rice 159, 166
Riḍwān Agha *see* Riḍwān Beg (Egyptian Mamluk)
Riḍwān Beg (Egyptian Mamluk) 11f, 114f, 117–19, 197
Riḍwān Beg (Egyptian Mamluk, founder of Ḳaṣaba Riḍwān) 66, 204
Riḍwān Beg (governor of Gaza) 61f
robe of honour 39, 66f, 118, 151
Roxolana *see* Khurrem Sultan
Rūm 83
Rumelia(n) 5, 9, 33, 41, 51, 76, 82ff, 89, 96, 102, 107, 125, 146, 153, 169, 172, 182, 186; *see also* Balkans
Russia(n) 13, 139
Rutter, Eldon 175

rūznāmdje 47

Sa'd b. Zaid *see* Sherif Sa'd
ṣadaḳa see alms
Ṣafā 15, 20, 30, 106, 112
Ṣafawī order 135
Safawids 33, 74, 87, 131, 134, 136, 138f, 141, 144f
safe conduct 128f, 132f, 207f
Safed 48, 69
Saladin *see* Ṣalāḥ al-Dīn Ayyūbī
Ṣalāḥ al-Dīn Ayyūbī 16f
Salāma (tribe) 57
Salāma (proper name) 64
salary *see 'ulūfe*
Salīma 129, 131
Salomon 120
Salonica 84
Samokov 95
Samarkand 128, 139
Samsun 140
sandjaḳbegi 148
Saydā (Sidon) 48, 96
Selīm I 3, 31, 80, 83, 85, 134, 147, 148
Selīm II 70, 80, 97, 101, 110, 122, 133, 141
Selmān Re'īs 147f
Seyyid Shaykh Ibrāhīm 68
Shāfi'ī 100
Shāfi'ī *müftī*s 115
Shāhdjahān 159
Shāh of Iran 127, 134–6, 139, 184
Shāh Ismā'īl I 134
Shāh Ismā'īl II 129, 138, 152f
Shāhrukh (son and successor of Timur Lenk) 28, 193
Shāh Sulṭān 129
Shāh Ṭahmāsp 129, 136, 138
shaykh al-ḥaram 142, 153f
sherī'at 152
Sherif(s) of Mecca 7f, 28f, 31f, 38, 42, 52, 58f, 66f, 75ff, 89, 111f, 114f, 117–19, 125, 130, 132, 143, 146f, 149–54, 156–8, 161–3, 166, 169f, 172, 179f, 184f, 197, 200, 206
Sherif Abū Numayy b. Barakāt 148, 157
Sherif Barakāt 148
Sherif Mas'ūd 114
Sherif Sa'd b. Zaid 67, 69, 166f, 179
Shi'is(m) 14f, 17, 87, 127, 134f, 137f, 154, 184, 207
shipping on the Rea Sea 164f
sikke-i ḥasene 56f
silver 96, 99, 122, 167
Sinai 16
Sinān the architect 116
Sinān Pasha 157
Sinop 140
Sivas 84
slaves 22, 88, 97, 109, 133, 167, 170, 201
Snouck Hurgronje 96
Soḳollu Meḥmed Pasha 106f, 109, 200
soldiers 34f, 37f, 42ff, 48, 50, 60, 66, 68ff, 85, 116, 169, 198
spies 127, 136f
strikes 97
soup kitchens 80, 88, 94, 98, 106f, 110, 123, 138
St John, the Knights of 32
stonecutters 97, 109, 121
ṣūbāshı 36
subsidies 34, 38, 44, 54ff, 72, 75ff, 80, 83, 85–8, 90, 131, 150, 164, 168, 185, 199f
Suez 157f, 164–6
Suez Canal 5, 34, 133
Surat 158f
Süheylī 11, 113f, 116, 119ff, 175, 204
Süleymān I (the Lawgiver, the Magnificent) 6, 8, 12, 32, 69f, 75, 80, 87f, 97, 100, 103f, 106, 109f, 120, 127f, 131, 133, 138, 185, 203
Süleymān Pasha 109
Süleymāniye 97–9, 101, 202f
Sultān, pilgrims in the name and place of 154
ṣürre 54, 56ff, 58f, 65ff, 71, 79, 107, 154; *see also* subsidies
Syria(n) 9–11, 16, 26, 32, 35, 37, 53f, 56, 58, 62–4, 67–70, 72–4, 83, 86f, 90, 96, 115, 122, 147, 166–8, 199, 201
Syrian caravan *see* Damascus caravan

Syrian market *see* Damascus market

Tabūk 41
Tamerlan *see* Timur Lenk
Tangier 127
Tanta 169
Tashkent 128, 130
Tatar Khān of the Crimea 140–43
Tatar pilgrims 140, 142
Tatars 13
Taurus 32
ṭawāf al-ifāda 23
taxation 136, 140, 143, 167
tax revenues 60, 70, 78, 80, 90, 96
teakwood 20, 92, 94f, 116; *see also* timber
theological school *see madrasa*
timār see military prebends
timber 28, 30, 94, 97, 101, 114, 120f, 165; *see also* teakwood
Timur Lenk 28, 141
Timurid 131, 139
Tokat 84
tolls 47, 89f
Topkapı Palace 96
torchbearers 34
town planning *see* urban planning
trade, conducted by pilgrims as a sideline 160, 169, 183
traders 34, 44, 46f, 49, 65, 72f, 85, 133, 137, 141, 158ff, 163, 167, 169, 171, 196
Transoxania(n) 140f, 184
Tripoli 16, 48
Ṭūmānbāy 147
Tunisia(n) 16

'ulemā 148f, 153, 186
'ulūfe (salary) 88, 91, 109
'Umar, caliph 26, 92, 137, 141
'Umar b. 'Abd al-'Azīz 120
Ummayads 7, 13, 27, 93, 101, 137
'umra 18, 20f
urban planning 93, 107ff, 112, 125, 132
Üsküdar 32
'Uthmān, caliph 122, 137
'Uyūn al-Tudjdjār 72
Uzbeks 134, 139, 144
Uzunçarşılı, Ismail Hakkı 156

Venice, Venetians 76, 84, 94, 133, 170, 183
Vereenigde Oostindische Compagnie 159
Via Egnatia 41
Vize 69
votive gifts 139, 143

wādjib al-re'āyet 44, 194
Wahabi(s) 9, 122, 179f
Wahīdāt 56
waḳfa 21–3, 25
Walīd b. 'Abd al-Malik, caliph 27
water, water supply 5f, 9, 22, 28, 34–6, 41f, 54, 67, 71, 75, 93, 98f, 103, 108–10, 123, 143, 182, 185, 198, 204
weapons 69ff
wells in the desert 42, 71
well Zamzam *see* Zamzam
white covering of the Ka'aba 105
wives, taken or not taken on the pilgrimage 7
wood *see* teakwood; timber

Yalamlam 19
Yaman 64
Yanbu' 9, 67, 77, 86, 98, 154, 165
Yazīd 137
Yemen(i) 5, 21f, 25, 29f, 33, 50, 54, 61f, 66, 135, 146, 151, 157f, 162f, 169f, 172, 183, 207
Yeni Djāmi' 125
Yenidje Vardar 84
yol emri 128–30, 141f

Zamzam, well 2, 20, 92
ze'āmet see military prebends
Zefat *see* Safed
Zubayda 8, 22